LLEWELLYN'S 2013

Daily Planetary Guide

ISBN: 978-0-7387-1519-3. Astrological calculations compiled and programmed by Rique Pottenger based on the earlier work of Neil F. Michelsen.

Astrological proofreading by Jim Shawvan and Ana Ruiz
Cover design by Lisa Novak
Cover photo © Photodisc Spacescapes
Edited by Andrea Neff

Llewellyn Worldwide Ltd.
2143 Wooddale Drive
Woodbury, MN 55125-2989
www.llewellyn.com

2012

SEPTEMBER

S	M	T	W	T	F	S
						1
2	3	4	5	6	7	8
9	10	11	12	13	14	15
16	17	18	19	20	21	22
23	24	25	26	27	28	29
30						

OCTOBER

S	M	T	W	T	F	S
	1	2	3	4	5	6
7	8	9	10	11	12	13
14	15	16	17	18	19	20
21	22	23	24	25	26	27
28	29	30	31			

NOVEMBER

S	M	T	W	T	F	S
				1	2	3
4	5	6	7	8	9	10
11	12	13	14	15	16	17
18	19	20	21	22	23	24
25	26	27	28	29	30	

DECEMBER

S	M	T	W	T	F	S
						1
2	3	4	5	6	7	8
9	10	11	12	13	14	15
16	17	18	19	20	21	22
23	24	25	26	27	28	29
30	31					

2013

JANUARY

S	M	T	W	T	F	S
		1	2	3	4	5
6	7	8	9	10	11	12
13	14	15	16	17	18	19
20	21	22	23	24	25	26
27	28	29	30	31		

FEBRUARY

S	M	T	W	T	F	S
					1	2
3	4	5	6	7	8	9
10	11	12	13	14	15	16
17	18	19	20	21	22	23
24	25	26	27	28		

MARCH

S	M	T	W	T	F	S
					1	2
3	4	5	6	7	8	9
10	11	12	13	14	15	16
17	18	19	20	21	22	23
24	25	26	27	28	29	30
31						

APRIL

S	M	T	W	T	F	S
	1	2	3	4	5	6
7	8	9	10	11	12	13
14	15	16	17	18	19	20
21	22	23	24	25	26	27
28	29	30				

MAY

S	M	T	W	T	F	S
			1	2	3	4
5	6	7	8	9	10	11
12	13	14	15	16	17	18
19	20	21	22	23	24	25
26	27	28	29	30	31	

JUNE

S	M	T	W	T	F	S
						1
2	3	4	5	6	7	8
9	10	11	12	13	14	15
16	17	18	19	20	21	22
23	24	25	26	27	28	29
30						

JULY

S	M	T	W	T	F	S
	1	2	3	4	5	6
7	8	9	10	11	12	13
14	15	16	17	18	19	20
21	22	23	24	25	26	27
28	29	30	31			

AUGUST

S	M	T	W	T	F	S
				1	2	3
4	5	6	7	8	9	10
11	12	13	14	15	16	17
18	19	20	21	22	23	24
25	26	27	28	29	30	31

SEPTEMBER

S	M	T	W	T	F	S
1	2	3	4	5	6	7
8	9	10	11	12	13	14
15	16	17	18	19	20	21
22	23	24	25	26	27	28
29	30					

OCTOBER

S	M	T	W	T	F	S
		1	2	3	4	5
6	7	8	9	10	11	12
13	14	15	16	17	18	19
20	21	22	23	24	25	26
27	28	29	30	31		

NOVEMBER

S	M	T	W	T	F	S
					1	2
3	4	5	6	7	8	9
10	11	12	13	14	15	16
17	18	19	20	21	22	23
24	25	26	27	28	29	30

DECEMBER

S	M	T	W	T	F	S
1	2	3	4	5	6	7
8	9	10	11	12	13	14
15	16	17	18	19	20	21
22	23	24	25	26	27	28
29	30	31				

2014

JANUARY

S	M	T	W	T	F	S
			1	2	3	4
5	6	7	8	9	10	11
12	13	14	15	16	17	18
19	20	21	22	23	24	25
26	27	28	29	30	31	

FEBRUARY

S	M	T	W	T	F	S
						1
2	3	4	5	6	7	8
9	10	11	12	13	14	15
16	17	18	19	20	21	22
23	24	25	26	27	28	

MARCH

S	M	T	W	T	F	S
						1
2	3	4	5	6	7	8
9	10	11	12	13	14	15
16	17	18	19	20	21	22
23	24	25	26	27	28	29
30	31					

APRIL

S	M	T	W	T	F	S
		1	2	3	4	5
6	7	8	9	10	11	12
13	14	15	16	17	18	19
20	21	22	23	24	25	26
27	28	29	30			

MAY

S	M	T	W	T	F	S
				1	2	3
4	5	6	7	8	9	10
11	12	13	14	15	16	17
18	19	20	21	22	23	24
25	26	27	28	29	30	31

JUNE

S	M	T	W	T	F	S
1	2	3	4	5	6	7
8	9	10	11	12	13	14
15	16	17	18	19	20	21
22	23	24	25	26	27	28
29	30					

JULY

S	M	T	W	T	F	S
		1	2	3	4	5
6	7	8	9	10	11	12
13	14	15	16	17	18	19
20	21	22	23	24	25	26
27	28	29	30	31		

AUGUST

S	M	T	W	T	F	S
					1	2
3	4	5	6	7	8	9
10	11	12	13	14	15	16
17	18	19	20	21	22	23
24	25	26	27	28	29	30
31						

Contents

Introduction to Astrology

by Kim Rogers-Gallagher

Your horoscope is calculated using the date and time you were born from the perspective of your birth location. From this information, a clock-like diagram emerges that shows where every planet was located at the moment you made your debut. Each chart is composed of the same elements, rearranged, so everyone has one of everything, but none are exactly alike. I think of planets, signs, houses, and aspects as the four astrological building blocks. Each block represents a different level of human existence.

The eight planets along with the Sun and Moon are actual physical bodies. They represent urges or needs we all have. Chiron also falls into this category. The twelve signs of the zodiac are sections of the sky, and each is 30 degrees. The signs describe the behavior a planet or house will use to express itself. The twelve houses in a chart tell us where our planets come to life. Each house represents different life concerns—values, communication, creativity, and so on—that we must live through as life and time progress.

Basically, aspects are angles. Some of the planets will be positioned an exact number of degrees apart, forming angles to one another. For example, 180 degrees is a circle divided by two and is called an opposition. A square is 90 degrees and divides the circle by four. A trine is 120 degrees and divides the circle by three, and so forth. Aspects show which planets will engage in constant dialogue with one another. The particular aspect that joins them describes the nature of their "conversation." Not all planets will aspect all other planets in the houses.

Planets: The First Building Block

Each planet acts like the director of a department in a corporation, and the corporation is, of course, you. For example, Mercury directs your Communications Department and Jupiter oversees your Abundance and Growth Department. When you have the need to communicate, you call on your Mercury; when it's time to take a risk or grow, you use your Jupiter. Let's meet each of the planets individually and take a look at which job duties fall under each planet's jurisdiction.

The Sun

☉ Every corporation needs an executive director who makes the final decisions. The Sun is your Executive Director. The Sun in your chart is your core, your true self. Although each of the planets in your chart is important in its own right, they all "take their orders," figuratively speaking, from the Sun.

Everyone's Sun has the same inner goal: to shine. The house your Sun is in shows where you really want to do good, where you want to be appreciated and loved. Your Sun is your inner supply of pride and confidence, your identity. The Sun is you at your creative best, enjoying life to the fullest.

The Sun shows the focus of the moment, where the world's attention will be directed on that particular day. In fact, in horary and electional astrology, the two branches that pertain most to timing and prediction, the Sun represents the day, the Moon the hour, and the Midheaven the moment. In the physical body, the Sun rules the heart, upper back, and circulatory system.

The Moon

☽ Speaking of the Moon, a good place to meet her and begin to understand her qualities is by the water on a clear night when she's full. Whether you're looking up at her or at that silvery patch she creates that shivers and dances on the water, take a deep breath and allow yourself to be still. She represents the soft interior of each of us that recalls memories, that fears and dreams.

She's a lovely lady who oversees the Department of Feelings; she's the bringer of "moods" (a great Moon word). Her house and placement in your chart reveal how your intuition works, what your emotional needs are, and how you want your needs met. She is the ultimate feminine energy, the part of you that points both to how you were nurtured and to how you will nurture others. In the body, the Moon has jurisdiction over the breasts, ovaries, and womb. She also rules our body fluids, the internal ocean that keeps us alive.

Mercury

☿ Back when gods and goddesses were thought to be in charge of the affairs of humanity, Mercury shuttled messages between the gods and mortals. In today's world, Mercury is the computer, the telephone, and the Internet. He's the internal computer that constantly feeds you data about the world. His position and house in your chart show how you think and reason, and how you express yourself to others. You'll recognize him in your speech patterns, your handwriting, and in the way you walk, because moving through your environment means communicating with it. He operates through your five senses and your brain, and makes you conscious of opposites—light and dark, hot and cold, up and down. He's what you use when you have a conversation, exchange a glance, gesture, or interpret a symbol. Mercury represents the side of you living totally in the present.

If you've ever tried to collect mercury after it escaped from a broken thermometer, you've learned something about Mercury. Just as your Mercury never stops collecting data, those tiny beads you tried so hard to collect brought back a bit of everything they contacted—dog hair, crumbs, and grains of dirt. In the body, Mercury also acts as a messenger. He transmits messages through his function as the central nervous system that lets your eyes and hands collaborate, your eyes blink, and breathing continue.

Venus

♀ Venus spends her energy supplying you with your favorite people, places, and things. If you want chocolate, music, flannel sheets, or the coworker you've got a mad crush on, it's your Venus that tells you how to get it. Venus enjoys beauty and comfort. She shows how to attract what you love, especially people. When you're being charming, whether by using your manners or by adorning yourself, she's in charge of all behavior that is pleasing to others—social chitchat, smiles, hugs, and kisses. Whenever you're pleased, satisfied, or content enough to purr, it's your Venus who made you feel that way. Since money is one of the ways we draw the objects we love to us, she's also in charge of finances. Venus relates to your senses—sight, smell, taste, touch, and sound—the body's receptors.

After all, it's the senses that tell us what feels good and what doesn't. Venus responds to your desire for beautiful surroundings, comfortable clothing, and fine art.

Mars

♂ Mars is in charge of your Self-Defense and Action Department. He's the warrior who fights back when you're attacked—your own personal SWAT team. Your Mars energy makes you brave, courageous, and daring. His placement in your chart describes how you act on your own behalf. He's concerned only with you, and he doesn't consider the size, strength, or abilities of whomever or whatever you're up against. He's the side of you that initiates all activity. He's also in charge of how you assert yourself and how you express anger.

"Hot under the collar," "seeing red," and "all fired up" are Mars phrases. Mars is what you use to be passionate, adventurous, and bold. But he can be violent, accident-prone, and cruel, too. Wherever he is in your chart, you find constant action. Mars pursues. He shows how you "do" things. He charges through situations. This "headstrong" planet corresponds to the head, the blood, and the muscles.

Jupiter

♃ Jupiter is called "the Greater Benefic," and he heads the Department of Abundance and Growth. He's the side of you that's positive, optimistic, and generous. He's where you keep your supply of laughter, enthusiasm, and high spirits. It's Jupiter's expansive, high-spirited energy that motivates you to travel, take classes, and meet new people. Wherever he is in your chart is a place where you'll have an extensive network of friends and associates—folks you can visit, count on, and learn from. Jupiter is the side of you that will probably cause you to experience the "grass is greener" syndrome. Your Jupiter is also what you're using when you find yourself being excessive and wasteful, overdoing, or blowing something out of proportion. Words like "too" and "always" are the property of Jupiter, as are "more" and "better." In general, this planet just loves to make things bigger. In the body, Jupiter corresponds with the liver, the organ that filters what you take in and rids your body of excess. Jupiter also handles physical growth.

Saturn

♄ Saturn represents withholding and resistance to change. He heads the Boundaries and Rules Department. Locate Saturn in your chart to find out where you'll build walls to keep change out, where you may segregate yourself at times, where you'll be most likely to say no. Your Saturn is the authority inside you, the spot where you may inhibit or stall yourself throughout life—most often because you fear failure and would rather not act at all than act inappropriately. This planet teaches you to respect your elders, follow the rules, and do things right the first time. Wherever Saturn is in your chart is a place where you'll feel respectful, serious, and conservative. Your Saturn placement is where you'll know that you should never embellish the facts and never act until you're absolutely sure you're ready. Here is where you won't expect something for nothing. Saturn is also where you're at your most disciplined, where you'll teach yourself the virtues of patience, endurance, and responsibility. Because this planet is so fond of boundaries, it's also the planet in charge of organization, structures, and guidelines. In the physical body, Saturn correlates with the bones and the skin, those structures that hold your body together.

Uranus

♅ There's a spot in everyone's chart where independence is the order of the day, where rules are made specifically to be broken, and where personal freedom is the only way to go, regardless of the consequences. Here's where you'll surprise even yourself at the things you say and do. Meet Uranus, head of the Department of One Never Knows, the place in your chart where shocks, surprises, and sudden reversals are regular fare.

Your Uranus energy is what wakes you up to how confined you feel, breaks you out of the rut you're in, and sets you free. He's a computer wizard and involved in mass communications. Where he's strong in your chart, you will be strong, too. Here is where you'll have genius potential, where you'll be bold enough to ignore the old way to solve a problem and instead find a whole new way. Major scientific and technological breakthroughs like the space program and the Internet were inspired by Uranus. In the body, Uranus rules the lower part of the legs, including the calves and ankles, and it co-rules with Mercury the central nervous system.

Neptune

♆ Next time you hear yourself sigh or feel yourself slip into a day-dream, think of Neptune. This is the planet in charge of romance, nostalgia, and magic. Although her official title is head of the Department of Avoidance and Fantasy, she's also one of the most creative energies you own. Wherever she is in your chart is where you're psychic. It's also where you're capable of amazing compassion and sensitivity for beings and creatures less fortunate than yourself. It's where you'll be drawn into charity or volunteer work because you realize that we're all part of a bigger plan, that there are no boundaries between you and what's out there.

This combination of sensitivity and harsh reality doesn't always mix well. This may also be a place where you'll try to escape. Sleep, meditation, and prayer are the highest uses of her energies, but alcohol and drugs are also under her jurisdiction. Neptune's place in your chart is where you're equally capable of fooling all of the people all of the time, and of being fooled yourself. In the body, Neptune and the Moon co-rule fluids. Neptune also has a connection with poisons and viruses that invisibly infiltrate our bodies and with the body's immune system, which is how we keep our barriers intact.

Pluto

♇ Pluto is head of the Department of Death, Destruction, and Decay. He's in charge of things that have to happen, and he disposes of situations that have gone past the point of no return, where the only solution is to "let go." He also oversees sex, reincarnation, recycling, regeneration, and rejuvenation. Pluto's spot in your chart is a place where intense, inevitable circumstances will arrive to teach you about agony and ecstasy. Pluto's place in your chart is where you'll be in a state of turmoil or evolution, where there will be ongoing change. This is the side of you that realizes that, like it or not, life goes on after tremendous loss. It is the side of you that will reflect on your losses down the road and try to make sense of them. Most importantly, since Pluto rules life, death, and rebirth, here's where you'll understand the importance of process. You'll be amazingly strong where your Pluto is—he's a well of concentrated, transforming energy. In the body, Pluto is associated with the reproductive organs since here is where the invisible process of life and death begins. He is also in charge of puberty and sexual maturity. He corresponds with plutonium.

Signs: The Second Building Block

Every sign is built of three things: an element, a quality, and a polarity. Understanding each of these primary building blocks gives a head start toward understanding the signs themselves, so let's take a look at them.

The Polarities: Masculine and Feminine

The words "masculine" and "feminine" are often misunderstood or confused in the context of astrology. In astrology, masculine means that an energy is assertive, aggressive, and linear. Feminine means that an energy is receptive, magnetic, and circular. These terms should not be confused with male and female.

The Qualities: Cardinal, Fixed, and Mutable

Qualities show the way a sign's energy flows. The cardinal signs are energies that initiate change. Cardinal signs operate in sudden bursts of energy. The fixed signs are thorough and unstoppable. They're the energies that endure. They take projects to completion, tend to block change at all costs, and will keep at something regardless of whether or not it should be terminated. The mutable signs are versatile, flexible, and changeable. They can be scattered, fickle, and inconstant.

The Elements: Fire, Earth, Air, and Water

The fire signs correspond with the spirit and the spiritual aspects of life. They inspire action, attract attention, and love spontaneity. The earth signs are solid, practical, supportive, and as reliable as the earth under our feet. The earth signs are our physical envoys and are concerned with our tangible needs, such as food, shelter, work, and responsibilities. Air signs are all about the intellectual or mental sides of life. Like air itself, they are light and elusive. They love conversation, communication, and mingling. The water signs correspond to the emotional side of our natures. As changeable, subtle, and able to infiltrate as water itself, water signs gauge the mood in a room when they enter, and operate on what they sense from their environment.

Aries: Masculine, Cardinal, Fire

♈ Aries is ruled by Mars and is cardinal fire—red-hot, impulsive, and ready to go. Aries planets are not known for their patience, and they ignore obstacles, choosing instead to focus on the shortest distance between where they are and where they want to be. Planets in Aries are brave, impetuous, and direct. Aries planets are often very good at initiating projects. They are not, however, as eager to finish, so they will leave projects undone. Aries planets need physical outlets for their considerable Mars-powered energy; otherwise their need for action can turn to stress. Exercise, hard work, and competition are food for Aries energy.

Taurus: Feminine, Fixed, Earth

♉ Taurus, the fixed earth sign, has endless patience that turns your Taurus planet into a solid force to be reckoned with. Taurus folks never, ever quit. Their reputation for stubbornness is earned. They're responsible, reliable, honest as they come, practical, and endowed with a stick-to-it attitude other planets envy. They're not afraid to work hard. Since Taurus is ruled by Venus, it's not surprising to find that these people are sensual and luxury-loving, too. They love to be spoiled with the best—good food, fine wine, or even a Renoir painting. They need peace and quiet like no other, and don't like their schedules to be disrupted. However, they may need a reminder that comfortable habits can become ruts.

Gemini: Masculine, Mutable, Air

♊ This sign is famous for its duality and love of new experiences, as well as for its role as communicator. Gemini is mutable air, which translates into changing your mind, so expect your Gemini planet to be entertaining and versatile. This sign knows a little bit about everything. Gemini planets usually display at least two distinct sides to their personalities, are changeable and even fickle at times, and are wonderfully curious. This sign is ruled by Mercury, so if what you're doing involves talking, writing, gesturing, or working with hand-eye coordination, your Gemini planet will love it. Mercury also rules short trips, so any planet in Gemini is an expert at how to make its way around the neighborhood in record time.

Cancer: Feminine, Cardinal, Water

♋ Cancer is cardinal water, so it's good at beginning things. It's also the most privacy-oriented sign. Cancer types are emotionally vulnerable, sensitive, and easily hurt. They need safe "nests" to return to when the world gets to be too much. Cancer types say "I love you" by tending to your need for food, warmth, or a place to sleep. The problem is that they can become needy, dependent, or unable to function unless they feel someone or something needs them. Cancer rules the home and family. It's also in charge of emotions, so expect a Cancer to operate from his or her gut most of the time.

Leo: Masculine, Fixed, Fire

♌ Leo is fixed fire, and above all else represents pride and ego. Sun-ruled Leo wants to shine and be noticed. Natural performers, people in this sign are into drama and attract attention even when they don't necessarily want it. Occasionally your Leo friends may be touchy and high maintenance. Still, they are generous to a fault. Leo appreciates attention and praise with lavish compliments, lovely gifts, and creative outings designed to amaze and delight. Leo's specialties are having fun, entertaining, and making big entrances and exits.

Virgo: Feminine, Mutable, Earth

♍ Virgo may seem picky and critical, but that may be too simplistic. As a mutable earth sign, your Virgo planet delights in helping, and it's willing to adapt to any task. Having a keen eye for details may be another way to interpret a Virgo planet's automatic fault-finding ability. When Virgo's eye for detail combines with the ability to fix almost anything, you have a troubleshooter extraordinaire. This sign practices discrimination—analyzing, critiquing, and suggesting remedies to potential problems. This sign is also wonderful at lists, agendas, and schedules. Keep your Virgo planet happy by keeping it busy.

Libra: Masculine, Cardinal, Air

♎ Libra adores balance, harmony, and equal give and take—no easy task. A more charming sign would be difficult to find, though. Libra's cardinal airy nature wants to begin things, and entertaining and socializing are high priorities. These expert people-pleasing Venus-ruled planets specialize in manners, courtesy, and small talk. Alone time may be shunned, and because they're gifted with the ability to pacify, they may sell out their own needs, or the truth, to buy peace and companionship. Seeing both sides of a situation, weighing the options, and keeping their inner balance by remaining honest may be Libra's hardest tasks.

Scorpio: Feminine, Fixed, Water

♏ Planets in this sign are detectives, excelling at the art of strategy. Your Scorpio planets sift through every situation for subtle clues, which they analyze to determine what's really going on. They're also gifted at sending subtle signals back to the environment, and at imperceptibly altering a situation by manipulating it with the right word or movement. Scorpio planets are constantly searching for intimacy. They seek intensity and may be crisis-oriented. They can be relentless, obsessive, and jealous. Remember, this is fixed water. Scorpios feel things deeply and forever. Give your Scorpio planets the opportunity to fire-walk, to experience life-and-death situations.

Sagittarius: Masculine, Mutable, Fire

♐ The enthusiasm of this mutable fire sign, ruled by Jupiter, spreads like a brushfire. These planets tend to never feel satisfied or content, and to always wonder if there's something even more wonderful over the next mountain. Your Sagittarius planets are bored by routine; they're freedom oriented, generous, and optimistic to a fault. They can be excessive and overindulgent. They adore outdoor activities and foreign places and foreign people. They learn by first having the big picture explained. They're only too happy to preach, advertise, and philosophize. Sagittarius planets can be quite prophetic, and they absolutely believe in the power of laughter, embarrassing themselves at times to make someone laugh.

Capricorn: Feminine, Cardinal, Earth

♑ Your Capricorn planets, ruled by Saturn, have a tendency to build things, such as erecting structures and creating a career for you. Saturn will start up an organization and turn it into the family business. These planets automatically know how to run it no matter what it is. They're authority figures. They exercise caution and discipline, set down rules, and live by them. Capricorn is the sign with the driest wit. Here's where your sense of propriety and tradition will be strong, where doing things the old-fashioned way and paying respect to the elders will be the only way to go. They want a return for the time they invest, and don't mind proving how valuable they are.

Aquarius: Masculine, Fixed, Air

♒ Aquarian planets present some unexpected contradictions because they are fixed air and unpredictable. This sign's ruler, Uranus, gets the credit for Aquarius's tumultuous ways. Aquarian energy facilitates invention and humanitarian conquests, to the amazement of the masses, and planets in this sign are into personal freedom like no other. They create their own rules, fight city hall whenever possible, and deliberately break tradition. They adore change. Abrupt reversals are their specialty, so others often perceive them as erratic, unstable, or unreliable. But when Aquarius energy activates, commitment to a cause or an intellectual ideal has a steadfastness like no other sign possesses.

Pisces: Feminine, Mutable, Water

♓ Mutable Pisces can't separate itself emotionally from whatever it's exposed to. While this is the source of Pisces' well-deserved reputation for compassion, it's also the source of a desire to escape reality. Planets in this sign feel everything—for better or worse—so they need time alone to unload and reassemble themselves. Exposure to others, especially in crowds, is exhausting to your Pisces planets. Here is where you may have a tendency to take in stray people and animals and where you'll need to watch for the possibility of being victimized or taken advantage of in some way. Pisces planets see the best in people or situations, and they can be disappointed when reality sets in. These planets are the romantics of the zodiac. Let them dream in healthy ways.

Houses: The Third Building Block

Houses are represented by twelve pie-shaped wedges in a horoscope chart. (See blank chart on page 189.) They're like rooms in a house, and each reflects the circumstances we create and encounter in a specific area of life. One room, the Sixth House, relates to our daily routine and work, while the Eleventh House relates to groups we may be affilliated with, for example. The sign (Aries, Taurus, etc.) on the cusp of each house tells us something about the nature of the room behind the door. Someone with Leo on the Sixth House cusp will create different routines and work habits than a person with Capricorn on that cusp. The sign influences the type of behavior you'll exhibit when those life circumstances turn up. Since the time of day you were born determines the sign on each of the houses, an accurate birth time will result in more accurate information from your chart.

The Twelve Houses

The First House

The First House shows the sign that was ascending over the horizon at the moment you were born. Let's think again of your chart as one big house and of the houses as "rooms." The First House symbolizes your front door. The sign on this house cusp (also known as the Rising Sign or Ascendant) describes the way you dress, move, and adorn yourself, and the overall condition of your body. It relates to the first impression you make on people.

The Second House

This house shows how you handle the possessions you hold dear. That goes for money, objects, and the qualities you value in yourself and in others. This house also holds the side of you that takes care of what you have and what you buy for yourself, and the amount of money you earn. The Second House shows what you're willing to do for money, too, so it's also a description of your self-esteem.

The Third House

This house corresponds to your neighborhood, including the bank, the post office, and the gym where you work out. This is the side of you that performs routine tasks without much conscious thought. The Third House also refers to childhood and grammar school, and it shows our relationships with siblings, our communication style, and our attitude toward short trips.

The Fourth House

This house is the symbolic foundation brought from your childhood home, your family, and the parent who nurtured you. Here is where you'll find the part of you that decorates and maintains your nest. It decides what home in the adult world will be like and how much privacy you'll need. The Fourth House deals with matters of real estate. Most importantly, this house contains the emotional warehouse of memories you operate from subconsciously.

The Fifth House

Here's the side of you that's reserved for play, that only comes out when work is done and it's time to party and be entertained. This is the charming, creative, delightful side of you, where your hobbies, interests, and playmates are found. If it gives you joy, it's described here. Your Fifth House shines when you are creative, and it allows you to see a bit of yourself in those creations—anything from your child's smile to a piece of art. Traditionally this house also refers to speculation and gambling.

The Sixth House

This house is where you keep the side of you that decides how you like things to go along over the course of a day, the side of you that plans a schedule. Since it describes the duties you perform on a daily basis, it also refers to the nature of your work, your work environment, and how you take care of your health. It's how you function.

Pets are also traditionally a Sixth House issue, since we tend to them daily and incorporate them into our routine.

The Seventh House

Although it's traditionally known as the house of marriage, partnerships, and open enemies, the Seventh House really holds the side of you that only comes out when you're in the company of just one other person. This is the side of you that handles relating on a one-to-one basis. Whenever you use the word "my" to describe your relationship with another, it's this side of you talking.

The Eighth House

Here's the crisis expert side of you that emerges when it's time to handle extreme circumstances. This is the side of you that deals with agony and ecstasy, with sex, death, and all manner of mergers, financial and otherwise. The Eighth House also holds information on surgeries, psychotherapy, and the way we regenerate and rejuvenate after loss.

The Ninth House

This house holds the side of you that handles new experiences, foreign places, long-distance travel, and legal matters. Higher education, publishing, advertising, and forming opinions are handled here, as are issues involving the big picture, such as politics, religion, and philosophy.

The Tenth House

This spot in your chart describes what the public knows about you. Your career, reputation, and social status are found here. This is the side of you that takes time to learn and become accomplished. It describes the behavior you'll exhibit when you're in charge, and also the way you'll act in the presence of an authority figure. Most importantly, the Tenth House describes your vocation or life's work—whatever you consider your "calling."

The Eleventh House

Here's the team player in you, the side of you that helps you find your peer groups. The Eleventh House shows the type of organizations you're drawn to join, the kind of folks you consider kindred spirits, and how you'll act in group situations. It also shows the causes and social activities you hold near and dear.

The Twelfth House

This is the side of you that only comes out when you're alone, or in the mood to retreat and regroup. Here's where the secret side of you lives, where secret affairs and dealings take place. Here, too, is where matters like hospital stays are handled. Most importantly, the Twelfth House is the room where you keep all the traits and behaviors that you were taught early on to stifle, avoid, or deny—especially in public. This side of you is very fond of fantasy, illusion, and pretend play.

Aspects and Transits: The Fourth Building Block

Planets form angles to one another as they move through the heavens. If two planets are 90 degrees apart, they form a square. If they're 180 degrees apart, they're in opposition. Planets in aspect have twenty-four-hour communication going on. The particular angle that separates any two planets describes the nature of their conversation. Astrologers use seven angles most often, each of which produces a different type of relationship or "conversation" between the planets they join. Let's go over the meaning of each of the aspects.

Ptolemic Aspects

The Conjunction: (0–8 degrees)

☌ When you hear that two things are operating "in conjunction," it means they're operating together. This holds true with planets as well. Two (or more) planets conjoined are a team, but some planets pair up more easily than others. Venus and the Moon work well together because both are feminine and receptive, but the Sun and Mars are both pretty feisty by nature, and may cause conflict. Planets in conjunction are usually sharing a house in your chart.

The Sextile: (60 degrees)

⚹ The sextile links planets in compatible elements. That is, planets in sextile are either in fire and air signs or earth and water signs. Since these pairs of elements get along well, the sextile encourages an active exchange between the two planets involved, so these two parts of you will be eager to work together.

The Square: (90 degrees)

□ A square aspect puts planets at cross-purposes. Friction develops between them and one will constantly challenge the other. You can see squares operating in someone who's fidgety or constantly restless. Although they're uncomfortable and even aggravating at times, your squares point to places where tremendous growth is possible.

The Trine: (120 degrees)

△ Trines are usually formed between planets of the same element, so they understand each other. They show an ease of communication not found in any of the other aspects, and they're traditionally thought of as "favorable." Of course, there is a downside to trines. Planets in this relationship are so comfortable that they can often get lazy and spoiled. (Sometimes they get so comfy they're boring.) Planets in trine show urges or needs that automatically support each other. The catch is that you've got to get them operating.

The Quincunx: (150 degrees)

⚻ This aspect joins two signs that don't share a quality, element, or gender, which makes it difficult for them to communicate with each other. It's frustrating. For that reason, this aspect has always been considered to require an adjustment in the way the two planets are used. Planets in quincunx often feel pushed, forced, or obligated to perform. They seem to correspond to health issues.

The Opposition: (180 degrees)

☍ When two planets are opposed, they work against each other. For example, you may want to do something, and if you have two opposing planets you may struggle with two very different approaches to getting the job done. If Mars and Neptune are opposing, you may struggle between getting a job done the quick, easy way or daydreaming about all the creative possibilities open to you. It's as if the two are standing across from one another with their arms folded, involved in a debate, neither willing to concede an inch. They can break out of their standoff only by first becoming aware of one another and then compromising. This aspect is the least difficult of the traditionally known "hard" aspects because planets "at odds" with one another can come to some sort of compromise.

Transits

While your horoscope (natal chart) reflects the exact position of planets at the time of your birth, the planets, as you know, move on. They are said to be "transiting." We interpret a transit as a planet in its "today" position making an aspect to a planet in your natal chart. Transiting planets represent incoming influences and events that your natal planets will be asked to handle. The nature of the transiting planet describes the types of situations that will arise, and the nature of your natal planet tells which "piece" of you you're working on at the moment. When a planet transits through a house or aspects a planet in your chart, you will have opportunities for personal growth and change. Every transit you experience adds knowledge to your personality.

Sun Transit

A Sun transit points to the places in your chart where you'll want special attention, pats on the back, and appreciation. Here's where you want to shine. These are often times of public acclaim, when we're recognized, congratulated, or applauded for what we've done. Of course, the ultimate Sun transit is our birthday, the day when we're all secretly sure that we should be treated like royalty.

Moon Transit

When the Moon touches one of the planets in our natal chart, we react from an emotional point of view. A Moon transit often corresponds to the highs and lows we feel that last only a day or two. Our instincts are on high during a Moon transit and we're more liable to sense what's going on around us than to consciously know something.

Mercury Transit

Transiting Mercury creates activity in whatever area of life it visits. The subject is communication of all kinds, so conversation, letters, and quick errands take up our time now. Because of Mercury's love of duality, events will often occur in twos—as if Hermes the trickster were having some fun with us—and we're put in the position of having to do at least two things at once.

Venus Transit

Transiting Venus brings times when the universe gives us a small token of warmth or affection or a well-deserved break. These are often sociable, friendly periods when we do more than our usual share of mingling and are more interested in good food and cushy conditions than anything resembling work. A Venus transit also shows a time when others will give us gifts. Since Venus rules money, this transit can show when we'll receive financial rewards.

Mars Transit

Mars transiting a house can indicate high-energy times. You're stronger and restless, or maybe you're cranky, angry, accident-prone, or violent. When Mars happens along, it's best to work or exercise hard to use up this considerable energy. Make yourself "too tired to be mad." These are super times to initiate projects that require a hard push of energy to begin.

Jupiter Transit

Under this transit you're in the mood to travel, take a class, or learn something new about the concerns of any house or planet Jupiter visits. You ponder the big questions. You grow under a Jupiter transit, sometimes even physically. Now is the time to take chances or risk a shot at the title. During a Jupiter transit you're luckier, bolder, and a lot more likely to succeed. This transit provides opportunities. Be sure to take advantage of them.

Saturn Transit

When Saturn comes along, we see things as they truly are. These are not traditionally great times, but they are often times when your greatest rewards appear. When Saturn transits a house or planet, he checks to see if the structure is steady and will hold up. You are then tested, and if you pass, you receive a symbolic certificate of some kind—and sometimes a real one, like a diploma. We will always be tested, but if we fail, life can feel very difficult. Firming up our lives is Saturn's mission. This is a great time to tap into Saturn's willpower and self-discipline to stop doing something. It is not traditionally a good time to begin new ventures, though.

Uranus Transit

The last thing in the world you'd ever expect to happen is exactly what you can expect under a Uranus transit. This is the planet of last-minute plan changes, reversals, and shock effects. So if you're feeling stuck in your present circumstances, when a Uranus transit happens along you won't be stuck for long. "Temporary people" often enter your life at these times, folks whose only purpose is to jolt you out of your present circumstances by appearing to provide exactly what you were sorely missing. That done, they disappear, leaving you with your life in a shambles. When these people arrive, enjoy them and allow them to break you out of your rut—just don't get comfortable.

Neptune Transit

A Neptune transit is a time when the universe asks only that you dream and nothing more. Your sensitivity heightens to the point that harsh sounds can actually make you wince. Compassion deepens, and psychic moments are common. A Neptune transit inspires divine discontent. We sigh, wish, feel nostalgic, and don't see things clearly at all. At the end of the transit, you realize that everything about you is different, that the reality you were living at the beginning of the transit has been gradually eroded or erased right from under your feet, while you stood right there upon it.

Pluto Transit

A Pluto transit is often associated with obsession, regeneration, and inevitable change. Whatever has gone past the point of no return, whatever is broken beyond repair, will pass from your life now. As with a Saturn transit, this time is not known to be wonderful, but when circumstances peel away everything from us and we're forced to see ourselves as we truly are, we do learn just how strong we are. Power struggles often accompany Pluto's visit, but being empowered is the end result of a positive Pluto transit. The secret is to let go, accept the losses or changes, and make plans for the future.

Retrograde Planets

Retrograde literally means "backwards." Although none of the planets ever really throw their engines in reverse and move backward, all of them, except the Sun and Moon, appear to do so periodically from our perspective here on Earth. What's happening is that we're moving either faster or slower than the planet that's retrograde, and since we have to look over our shoulder to see it, we refer to it as retrograde.

Mercury Retrograde: A Communication Breakdown

The way retrograde planets seem to affect our affairs varies from planet to planet. In Mercury's case, it means often looking back at Mercury-ruled things—communications, contracts, and so on. Keep in mind that Mercury correlates with Hermes, the original trickster, and you'll understand how cleverly disguised some of these errors can be. Communications become confused or are delayed. Letters are lost or sent to Auckland instead of Oakland, or they end up under the car seat for three weeks. We sign a contract or agreement and find out later that we didn't have all the correct information and what we signed was misleading in some way. We try repeatedly to reach someone on the telephone but can never catch them, or our communications devices themselves break down or garble information in some way. We feel as if our timing is off, so short trips often become more difficult. We leave the directions at home or write them down incorrectly. We're late for appointments due to circumstances beyond our control, or we completely forget about them.

Is there a constructive use for this time period? Yes. Astrologer Erin Sullivan has noted that the ratio of time Mercury spends moving retrograde (backward) and direct (forward) corresponds beautifully with the amount of time we humans spend awake and asleep—about a third of our lives. So this period seems to be a time to take stock of what's happened over the past three months and assimilate our experiences.

A good rule of thumb with Mercury retrograde is to try to confine activities to those that have "re" attached to the beginning of a word: reschedule, repair, return, rewrite, redecorate, restore, replace, renovate, or renew, for example.

Retrogrades of the Other Planets

With Venus retrograde every eighteen months for six weeks, relationships and money matters are delayed or muddled.

With Mars retrograde for eleven weeks and then direct for twenty-two months, actions initiated are often rooted in confusion or end up at cross-purposes to our original intentions. Typically under a Mars retrograde, the aggressor or initiator of a battle is defeated.

Jupiter retrogrades for four months and is direct for nine months. Saturn retrogrades for about the same amount of time. Each of the outer planets, Uranus, Neptune, and Pluto, stays retrograde for about six or seven months of every year. In general, remember that actions ruled by a particular planet quite often need to be repeated or done over when that planet is retrograde. Just make sure that whatever you're planning is something you don't mind doing twice.

Moon Void-of-Course

The Moon orbits Earth in about twenty-eight days, moving through each of the signs in about two days. As she passes through the thirty degrees of each sign, she visits with the planets in order by forming angles, or aspects, with them. Because she moves one degree in just two to two and a half hours, her influence on each planet lasts only a few hours. As she approaches the late degrees of the sign she's passing through, she eventually forms what will be her final aspect to another planet before leaving the sign. From this point until she actually enters the new sign, she is referred to as being "void-of-course (v/c)."

The Moon symbolizes the emotional tone of the day, carrying feelings of the sign she's "wearing" at the moment. She rules instincts. After she has contacted each of the planets, she symbolically "rests" before changing her costume, so her instincts are temporarily on hold. It's during this time that many people feel fuzzy, vague, or scattered. Plans or decisions do not pan out. Without the instinctual knowing the Moon provides as she touches each planet, we tend to be unrealistic or exercise poor judgment. The traditional definition of the void-of-course Moon is that "nothing will come of this," and it seems to be true. Actions initiated under a void-of-course Moon are often wasted, irrelevant, or incorrect—usually because information needed to make a sound decision is hidden or missing or has been overlooked.

Now, although it's not a good time to initiate plans when the Moon is void, routine tasks seem to go along just fine. However, this period is really ideal for what the Moon does best: reflection. It's at this time that we can assimilate what has occurred over the past few days. Use this time to meditate, ponder, and imagine. Let your conscious mind rest and allow yourself to feel.

On the lighter side, remember that there are other good uses for the void-of-course Moon. This is the time period when the universe seems to be most open to loopholes. It's a great time to make plans you don't want to fulfill or schedule things you don't want to do. In other words, like the song says, "To everything, there is a season." Even void-of-course Moons.

The Moon's Influence

As the Moon goes along her way, she magically appears and disappears, waxing to full from the barest sliver of a crescent just after she's new, then waning back to her invisible new phase again. The four quarters—the New Moon, the second quarter, the Full Moon, and the fourth quarter—correspond to the growth cycle of every living thing.

The Quarters

First Quarter

This phase begins when the Moon and the Sun are conjunct one another in the sky. At the beginning of the phase, the Moon is invisible, hidden by the brightness of the Sun as they travel together. The Moon is often said to be in her "dark phase" when she is just new. The New Moon can't actually be seen until 5½ to 12 hours after its birth. Toward the end of the first quarter phase, as the Moon pulls farther away from the Sun and begins to wax toward the second quarter stage, a delicate silver crescent appears. This time corresponds to all new beginnings; this is the best time to begin a project.

Second Quarter

The second quarter begins when the Moon has moved 90 degrees away from the Sun. At this point the waxing Moon rises at about noon and sets at about midnight. It's at this time that she can be seen in the western sky during the early evening hours, growing in size from a crescent to her full beauty. This period corresponds to the development and growth of life, and with projects that are coming close to fruition.

Third Quarter

This phase begins with the Full Moon, when the Sun and Moon are opposite one another in the sky. It's now that the Moon can be seen rising in the east at sunset, a bit later each night as this phase progresses. This time corresponds to the culmination of plans and to maturity.

Fourth Quarter

This phase occurs when the Moon has moved 90 degrees past the full phase. She is decreasing in light, rises at midnight, and can be seen now in the eastern sky during the late evening hours. She doesn't reach the highest point in the sky until very early in the morning. This period corresponds to "disintegration"—a symbolic "drawing back" to reflect on what's been accomplished. It's now time to reorganize, clear the boards, and plan for the next New Moon stage.

The Moon Through the Signs

The signs indicate how we'll do things. Since the Moon rules the emotional tone of the day, it's good to know what type of mood she's in at any given moment. Here's a thumbnail sketch to help you navigate every day by cooperating with the Moon no matter what sign she's in.

Aries

☽♈ The Moon in Aries is bold, impulsive, and energetic. It's a period when we feel feisty and maybe a little argumentative. This is when even the meekest aren't afraid to take a stand to protect personal feelings. Since Aries is the first sign of the zodiac, it's a natural starting point for all kinds of projects, and a wonderful time to channel all that "me first" energy to initiate change and new beginnings. Just watch out for a tendency to be too impulsive and stress-oriented.

Taurus

☽♉ The Moon in Taurus is the Lady at her most solid and sensual, feeling secure and well rooted. There's no need to stress or hurry—and definitely no need to change anything. We tend to resist change when the Moon is in this sign, especially change that's not of our own making. We'd rather sit still, have a wonderful dinner, and listen to good music. Appreciating the beauty of the earth, watching a sunset, viewing some lovely art, or taking care of money and other resources are Taurus Moon activities.

Gemini

☽♊ This mutable air sign moves around so quickly that when the Moon is here we're a bit more restless than usual, and may find that we're suddenly in the mood for conversation, puzzles, riddles, and word games. We want two—at least two—of everything. Now is a great time for letter writing, phone calls, or short trips. It's when you'll find the best shortcuts, and when you'll need to take them, too. Watch for a tendency to become a bit scattered under this fun, fickle Moon.

Cancer

☽♋ The Moon in this cardinal water sign is at her most nurturing. Here the Moon's concerns turn to home, family, children, and mothers, and we respond by becoming more likely to express our emotions and to be sympathetic and understanding toward others. We often find ourselves in the mood to take care of someone, to cook for or cuddle our dear ones. During this time, feelings run high, so it's important to watch out for becoming overly sensitive, dependent, or needy. Now is a great time to putter around the house, have family over, and tend to domestic concerns.

Leo

☽♌ The Leo Moon loves drama with a capital *D*. This theatrical sign has long been known for its big entrances, love of display, and need for attention. When the Moon is in this sign, we're all feeling a need to be recognized, applauded, and appreciated. Now, all that excitement, pride, and emotion can turn into melodrama in the blink of an eye, so it's best to be careful of overreacting or being excessively vain during this period. It's a great time to take in a show (or star in one), be romantic, or express your feelings for someone in regal style.

Virgo

☽♍ The Moon is at her most discriminating and detail-oriented in Virgo, the sign most concerned with fixing and fussing. This Moon sign puts us in the mood to clean, scour, sort, troubleshoot, and help. Virgo, the most helpful of all the signs, is also more health conscious, work-oriented, and duty bound. Use this period to pay attention to your diet, hygiene, and daily schedules.

Libra

☽♎ The Libra Moon is most oriented toward relationships and partnerships. Since Libra's job is to restore balance, however, you may find yourself in situations of emotional imbalance that require a delicate tap of the scales to set them right. In general, this is a social, polite, and friendly time, when others will be cooperative and agree more easily to compromise. A Libra Moon prompts us to make our surroundings beautiful, or to put ourselves in situations where beauty is all around us. This is a great time to decorate, shop for the home, or visit places of elegant beauty.

Scorpio

☽♏ Scorpio is the most intense sign, and when the Moon is here, she feels everything to the nth degree—and needless to say, we do, too. Passion, joy, jealousy, betrayal, love, and desire can take center stage in our lives now, as our emotions deepen to the point of possible obsession. Be careful of a tendency to become secretive or suspicious, or to brood over an offense that was not intended. Now is a great time to investigate a mystery, do research, "dig"—both figuratively and literally—and allow ourselves to become intimate with someone.

Sagittarius

☽♐ The Moon is at her most optimistic and willing to let go of things in Sagittarius. Jupiter, the planet of long-distance travel and education of the higher mind, makes this a great time to take off for adventure or attend a seminar on a topic you've always been interested in—say, philosophy or religion. This is the sign with the gift of prophecy and wisdom. When the Moon is in this sign, spend time outdoors, be spontaneous, and laugh much too loudly; just watch for a tendency toward excess, waste, and overdoing.

Capricorn

☽♑ The Moon is at her most organized, practical, and businesslike in Capricorn. She brings out the dutiful, cautious, and pessimistic side of us. Our goals for the future become all-important. Now is the time to tend to the family business, act responsibly, take charge of something, organize any part of our lives that has become scattered or disrupted, set down rules and guidelines, or patiently listen and learn. Watch for the possibility of acting too businesslike at the expense of others' emotions.

Aquarius

☽♒ The Aquarius Moon brings out the rebel in us. This is a great time to break out of a rut, try something different, and make sure everyone sees us for the unique individuals we are.

This sign is ruled by Uranus, so personal freedom and individuality are more important than anything now. Our schedules become topsy-turvy, and our causes become urgent. Watch for a tendency to become fanatical, act deliberately rebellious without a reason, or break tradition just for the sake of breaking it.

Pisces

☽♓ When the Moon slips into this sign, sleep, meditation, prayer, drugs, or alcohol is often what we crave to induce a trancelike state that will allow us to escape from the harshness of reality. Now is when we're most susceptible to emotional assaults of any kind, when we're feeling dreamy, nostalgic, wistful, or impressionable. Now is also when we're at our most spiritual, when our boundaries are at their lowest, when we're compassionate, intuitive, and sensitive to those less fortunate. This is the time to attend a spiritual group or religious gathering.

2013 Eclipse Dates

Times are in Eastern Time and are rounded off to the nearest minute. The exact time of an eclipse generally differs from the exact time of a New or Full Moon. For solar eclipses, "greatest eclipse" represents the time (converted from Local Mean Time) of the Moon's maximum obscuration of the Sun as viewed from the earth in right ascension. For lunar eclipses, the time shown is when the Moon reaches the centermost point of its journey through the shadow cast by the earth passing between it and the Sun. Data is from *Astronomical Phenomena for the Year 2013,* prepared by the United States Naval Observatory and Her Majesty's Nautical Almanac Office (United Kingdom).

April 25

Partial Lunar Eclipse at 4:07 P.M. EDT— 5° ♏ 51'

May 9

Annular Solar Eclipse at 10:55 p.m. EDT— 19° ♉ 33'

May 25

Penumbral Lunar Eclipse at 12:10 a.m. EDT—3° ♐ 58'

October 18

Penumbral Lunar Eclipse at 7:50 p.m. EDT—25° ♈ 51'

November 3

Total Solar Eclipse at 7:46 a.m. EST—11° ♏ 16'

2013 Retrograde Planets

Planet	Begin	Eastern	Pacific	End	Eastern	Pacific
Jupiter	10/04/12	9:18 am	**6:18 am**	01/30/13	6:37 am	**3:37 am**
Saturn	02/18/13	12:02 pm	**9:02 am**	07/07/13		**10:12 pm**
Saturn	02/18/13	12:02 pm	**9:02 am**	07/08/13	1:12 am	
Mercury	02/23/13	4:41 am	**1:41 am**	03/17/13	4:03 pm	**1:03 pm**
Pluto	04/12/13	3:34 pm	**12:34 pm**	09/20/13	11:29 am	**8:29 am**
Neptune	06/07/13	4:24 am	**1:24 am**	11/13/13	1:42 pm	**10:42 am**
Mercury	06/26/13	9:08 am	**6:08 am**	07/20/13	2:22 pm	**11:22 am**
Uranus	07/17/13	1:20 pm	**10:20 am**	12/17/13	12:40 pm	**9:40 am**
Mercury	10/21/13	6:29 am	**3:29 am**	11/10/13	4:12 pm	**1:12 pm**
Jupiter	11/06/13		**9:03 pm**	03/06/14	5:42 am	**2:42 am**
Jupiter	11/07/13	12:03 am		03/06/14	5:42 am	**2:42 am**
Venus	12/21/13	4:53 pm	**1:53 pm**	01/31/14	3:49 pm	**12:49 pm**

Eastern Time in plain type, **Pacific Time in bold type**

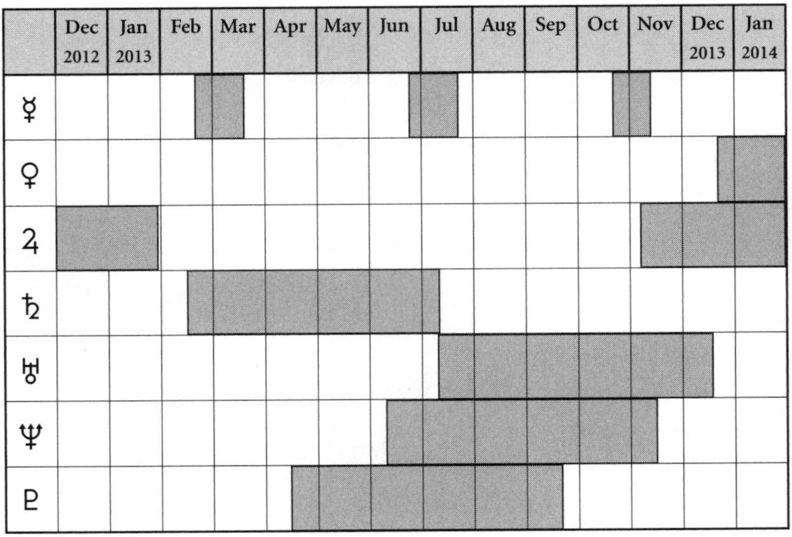

	Dec 2012	Jan 2013	Feb	Mar	Apr	May	Jun	Jul	Aug	Sep	Oct	Nov	Dec 2013	Jan 2014
☿														
♀														
♃														
♄														
♅														
♆														
♇														

2013 Planetary Phenomena

Information on Uranus and Neptune assumes the use of a telescope. Resource: *Astronomical Phenomena for the Year 2013*, prepared by the U.S. Naval Observatory and the Royal Greenwich Observatory. The dates are expressed in Universal Time and must be converted to your Local Mean Time. (See the World Map of Time Zones on page 191.)

Planets Visible in Morning and Evening

Planet	Morning	Evening
Venus	Jan 1–Feb 16	May 7–Dec 31
Mars	June 20–Dec 31	Jan 1–Feb 9
Jupiter	July 4–Dec 31	Jan 1–June 5
Saturn	Jan 1–April 28 Nov 24–Dec 31	April 28–Oct 20

Mercury

Mercury can only be seen low in the east before sunrise or low in the west after sunset. It is visible in the mornings between the following approximate dates: January 1 to January 2, March 11 to May 4, July 19 to August 16, and November 8 to December 12.

Venus

Venus is a brilliant object in the morning sky from the beginning of the year until mid-February, when it becomes too close to the Sun for observation. At the end of the first week of May it reappears in the evening sky, where it stays until the end of the year.

Mars

Mars can be seen in the evening sky in Capricornus and Aquarius from late January until the second week of February, when it becomes too close to the Sun for observation. It reappears in the morning sky during the second half of June in Taurus and moves into Gemini from mid-July. It remains in the morning sky for the rest of the year, moving into Cancer in late August, Leo in late September, and Virgo at the end of November.

Jupiter

Jupiter is in Taurus at the beginning of the year and can be seen for more than half the night until late February, after which it can be seen only in the evening sky. In the first week of June it becomes too close to the Sun for observation. It reappears in the morning sky in early July in Gemini, where it remains for the rest of the year.

Saturn

Saturn rises shortly after midnight at the beginning of the year in Libra, passes into Virgo in mid-May, and re-enters Libra in early September. It is at opposition on April 28, when it can be seen throughout the night, and is visible only in the evening sky from late July until mid-October. It then becomes too close to the Sun for observation until it reappears in the second half of November and can be seen in the morning sky for the rest of the year.

Uranus

Uranus is visible at the beginning of the year in the evening sky in Pisces. It moves into Cetus in the first week of March and then becomes too close to the Sun for observation. In mid-April it reapears in the morning sky in Pisces, close to the border with Cetus. For the remainder of the year Uranus can be found along the border of Cetus and Pisces.

Neptune

Neptune is visible at the beginning of the year in the evening sky in Aquarius and remains in the constellation throughout the year. At the beginning of February it becomes too close to the Sun for observation and reappears in mid-March in the morning sky. From late November it can be seen only in the evening sky.

2013 Weekly Forecasts

by Pam Ciampi

Overview of 2013:
Water, Water Everywhere and the Saving Grace of Feminine Energy

In 2013 a majority of planets will be traveling through the zodiac in water signs: Cancer, Scorpio, and Pisces. Water is the essential ingredient of every life form on earth. It not only covers 70 percent of the earth's surface, it also makes up 70 percent of the human body. Astrological wisdom tells us that the element of water symbolizes the feminine or lunar side of life, the side that calls attention to inner wisdom, women, and healing. The majority of planets in water energies in 2013 is an indication of a major shift away from solar/masculine power towards lunar/feminine power. This water emphasis also signals that women (or men with a prominent feminine component) will rise to positions of power this year. Other possibilities of this water emphasis include global healing, rising sea levels and flooding, and skyrocketing prices of liquids like oil, gas, and water.

Planets and Points in Feminine/Water Signs This Year

- Moon's North Node in Scorpio, all year
- Mercury retrogrades in Pisces, Cancer, Scorpio
- Jupiter in Cancer, half the year
- Saturn in Scorpio until 2015
- Neptune in Pisces until 2026
- Grand Sextile in earth and water signs in July

Although the Moon's nodes are not planets, they represent important Sun/Moon crossing points. Traditionally the Moon's North Node points to the future. When the North Node is in watery Scorpio, as it is this year, it indicates that we are reaching an intensely powerful and serious crisis point where change is inevitable.

The Mercury retrogrades in water this year will triple the time Mercury spends in water signs, where our mental energy and style of communication are based on emotions rather than reason.

Although Jupiter in watery Cancer gives a boost to women, families, and the real estate market, Saturn in Scorpio symbolizes continued economic contraction and tough austerity measures. In a watery zodiac sign like Scorpio, Saturn raises the possibility of intense behind-the-scenes power struggles involving liquid resources like oil, gas, and water.

Neptune's long journey through watery Pisces (2011–2026) continues to highlight national healthcare, big pharmeutical companies, and liquid resources. Neptune in Pisces will also affect (for good or ill) floods, films, spirituality, religious convictions, mental health disorders, and, most dangerously, the capacity for denial.

The year 2013 will also be host to three (of twelve) Uranus/Pluto firefights that began last year and will continue until 2015. These Uranus/Pluto squares indicate a continuation of global protests and political rebellions that have already characterized the past few years. With an overemphasis on emotions combined with unpredictable violence, it's not hard to see that 2013 could possibly be a year when the floodgates open. But every dark cloud has a silver lining, and there is a very, very bright sign in the sky to look forward to at the end of July. That's when a rare alignment called a Grand Sextile will occur. Seven out of ten planets will be actively involved in this positive design. The Grand Sextile is composed of six sextiles, two easy Grand Trines, and three oppositions. Since all the players in this Grand Sextile are either in earth or water signs, this alignment is a sign that the feminine force is gracing the planet with a tremendous flow of healing energy. In ancient tradition, water was ritualistically used to wash away the sins of the past. If all goes well, this will be done in a gentle manner, so there won't be a need to recreate Noah's ark!

Note to 2013 wedding planners: Avoid the middle to end of December 2013 when Venus is retrograde as well as in a noncompatible sign.

Similarities in Planetary Line-ups in 1965 and 2013

1965 Uranus conjunct Pluto in Virgo (feminine)
Neptune in Scorpio (feminine)
Saturn in Pisces (feminine)

2013 Uranus square Pluto in Capricorn (feminine)
Neptune in Pisces (feminine)
Saturn in Scorpio (feminine)

January 1–5

As seen in the overview, 2013 looks like a year filled with geopolitical transitions, continuing financial and health crises, and environmental changes that have been rocking the world since the beginning of the twenty-tens. That's why it's wonderful news that Friday, January 4, is host to an easy trine between fearless Mars and optimistic Jupiter. Both Mars and Jupiter are in air signs, and this type of fortunate aspect sends out a special blend of inner hope and faith that, as bad as it seems, everything can and will work out in the end. The musical *Hair* back in the sixties said it all: "... when Jupiter aligns with Mars, then peace will guide the planets and love will steer the stars." Although Jupiter is retrograde, in only a few more weeks it will begin to move forward again.

January 6–12

If last week was full of hope, this week is full of challenges. With a Mercury/Pluto connection, a difficult sign change for Venus, and a somber New Moon on tap, this is a week to get with the program and activate your common sense button. On Sunday, January 6, when Mercury joins with secretive Pluto, it's time to deal with those skeletons that are lurking in your psychological closet. Then on Tuesday, January 8, naturally sensuous Venus begins a four-week period of cooling its heels in somber Capricorn. Venus is uncomfortable in Capricorn, where its worth is judged on its usefulness rather than on its beauty. The Capricorn New Moon on Friday, January 11, rings the same practical, if joyless, note. Since this month's New Moon also has five planets in Capricorn, the emphasis is on being productive, but the pace this month is very down tempo. Every New Moon signifies a time when the unconscious lunar forces are at rest and at their monthly low. Since all seeds have a better chance of sprouting when the Moon is waxing, the two weeks following the New Moon are the best times of the month to initiate any kind of start-up. Since it takes time for any start-up to take root under a Capricorn New Moon, this is a month to move slowly and pace yourself. Success is merely delayed, not denied. If you don't happen to be near a calendar and are wondering how to tell if the Moon is waxing or waning, here's an easy solution. If you make a *C* with your right hand (by cupping your hand) and it fits around the crescent, the Moon is waxing and growing larger. This means it's a good time to do things that you want to grow and increase. If you make a *C* with your left hand and it fits around the crescent, the Moon is waning and decreasing. This is a good time to finish projects and to get rid of things you don't want.

January 13–19

This week features a dangerous meet-up of Mercury and the Sun, as well as sign changes for both. In the middle of the week on Wednesday, January 16, Venus takes the ball from Mercury and gets its turn at a match-up with Pluto. This Venus/Pluto combination sends love, money, and other things you value into crisis mode. Whenever Venus and Pluto get together there can be emotional eruptions, so it's important to keep your wits about you and try to stay the course. Mercury's style of communication leaves Capricorn doom and gloom behind on Friday, January 18, and takes on a lighter, friendlier tone as it enters Aquarius and stays there for the next three weeks. On Saturday, January 19, the Sun puts out a public-spirited, altruistic energy as it also makes its entry into Aquarius. With the Sun in Aquarius for the next month, the spotlight is on inventions, technological and scientific advances, networking, and humanitarian pursuits. The unruly side of Aquarius can also encourage rebellions, group protests, and disturbances like flash mobs.

January 20–26

This is a busy week with a mixed bag of tricks. There's a difficult Moon/Mars square, followed by some happy Jupiter aspects, another Pluto-induced crisis, and a Full Moon. The inauguration of the President of the United States happens at noon Eastern Standard Time on Sunday, January 20. That's also the day when a rough-and-ready Aquarian Mars crosses swords as it squares the gentle Taurus Moon. While this Moon/Mars situation is not a total deal breaker, it can indicate unconventional or weird circumstances surrounding the inauguration. The forecast for the rest of the week is mostly sunshine with a chance of thunderstorms on Thursday, January 24. It's sunny skies on Monday, January 21, when Jupiter couples with the Moon and makes a trine to Mercury the next day. This inspiring trio signals that this will be a great week for the new President (or you) to schedule important meetings. The boom lowers on Thursday, January 24, when Pluto has a showdown with the Moon. Although this opposition is a recipe for sudden emotional upsets and possible crises, the good news is that it's only in play for a few days. In the meantime sunny skies are back on Friday, January 25, when the Sun trines lucky Jupiter. The Leo Full Moon on Saturday, January 26, is a signal that the unconscious lunar forces have reached their monthly power peak. The two weeks following this lunar power day are the best times of the month to fast, detox, or get rid of bad habits. The theme of the Leo Full Moon is to find a balance between the needs of the group and your needs within the group. Although Saturn squares this Full Moon, both the Sun and Moon still enjoy good aspects with Jupiter. The mixed alignments this week are like a yellow traffic light: you're good to go, but use caution.

January 27–February 2

Because Jupiter changes direction and both Mars and Venus change zodiac signs to the tune of an easy Sun/Moon trine, this week looks like it's a good time for you to make some changes. It starts off on Wednesday, January 30, when Jupiter ends its retrograde and moves into forward gear. This positive movement is a sign of growth and increase. The Sun/Moon air trine on Thursday, January 31, adds

Aquarian innovation and Libran vision to this bit of Jupiter luck. Unfortunately the bad fairy crashes the party on Friday, February 1, when fiery Mars enters the hidden waters of Pisces. When a fiery planet like Mars enters a water sign, it creates a dangerous situation because water puts out fire. The aggressive energy of Mars goes underwater, where it is famous for hidden strategies, secret plans, and passive-aggressive behavior. This difficult dynamic will continue for the next six weeks. On that same day, February 1, Venus also changes sign and enters cool-headed Aquarius, so futuristic ideas and altruistic ideals will be on the front burner for the next month. Venus/Aquarius is a calming counterpoint to the Mars/Pisces combination and will help to keep things from reaching the boiling point.

February 3–9

The news this week includes a dangerous Pisces trio, a sign change for Mercury, and some helpful advice from Saturn. Danger is still in the air from the passive-aggressive energies of Mars in Pisces as it meets up with shadowy Neptune on Monday, February 4. For the most evolved souls among us this alignment may serve to strengthen spiritual muscles; for the rest of us this can be a week when fears run rampant and send us looking for the nearest guilty pleasure to ease the pain. Because Pisces rules the unseen world, this Mars/Neptune alignment carries a warning label to be extra careful around drugs, alcohol, and other harmful chemicals or toxic gases. Mercury puts its two cents into this mix on Tuesday, February 5, when it joins the Pisces show and communications turn to pea soup. Reasonable Mercury is the most uncomfortable in emotional Pisces of all the zodiac signs. That's a crying shame, because due to a retrograde later on this month, Mercury's murky trek through Pisces will be extended from three weeks to over two months. A square from Jupiter to this Mercury/Mars/Neptune trio on Saturday, February 9, makes it even easier to shut our eyes to reality and to be infused with a magical, if unrealistic, optimism. The planetary antidote for making sense of all this confusion is (surprise) poor old much-maligned Saturn. The best of Saturn in Scorpio is like a Navy SEAL: unbelievably tough, brave, and willing to take risks in confusing and dangerous waters.

If you use this side of Saturn, you'll be cool enough to see through the Pisces veil of illusions and denial and tough enough to get the job done.

February 10–16

Fireworks are on tap this week when the New Moon on Sunday, February 10, welcomes in the Chinese Year of the Fire Snake. In Chinese astrology the new year is always celebrated at the Aquarius New Moon. The date for Chinese New Year is different every year, because the Aquarius New Moon takes place on different days and sometimes even in different months. Besides being the Year of the Fire Snake, 2013 is also a water year in Chinese astrology. Because feminine water puts out fire, the masculine power of the Fire Snake is said to be weak this year. How this will play out is anyone's guess, but the Fire Snake/water year combination is exactly in synch with the concept put forth in this year's overview: 2013 is a year when the masculine/yang tide is waning and the feminine/yin is increasing. The Aquarius New Moon signifies a time when the unconscious lunar forces are dark and at a monthly low. Since all seeds have a better chance of sprouting when the Moon is waxing, the two weeks following the New Moon are the best times of the month for any kind of groundbreaking start-up. Be sure to sign all papers to get any new project up and running before the Mercury retrograde next Saturday, February 23.

February 17–23

This week features a sign change for the Sun that takes you out of your head and into your heart, as well as directional changes for both Saturn and Mercury that have warnings for new projects. This week the fiery Sun adds more fuel to the fire-under-water idea when it dives into the emotional depths of Pisces on Monday, February 18. This movement indicates a shift toward using (or being used by) your sixth sense for the next month. Although the Sun in Pisces is at its most positive when engaged in compassionate service, spirituality, and the creative arts, it also brings to the fore a big fantasy factor, including all forms of addiction and escapism. On the same day the Sun enters Pisces, February 18, Saturn turns retrograde for the next five months. This U-turn indicates that at some time between now and July it would be best to review and reassess your accomplishments. Since you are going to be looking backwards, this is not the time to take on any new projects and especially any unnecessary responsibilities. If you've made commitments that are not in your best interest, this is the time to back out gracefully. On Thursday, February 21, the Pisces Sun merges with the ruler of Pisces, Neptune, which doubles the Pisces vibration mentioned earlier. Then on Saturday, February 23, Mercury follows Saturn's lead when it turns retrograde for the first time this year. Mercury will retrograde three times this year, in February, June, and October. All retrogrades signal a time-out. If you're a Type A personality who considers that unthinkable, then make sure that whatever you're doing during a Mercury retrograde starts with the prefix "re," as in rethink, refine, or repair. Since you'll be in redo mode, the next three weeks are not good days to start something new or sign important papers. This retrograde stalls Mercury and will add another seven weeks to the time it will be slogging through the murky waters of emotional Pisces.

February 24–March 2

Busy, busy. Besides the continuing Mercury retrograde, there's a hypersensitive Full Moon, a foggy Venus/Neptune aspect, plus a Sun/Moon trine to make you smile this week. Because Mercury is retrograde, communications are on the hot seat. Don't be surprised if electronic equipment and gadgets seem to be full of little gremlins that make your life difficult. Expect misunderstandings, missed calls, texts routed into cyberspace, and appointment mix-ups to be as common as a cold. But Tuesday, February, 26, is the real problem child of the week when Mercury backs up and merges with red-hot Mars, and you will see tempers flare. There is a Full Moon on Monday, February 25, in Virgo. The theme of the Virgo Full Moon is to find the delicate balance between being hypersensitive and obsessive-compulsive. As hard as that may be, this Full Moon also comes with a particular challenge because the Sun/Moon are both involved in a T-square with Jupiter. Because Sun/Moon/Jupiter are in flexible signs, this T-square is not as difficult as it sounds. You will have a choice to either (a) make changes in your life or (b) go completely off the rails. In general, every Full Moon signifies the time of the month when the lunar or unconscious forces are at the peak of their power. The two weeks following the Full Moon are good times to wrap things up, get rid of bad habits, and put the finishing touches on projects that are in the works. Later that same day, February 25, ladylike Venus enters feminine Pisces, where it will be an honored guest for the next four weeks. Then on Thursday, February 28, enchanting Venus teams up with dreamy Neptune, which ramps up romance, spirituality, artistic creativity, and feelings of compassion. Unfortunately this is also a time to watch your wallet, because this position indicates a nebulous approach to money. Hands down the calmest day of this week is Saturday, March 2, when the Sun and Moon/Saturn form an emotional water trine. Take advantage of this sweet alignment and make plans to visit a spa, go on a retreat, or get away for a romantic weekend.

March 3–9

Get ready to enjoy yourself this week since there's no astrological weather to worry about. All the planets are in the same signs, with no plans for any of them to change direction. Plus there are no New or Full Moons to power you up or down and no planets crossing swords to worry about. Although Mercury remains retrograde, and all retrograde suggestions from last week still apply, even Mercury gets lucky with a meet-up and a trine at mid-week. On Wednesday, March 6, Mercury meets sensuous Venus and together they form a water trine with Saturn in creative water signs. The best part of Saturn is the ability to create structures and boundaries that form a strong foundation. Combined with a talented duo like Mercury/Venus, this trine opens the door for creativity in literature and the arts, spirituality, and charity events. This unique opportunity lasts only until the end of this week, so if you want to make something happen you'll have to jump on it. Daylight Saving Time begins on Sunday, so turn your clocks ahead one hour before you go to bed on Saturday, March 9.

March 10–16

Astrology is all about timing, and this week there's a time change, a New Moon, and a Mars/Moon storm front heading your way. Daylight Saving Time goes into effect at 2:00 AM Local Time on Sunday, March 10, for all states in the U.S. except Arizona and Hawaii. The catchphrase is "spring ahead, fall back," so make sure your clocks are set ahead one hour. Spring is in the air and the Pisces New Moon on Monday, March 11, says it's time to start thinking about planting something new, whether it's a project in a garden, in a family business, or just in your mind. Every New Moon signifies the time of the month when the nights are dark and the unconscious lunar forces are resting. Since all seeds grow better when planted during the waxing Moon, the two weeks following the New Moon are the best times of the month for start-ups. Because Pisces is a flexible water sign, the focus for this Pisces New Moon will be on making adjustments. Because Pisces also rules hidden worlds within, this New Moon calls into play the arts and alternative healing modes like energy medicine. On the same day, March 11, there's also a planet sign change when manly Mars enters Aries. Mars has home field advantage in Aries because that's the sign where testosterone is king. There's a storm front heading in on Tuesday, March 12, when this pumped-up Mars meets the Moon. This fiery alignment will create some sparks, but it's short-lived and will be in play for only a day or two. Its real significance is that it's a harbinger of things to come next week when Mars meets Uranus and the sparks will really start to fly. This is also the last week of the Mercury retrograde.

March 17–23

This week begins with two planetary movements that will make you smile and ends with one that won't. The good news starts on Sunday, March 17, with the end of Mercury retrograde. This about-face means that communications will return to normal and it's safe to begin new projects. The positive energy extends into Wednesday, March 20, when the Sun enters Aries and marks the first day of spring. This day of equal light and dark is the first of four stopping points (spring, summer, fall, and winter) in the earth's yearly journey around the Sun. Also known as the spring equinox, the first day of spring is a wake-up call that it's time to map out your growth plan for 2013. This is the best time of the year to plant the right seeds to bring something new into your life, whether it's a garden, bank account, career, or relationship. Because this is the day when there is an equal balance between light and dark throughout the world, it's also a reminder to examine the balance in your life before springing into action. The next day, Thursday, March 21, Venus enters Aries. This is a difficult combination because it's hard for a girly planet like Venus to be ladylike in a manly sign like Aries. For the next month there will be a general urge to deal more aggressively than usual with issues related to love and money. The trouble escalates on Friday, March 22, when Mars meets up with Uranus and they come close enough to square Pluto. Bad boys Mars and Uranus pack such a strong punch that it's wise to take them very seriously. Adding Pluto to the mix creates scenarios that could include sudden or unexpected events with machinery, technology, electricity, acts of God, and weapons. This unholy alignment continues into next week, and although Mars will bow out for the time being, Uranus/Pluto will continue fighting this battle on and off until 2015! This is one of those years when it's good to bear in mind that "the stars impel, they do not compel." Come what may, we always have the free will to tap into the higher octaves of being human to soften or dissolve the karma of difficult aspects.

March 24–30

The skies continue to be stormy this week under the light of a difficult Full Moon as the major Uranus/Pluto firefight (2012–2015) escalates. The Libra Full Moon on Wednesday, March 27, signifies that the unconscious lunar forces have reached their monthly power peak. The two weeks following the Libra Full Moon are the best times to detox, wrap things up, or end bad habits. The theme of the Libra Full Moon is finding a balance between what is best for you and what is best for the other in your life. But because the Sun is sandwiched in between an aggressive Venus on one side and a volatile Uranus/Mars on the other, finding that sweet spot this month might be especially hard to do. Although Aries is competitive by nature, this is a week when it seems like whatever you do, you just can't win. By Thursday, March 28, the Moon has moved out of the picture, but intense Pluto moves in as its replacement as it squares the Sun/Venus/Uranus/Mars quartet for the next three weeks. This square symbolizes a fearful old guard (Pluto in Capricorn) digging in its heels in an attempt to retain the status quo, and the Uranian new guard fighting (Mars) to try to get the establishment to change its evil ways. Unless you have recently attained Buddha-hood, you can expect life to include at least one action-packed battle scene over the next three weeks.

March 31–April 6

The Christian holiday of Easter starts off the week on Sunday, March 31, with a reminder that there is light at the end of every tunnel. Christianity is a solar-based religion and Easter is always on a Sunday, but it can fall on any Sunday between the spring equinox on March 20 (early) and April 20 (late). The formula to find the date for Easter each year is to mark it as the first Sunday, after the first Full Moon, after the spring equinox (March 20). This Easter is home to a radiant fire trine between an energetic Sun and Moon. You can take advantage of this positive symbol of new life rising from the ashes by letting go of the past and moving on to something new and exciting this week. Monday, April 1, is April Fools' Day and also marks the beginning of the first eclipse season of the year. There will be one Lunar Eclipse in April and both a Lunar and a Solar Eclipse in May. No fooling around there.

April 7–13

This week is all about doing something new and different with a New Moon, a change of direction for Pluto that might make you think twice, and a sign change for Mercury that gets you moving. The fiery Aries New Moon on Wednesday, April 10, is the first sign that it's time to get out and start something new. Every New Moon signifies the time of the month when the nights are dark and the unconscious lunar forces are taking a rest. Since all seeds grow better when planted during the waxing Moon, the two weeks following the active Aries New Moon are the best times of the month to launch a product or project, schedule an opening, or start a relationship. But there's a completely different message on the radar when intense Pluto turns retrograde on Friday, April 12. This U-turn from the Mighty Mouse of the zodiac launches a five-month period of examining your navel. This long-range forecast gives you time from now until September to detoxify your physical body, clear out your memory bank, and recycle or discard anything that's not being used. The message of the creative Aries New Moon and the navel-gazing Pluto retrograde is that it's okay to start something as long as you keep in mind the long-range forecast to dig deeply. The last piece of this week's puzzle falls into place on Saturday, April 13, when Mercury makes a sign swap that kick-starts the action again as it enters Aries. Communications can get hot for the next three weeks when the lightning speed of Aries fire combines with Mercury's weakness for speaking first and thinking later.

April 14–20

This week Mercury/Aries will join up with exciting Uranus, but Taurus is the real star of the show with three planets moving into its territory. Sensuous Venus starts things off as it enters Taurus on Monday, April 15, where it will enjoy home field advantage for the next month. Venus and Taurus are simpatico because they share the same love for art and music, harmony, natural beauty, and personal security. This is a planet/sign combo that could give a course on how to hold on to things and people you love—in the nicest way possible! At the end of the week on Friday, April 19, the Sun also enters earthy Taurus. Like a bull, the Sun in Taurus is extremely powerful but is slow to change direction and set in its ways. Because creativity is high and very focused, the next month while the Sun is in Taurus is a great time for being productive. Mercury joins together with Uranus early on Saturday, April 20, which should electrify your brainwaves as well as the airwaves. On that same day Mars also enters Taurus, where unfortunately it doesn't make as pretty a picture as Venus and the Sun. Although willing to work hard and tow the line, manly Mars is like a bull in a china shop in this ladylike sign. Aggressive energies can be stubborn and turn ugly with this placement in play for the next six weeks.

April 21–27

A Saturn/Venus showdown and a Lunar Eclipse are the big newsmakers this week. The showdown between a strong Venus in its own sign and a grim Saturn on Monday, April 22, will make for a difficult two weeks ahead. Because the Venus/Saturn opposition signifies loss and fear of loss, this combination can also bring a tendency to be closed and selfish with the things you value most, like love and money. So while you're busy concentrating on watching your wallet, don't forget to keep on eye on the door to your heart. The Scorpio Full Moon on Thursday, April 25, signifies the time of the month when the lunar forces are at their power peak. In Scorpio this Full Moon gives you an opportunity to find a balance point between dealing with the transformative experiences confronting the world today and trying to make your life secure. This Full Moon is very special because it's also the first Lunar Eclipse of the year. Eclipses are rare and take place only when the Sun/Moon/Earth are in a unique alignment that results in a darkening of the Moon. The path of this eclipse will be visible from Europe, Africa, Asia, and Australia. Eclipses are very powerful Full Moons that open up times when change can occur. Although Lunar Eclipses don't have as strong an influence as Solar Eclipses, if your birthday is today (April 25) or October 25, this eclipse could be a sign that there will be an important turning point in your life during the next six months.

April 28–May 4

This busy week starts off with Saturn making its closest approach to Earth this year, an unusual number of sign changes on tap for Mercury, and one window of opportunity. On Sunday, April 28, serious Saturn sits opposite the Sun as it makes its once-a-year closest approach to Earth. While this Saturn/Sun showdown does not deny success, it is an indication of blockages or a slowdown in general affairs. Keep this in mind when the first window of opportunity to solve your problems opens up the next day. On Monday, April 29, the Sun and Moon form a productive earth trine that makes it easy to take advantage of the flow of energy and to calmly and rationally address any obstacles in your path. Communications and business transactions will be in a constant state of flux for the next four weeks because on Wednesday, May 1, speedy Mercury moves into Taurus for the first of its three sign changes this month. Mercury will hit this triple-header this year during three different months—May, September, and December! Is it any wonder that it seems like time is going by faster and faster? With changeable Mercury revving into so many different gears, this is probably *not* a good month to set anything in stone.

May 5–11

All the significant events of this week happen on Thursday, May 9. The first act is a sign change for Venus, and the main event is the first Solar Eclipse of the year. Early on Thursday, Venus moves out of earthy Taurus and into airy Gemini. Because Gemini has a much lighter energy, it also has a much shorter attention span. Venus in Gemini focuses values on change, whether it's a new look or new neighbors, siblings, roommates, jobs, or short trips. Since Gemini is a dual sign with two different sides, it will be easier for the next four weeks to do two things than to concentrate on one. Later that day, May 9, there will be a difficult Solar Eclipse on the Taurus New Moon. A Solar Eclipse is special kind of New Moon where the Sun/Moon/Earth are in a unique alignment that causes the Moon to cast a shadow on the Sun. This Solar Eclipse is expected to be more powerful than the Lunar Eclipse on April 25 because its influence also extends to global leaders, nobility, and heads of state. In general, the Taurus New Moon focuses Sun/Moon energy on the natural environment and on finding new ways to be secure. But because Saturn is involved and because this New Moon is also a Solar Eclipse, this is an indication that deep-seated fears about economic security are on the rise all over the world. This is an annular eclipse, which means that the Moon will not completely cover the Sun. The shadow cast by this eclipse will pass over Australia, New Zealand, and the Central Pacific, where it is expected to have the greatest influence. If your birthday is today (May 9) or November 9, this eclipse could indicate an important turning point in your life sometime in the next twelve months.

May 12–18

News flash: scientists have predicted that solar flares will reach an eleven-year peak of solar surges during May. If the outbursts of predicted electromagnetic energy reach the earth's magnetic field, the power surge could cause chaos through extensive damage to electronic and wireless infrastructures throughout the world. It is also a possibility that such a heavy surge could cause blackouts, electric grid failures, loss of GPS tracking systems, and loss of cell phone towers and satellite communications across the globe. Such a phenomenon occurs about once every 100 years. The last big flare was called the "Carrington Event" in 1859, but of course at that time we weren't tied into the grid as we are these days, when it would be a global catastrophe. While it's impossible to know if the flares will be as severe as predicted, you might want to follow the advice of a top NASA representative: "Go ahead and mark your calendar for May 2013, but you might want to use a pencil." In other news this week, Mercury enters Gemini on Wednesday, May 15, for a quick two weeks. Mercury and Gemini are like two peas in a pod: witty, charming, talkative, easily bored, and restless. The only thing that's missing when these two get together is the ability to be quiet and sit still.

May 19–25

With a sign change for the Sun and a Full Moon Lunar Eclipse this week, it looks like Gemini is getting crowded. First Venus moved into the sign of the Twins, then Mercury followed suit, and now on Monday, May 20, the Sun begins its four-week journey in the sign of youthful enthusiasm. Restless, easily bored, and a fantastic multitasker, Gemini is one of the most flexible signs of the zodiac. This means that the next four weeks are a great time to make changes in your life. The Gemini Sun shares the stage with the Sagittarius Moon on Saturday, May 25, at the Full Moon Lunar Eclipse. While every Full Moon signifies that the lunar forces are in control, this

Sagittarius Full Moon also gives you a chance to find a balance point between being current with the latest and greatest trends and being wise. The two weeks following the Full Moon are the best times to wrap things up or to end bad habits. This is a particularly special Full Moon because it is also a Lunar Eclipse. Eclipses are rare and powerful Full Moons that open up times when major changes occur. A Lunar Eclipse occurs when there is a unique alignment between the Sun/Moon/Earth that causes the earth to block the light of the Sun and cast a shadow on the Moon. The path of this eclipse will pass over the Americas and Africa, where it is expected to have the greatest influence. This Lunar Eclipse could be a tricky one because foggy Neptune is involved in a T-square with both the Sun and the Moon. Neptune's influence tends to muddy the waters, which makes it hard to figure out what's going on. The good news is that all three planets are in flexible signs. This means that if you can cut through Neptune's fog and make the correct adjustments, most problems can be easily solved. The influence of this Lunar Eclipse is not as strong as that of the Solar Eclipse on May 9, but if your birthday is either today (May 25) or November 25, this eclipse could mean that there will be a significant turning point or milestone in your life during the next six months.

May 26–June 1

The major events this week are two easy trines and two planetary sign changes. On Wednesday, May 29, the Sun/Moon form an airy trine that makes it easy to communicate radical and inventive messages by using all forms of wireless communication. This trine is also good for old-fashioned low-tech messaging devices like channeling and prayer. Then the Saturn/Neptune water trine moves into exact aspect on Thursday, May 30, showering its healing waters on one and all. On Friday, May 31, restless Mercury moves into sensitive Cancer to make its third, and last, zodiac sign change this month. Mercury/Cancer is not the best partnership because Cancer is an emotional water sign and Mercury is a rational planet. So while the style of communication is kinder and more sensitive in Cancer, when push comes to shove it can also rear up and use those crab claws to start pinching. You may as well get used to this mode of operation. Mercury retrogrades next month, which means that this Mercury/Cancer combo will continue vacillating between sweet and crabby until mid-August. Later the same day, May 31, the pace picks up as fiery Mars moves into Gemini. This combination can produce a lot of hot air, and you might find yourself in conversations with lots of talking and little results, as well as having disagreements with close friends, relatives, and neighbors. But by mid-July, when all is said and done there won't be any hard feelings. Mars/Gemini is a combination that's too impatient to get on to the next thing to hang around and be upset. The big challenge will be to stay on task over the next six weeks.

June 2–8

You'll be hard pressed to find a quiet moment this week with Venus mimicking last month's Mercury, as well as a Grand Trine, a Neptune U-turn, and a New Moon. Time speeds up as Venus follows Mercury's speedy sign changes by traveling through three different signs this month. On Sunday, June 2, Venus exits Gemini and moves into Cancer for a quick trip of twenty-four days before hitting Leo. These speedy shifts mean that your feelings about what is most valuable in your life are liable to change very quickly, from carefree Gemini to emotional Cancer to dramatic Leo—all from the beginning to the end of June. Since June is the traditional wedding month and Venus rules marriage, these quick shifts are a warning to all June brides that your wedding plans may go through several changes before the Big Day. The next day, Monday, June 3, Mercury joins in the Saturn/Neptune trine already in place to make it a three-way, or Grand, trine. This type of trine makes this week an easy time to make your dreams comes true. Then on Friday, June 7, Neptune goes into a stall and turns backwards until November. Because sensitivity as well as intuition are heightened during a Neptune retrograde, this can actually be a positive time when it's possible to see things that were previously invisible. A Neptune retrograde is a time to face the music and get real. Unfortunately for some this reality may be too painful and they will choose various Neptune escape tactics to opt out and row on the river of denial. Another point to remember is that Neptune always carries a hint of scandal, and this retrograde may bring up a number of scandals. On Saturday, June 8, the Gemini New Moon marks the time of the month when the nights are dark and the unconscious lunar forces are at rest. Because all seeds grow better when planted during the waxing Moon, the two weeks following the New Moon are the best times of this month to get married. That way as the Moon grows bigger, the marriage will also take root and grow stronger. Since Gemini is a dual sign that loves change and new experiences, the Gemini New Moon is somewhat scattered and not as focused as some of the other New Moons. With this in mind it might not be a bad idea to have a couple of different options for whatever intention you make during this New Moon.

June 9–15

This week is a mixed bag of fortunate and unfortunate events. On Tuesday, June 11, and Wednesday, June 12, Venus gets caught between Pluto and Uranus, but at the same time there's also a Saturn/Neptune trine that might be able to save the day. While Venus is trekking through Cancer, it gets involved in a challenging T-square with game-changer Pluto and unpredictable Uranus early this week. Because all three planets are in cardinal signs (Aries, Cancer, Capricorn), the most positive way out of this tricky configuration is to take positive action. The potential for havoc and mayhem concerning your heart or your bank account related to this Uranus/Pluto/Venus combo can be offset by the gifts of the Saturn/Neptune water trine. If you keep your sights set on service to others, such as running a marathon for charity or donating to a nonprofit foundation, the trine will see you through the tricky landscape of the T-square. This continuing Saturn/Neptune trine is also the coming attraction for the really big event of 2013: the Grand Sextile. Watch for more on the worldwide premiere of this amazing celestial event at the end of July!

June 16–22

Talk about being lucky: on Wednesday, June 19, the Sun marks the last day of spring by getting together with buoyant Jupiter. Use this day for expansion and increase. The next day, Thursday, June 20, is the longest day of the year—the first day of summer. Also known as the summer solstice, this is the day when the Sun enters Cancer and comes to an official standstill for a few days. This is also a signal that it's time for you to come to a personal standstill by taking a break from your busy schedule. The Sun's movement into Cancer marks the second of four stopping points in the earth's seasonal journey around the Sun (spring, summer, fall, and winter). Since summer is the peak of the growing season and the time when the seeds planted last spring are at maximum growth, it's a good time to ask yourself a few questions like: How is my personal garden growing? Does it need any additional fertilizer to reach its fullest potential? With the Sun in Cancer for the next four weeks, there is a crab-like tendency to withdraw at the slightest hint of aggression as well as the inclination to achieve your goals by moving sideways. As a water sign, Cancer operates under the radar, but because it's also active, it usually gets its way, usually by endplaying the opposition. Remember to get ready for the Mercury retrograde next week by taking care of business now. Plan to get new projects up and running and sign important papers before Mercury goes retrograde next Wednesday, June 26.

June 23–29

Don't be surprised if your calendar fills up quickly for this week. It starts off strong with a Full Moon and ends with a gentle three-way trine, and in between these two events there's one planet changing direction and another changing signs. It all begins on Sunday, June 23, with the Capricorn Full Moon. The theme of the Capricorn Full Moon is to find a balance between your public image and your private life. Every Full Moon signifies a time when the unconscious lunar forces have reached their monthly power peak. The two weeks following the Full Moon are the best times to wrap things up or to get rid of bad habits. On Tuesday, June 25, Jupiter moves into watery Cancer, where it will stay for the rest of the year. Benevolent Jupiter and nurturing Cancer are a happy match-up, but even Jupiter has its negative side. Jupiter's unfortunate habit of going over the top also brings up the possibility of an overflow. In a water sign like Cancer, Jupiter energy can mean an increased danger of rain and flooding.

Miscommunication and confusion are the name of the game for the next three weeks as Mercury goes retrograde on Wednesday, June 26. This is a reminder not to start anything new or sign important papers for the next three weeks. Although that may put a wrench in your plans, a Mercury retrograde period also has its perks if you can push the pause button and look back at what's happened over the last three months. Emotions, women, home, and family are some of the topics that will come under review, with home or personal makeovers, refinancing, and retreats at the top of the to-do list. On the same day, June 26, the Cancer Sun forms a three-way water trine with Saturn and Neptune, giving you yet another opportunity to use your intuition to make your dreams come true. On Thursday, June 27, the Moon, holding tight to Neptune's trident, also enters Pisces to make this trine a powerful foursome for a day or two. Later that same day, June 27, Venus enters bold and playful Leo, where hearts beat to a fiery drum. When Venus is in Leo, love and money are viewed as creative outlets and opportunities for play. Although the next three-plus weeks will be full of fun, there's also a tendency to be generous to a fault and somewhat impractical. Enjoy!

June 30–July 6

This could be a tricky week to navigate, with a Venus/Saturn square and a Sun/Pluto showdown that both happen smack in the middle of the Mercury retrograde. The Venus/Saturn square on Monday, July 1, packs a powerful punch that can either take a big chunk out of your bank account or insert a permanent wrench into your love life. The Sun/Pluto showdown on the same day, July 1, adds power plays into the mix that could cause some fireworks before the Fourth of July. The best news is that both aspects are short-lived and in play only until the end of this week. And on Thursday, July 4, Uranus throws its hat into the ring to form a Sun/Pluto/Uranus T-square. This is yet another skirmish in the ongoing battle, between the old guard and the changes that are destined to come, that has become the hallmark of these difficult times. Because Sun/Pluto/Uranus are in the elements of fire, earth, and water, this can also be a sign of increased danger from wildfires, violent windstorms, or earthquakes. Things begin to lighten up on the Fourth of July when the air Moon sextiles Venus and on Saturday, July 6, when the Moon joins together with optimistic Jupiter.

July 7–13

Mercury is still retrograde and this week's lineup includes three significant events that all take place in the element of the year: water. That includes a New Moon in watery Cancer, a change of direction for Saturn in Scorpio, and fiery Mars entering Cancer. On Monday, July 8, the Cancer New Moon symbolizes the time of year to find new places, people, or things that will give you the emotional security you crave. Every New Moon marks the time of the month when the nights are dark and the unconscious/lunar forces are at rest. Because all seeds grow better when planted during the waxing Moon, the two weeks following the New Moon are the best times of the month to start looking for your emotional security blanket. On the same day, July 8, Saturn ends its five-month retrograde and turns direct. This positive movement usually feels like a huge weight has lifted and it's time to get back to chipping away at your to-do list. Saturn will remain in forward motion for the rest of the year. Water puts out fire on Saturday, July 13, when feisty Mars enters emotional Cancer and puts a damper on aggressive energy being expressed outwardly. But even though this Mars won't attack except under extreme provocation, getting hit by a strong defense is not all that pleasant either. This placement is in effect until the end of August, so if you run into someone who's incredibly crabby, be sure to tread lightly. Even though the fires of this Mars are underwater, they can still knock you out with a gut punch.

July 14–20

This week is another mixed bag. First one planet shifts into reverse, then another moves into first gear, and finally a three-way water trine smoothes out the wrinkled edges. Wednesday, July 17, is the day Uranus begins its five-month retrograde period. Uranus retrogrades are times when the desire for sudden change takes a break, so it looks like you can look forward to a few months of calm in the eye of the hurricane. A Uranus retrograde is also an opportunity to process a sudden loss or separation that you haven't been able to come to terms with. You can circle Saturday, July 20, on your calendar because that's the end of another retrograde, but this time it's Mercury. You can now expect that communications will gradually return to normal and that it's safe to sign important documents as well as buy electronics or start something new. On that same day, July 20, Mars forms a three-way trine (Grand Trine) with Saturn/ Neptune. Although aggressive Mars and uptight Saturn are traditionally known as the bad guys of the zodiac, they play very nice when Neptune makes a trine with them. With Neptune playing the part of a beautiful lady whose very presence softens their hard edges, this three-way trine is about as good as it gets with Mars providing the necessary push to make Neptunian dreams come true (Saturn).

July 21–27

Monday and Saturday are the days to watch this week because they're chock full of important celestial events. On Monday, July 22, there will be a positive alignment between Mars and Jupiter, sign changes for both Venus and the Sun, and a Full Moon! Saturday, July 27, is quieter but is still host to a Sun/Moon trine and a showdown between Mars and Pluto. Early on Monday, July 22, Mars aligns with Jupiter for the second time this year (see the forecast for January 1–5). This time both planets are in emotional water signs, and the downside is a day when tears or fears may flood the atmosphere. A little later the same day, July 22, sexy Venus enters tidy Virgo, and love and money come under Virgo's critical looking glass where almost nothing measures up. Virgo, symbolized by the all-perfect Virgin, is the hardest sign of the zodiac to please. Any gains to be had in love or money during the next four weeks will come primarily through service to others. Later that same day, July 22, the Sun enters fiery Leo, the heart and joy of the zodiac. Leo is a totally charming and good-natured sign, even when it's being self-centered. Over the next four weeks you'll be looking for fun ways to express your heart's desire. The Aquarius Full Moon echoes these same sentiments later again on July 22 and symbolizes a time when the need for personal fun is balanced against the good of the group. Every Full Moon signifies that the lunar forces have reached their monthly power peak. The two weeks following the Full Moon are the best times to wrap things up or to get rid of bad habits. Saturday, July 27, is not quite as busy as Monday, but it's still a day that's smoking hot. With a dramatic Sun/Moon trine and a potentially violent Mars/Pluto showdown, it promises to be anything but dull. Even though the Sun/Moon trine is made up of benefic planets and is a so-called good configuration, it doesn't entirely cancel out the nasty opposition between prickly and aggressive Mars and powerful, pot-stirring Pluto. But hopefully the trine might soften some of the square's more violent effects. Saturday, July 27, is a day to be careful—very careful.

July 28–August 3:
The Saving Grace

Well, it's finally here: the long-awaited Grand Sextile! Everything else is overshadowed by this rare aspect configuration on Monday, July 29. Although it's not visible to the naked eye, its positive influence is still very strong. The Grand Sextile is a six-pointed star figure (hexagram) made up of two triangles, one pointing up and one pointing down, with different planets at each of the points. It is composed of six sextiles, six trines, and three oppositions. There are seven planets involved in this Grand Sextile, and they are all in feminine signs (water and earth). This emphasis symbolizes the return of feminine energy to the planet. The two Grand Trines are healing gifts in earth (Moon trine Venus trine Pluto) and water (Mars / Jupiter trine Saturn trine Neptune) signs. The sextiles have great but unrealized potential and are like trines-in-training. The three oppositions (Mars/Jupiter opposite Pluto, Moon opposite Saturn, and Venus opposite Neptune) are the engines that are needed to make the whole configuration sit up and come alive. The return of the feminine symbolized by this Grand Sextile is a gift from the heavens to help us regain the equilibrium (ecological, sociopolitical, and spiritual) that is out of balance in the world today. In the midst of the Uranus/Pluto battlefield (2012–15), this Grand Sextile is a saving grace that holds fantastic healing potential.

August 4–10

This week features a New Moon, a check-in on the ongoing Uranus/Pluto battle, and a sign change. The Leo New Moon starts it off on Tuesday, August 6, and marks the time of the month to find new ways to be creative. Every New Moon signifies a time of the month when the nights are dark and the unconscious lunar forces are at rest. Because all seeds grow better when planted during the waxing Moon, the two weeks after the New Moon are the best times of the month to start a creative project or relationship. As the Moon grows bigger, your creation will take root and grow. The Pluto/Uranus battlefield gets bigger on Wednesday, August 7, with the addition of Mars and Jupiter as the worldwide warfare that has been going on all year continues. Mercury enters fiery Leo on Thursday, August 8, for the next four weeks. When Mercury is in Leo, the style of communication is creative, charming, self-centered, stubborn, and dramatic. With the Sun, Moon, and Mercury in Leo this week, you will want to keep your creative fires burning brightly. It's also a good idea to make sure they don't get out of hand and burn down the house.

August 11–17

This week looks lovely and quiet. All the important action happens on Friday, August 16, when Venus changes sign and the Sun and Moon fire up their engines. Venus is all smiles when it enters harmonious and refined Libra, where it is at home because Venus/Libra speak the same language—artistic, refined, and beautiful. The urge to create harmonious relationships, whether it's being in love or loving your money, will be strong for the next four weeks. Later on that same day, August 16, the Moon moves into adventurous Sagittarius and forms a trine with a brave and bold Leo Sun. With both the solar and lunar forces in fire signs, the energy dial is pointing to High. While not known for being delicate or oversensitive, this Sun/Moon fire trine is creative, courageous, and inspirational. It's just what you need to get any job done with a little bit of drama and a lot of style.

August 18–24

This should be a busy week with one instant replay and two sign changes. The instant replay is on Tuesday, August 20, when there will be the second Aquarius Full Moon (see the forecast for July 21–27) of this year. Although this Full Moon is not a blue moon, it is unusual. Unlike the Sun, which can be counted on to shine with the same intensity day in and day out, the Moon hops around the sky like a rabbit, changing size as well as light. The only thing you can count on for sure with the inconstant Moon is that you can't count on it! The theme of the Aquarius Full Moon (once again) is finding a balance between doing what pleases you and doing what's good for the group. On Thursday, August 22, the Sun enters Virgo, and on Friday, August 23, Mercury follows suit. Because Virgo is Mercury's home field, this placement triples the Virgo effect over the next few weeks. The Sun in Virgo loves to sweat the small stuff and turn its beam on analyzing the details of everything that comes its way. When the Sun is in Virgo, it's the best time of year to get involved in clearing out your space. It's also time to focus on service to others, diet and personal hygiene, and your job.

August 25–31

Between a sign of a cross, a close call, and a fire planet entering a fire sign, this is a week you won't soon forget. It starts on Sunday, August 25, with a Grand Cross between four planets: Venus/Jupiter/Pluto/Uranus. As the new kids to the Grand Cross, Venus and Jupiter bring love and money and a larger-than-life viewpoint to the continuing Uranus/Pluto shootout. Since all the planets in the Grand Cross are in cardinal signs, the way out is to take some positive action. Because Venus/Jupiter are involved, that action may be pointed towards personal finances, the stock market, and/or international banking. Unfortunately it's a possibility that the call may not be heard, because there's another kind of call on Monday, August 26. That's when Neptune makes its closest approach to the earth and appears opposite the Sun. While there's no real danger of Neptune coming anywhere near the earth, nebulous Neptune opposite the Sun can either mean deception and denial or compassion and idealism.

Either way, between the Grand Cross and the Sun/Neptune showdown, nothing will be clear and simple this week. Things really get hot on Tuesday, August 27, when fiery Mars enters passionate Leo for the next six weeks. This fire planet/fire sign combination doubles the bet that you will spend most of that time putting out fire with fire, or heading towards a burnout.

September 1–7

All systems are go this week with a Sun/Pluto trine, a Moon/Mars meet-up, and a New Moon. The Sun makes a quick but powerful earth trine with tiny but mighty Pluto on Sunday, September 1. Although this aspect is in effect for only a day or two, if you're looking to make some big changes in your life this is the date. Your chances for success just doubled, because on the same day, September 1, there's a sizzling conjunction of Moon/Mars in Leo that adds more fuel to the Sun/Pluto fire. On Thursday, September 5, the hardworking Virgo New Moon is a sign that it's time to move in new directions at work, with your health, and towards helping others. At the New Moon the nights are dark because the unconscious lunar forces are at rest. All seeds have a better chance of growth when planted during the waxing Moon, and the two weeks following the New Moon are the best times of the month to start any activity. Because this Virgo New Moon is positively involved with Mercury as well as lucky Jupiter, it promises great things if you can resist getting stuck in the details and being too hard to please.

September 8–14

With two sign changes, a Mars/Saturn square, a Saturn/North Node meet-up, and a Mars/Uranus trine, if this week is any proof, September looks like another mind-bender. On Monday, September 9, Mercury enters Libra for the next three weeks. With this placement it may be harder than usual to make up your mind, but that's only because you will be mentally weighing everything and trying to find the right balance. Because Mercury will grace three different signs this month—first Virgo, now Libra, and Scorpio at the end of the month—it would probably be a good idea to avoid making any long-term commitments during September. Monday, September 9, is the same day bad boys Mars and Saturn get into a nasty square that symbolizes intense frustration, because Mars pushes forward while Saturn holds back. Since both planets are in fixed signs, where neither one will back down or take any prisoners, the best approach may be to lie low. There's a slight shift on Tuesday, September 10, but unfortunately it's not for the better. That's when Venus enters Scorpio, the place where it is most uncomfortable. Although the match-up of a feminine planet in a feminine sign seems benign, Scorpio's possessiveness and love for revenge are hard for harmonious Venus to take. With this in mind, the next four weeks may be hard times if you are the jealous type. Scorpio is a deep feeler, but like all the other water signs, it's not a talker. Its mode of operation is to quietly wait until it can't stand it anymore and then administer a "stinger." On Wednesday, September 11, the North Node meets up with Saturn, also in Scorpio. It's possible that this combination will bring back the unprecedented terror that Americans felt at being attacked on September 11, 2001. Saturn also emphasizes accountability for what has happened since. A trine between a feisty Mars and ingenious Uranus on Saturday, September 14, completes the week with a more than fifty percent chance for some abrupt and dynamic changes.

September 15–21

The three events that spell out the star forecast for this week are a meet-up between Venus/Saturn/North Node, a Full Moon, and a positive change of direction for Pluto. On Wednesday, September 18, Venus joins the Saturn/North Node conjunction (see the forecast for September 8–14). Unfortunately Venus's light, already dimmed by Scorpio, is not helped by Saturn and the North Node. Venus rules both love and money (and everything you value) and this picture looks like a time when one or the other could suffer a loss. Your best bet is to be sober and practical and not take any unnecessary chances. On Thursday, September 19, the Pisces Full Moon asks you to find a balance between focusing on details and seeing the whole picture. The Full Moon is a sign that the unconscious lunar forces have reached their monthly power peak. The two weeks after the Full Moon are the best times to wrap things up or end bad habits. Pluto ends its five-month retrograde period when it turns direct on Friday, September 20. This forward direction means that small but mighty Pluto is back online and ready to focus on all the hidden truths that have been mulled over during the last five months. But because Pluto rules the underworld, any truths that come to light may be coated with slime. Earth changes, insurance, national healthcare, and the global financial crisis are some of the topics that will be most affected.

September 22–28

The centerpiece this week is one of the four movements of the seasonal calendar. It happens on Sunday, September 22, as the Sun enters Libra and marks the first day of fall. This is the next-to-last stop on the earth's seasonal journey around the Sun. Because there is an equal balance between light and dark throughout the world on this day, it is also called the fall equinox. In the Northern Hemisphere this is harvest time, a time to gather together and bring in the crops. It's also a celestial reminder to check in with your personal harvest. Because the Scales symbolize the zodiac sign of Libra, this is the time of year to make sure your personal scales are in balance. Is there too much of this, too little of that? Did you meet the goals you set for yourself last spring at the spring equinox? (See the forecast for March 17–23.) The fall equinox reminds you take stock and evaluate whether you've reaped the seeds you sowed. Once you do that, then you can decide what to keep and what to discard. The next four weeks when the Sun is in Libra are marked by this same need to rebalance all the different elements in your life.

September 29–October 5

This week you'll be dealing with a sign change, a New Moon, and a close call. It all starts on Sunday, September 29, when Mercury enters secretive and slippery Scorpio. Mercury has been assigned an extended tour of duty in Scorpio until the beginning of December, because in the middle of its passage Mercury goes into a stall and turns retrograde. Although with Mercury in Scorpio the style of communication can be intense and sarcastic, the next nine weeks also offer an extended opportunity to push the reset button and deal with all the nasty little things that are hidden in the back of your emotional closet. The Libra New Moon on Friday, October 4, is a sign that it's time to find new points of balance in your life. Every New Moon signifies a time of the month when the nights are dark and the unconscious lunar forces are at rest. Because all seeds grow better when planted during the waxing Moon, the two weeks after the New Moon are the best times of the month to start any activity. On Thursday, October 3, Uranus makes its closest approach to the earth when it has a showdown with the Sun. Because this movement emphasizes Uranus's love of chaos through sudden reversals, this is a week when you need to be prepared for change.

October 6–12

All is quiet on the front this week with only one sign change and a notable conjunction. On Monday, October 7, Venus turns into a foxy lady when it enters rowdy Sagittarius for the next four weeks. Venus can play fast and loose with love and money when traveling through adventurous Sagittarius. Be sure to enjoy this playtime, because after its four weeks in Sagittarius, Venus will move into hyper-responsible Capricorn for the rest of the year. On Tuesday, October 8, Mercury joins Saturn in Scorpio for the first of their three scheduled meetings over the next six weeks. Mercury/Saturn meet-ups indicate a time when more dark and depressing thoughts than usual are floating around the ozone. The light at the end of the tunnel will begin to burn bright after these three meetings are over at Thanksgiving. In the meantime stay positive, be accountable, and continue to take care of business.

October 13–19

There's a full schedule on tap this week. It starts off with an easy air trine between the two Lights (Sun/Moon), followed by a Lunar Eclipse, and ending with a murky showdown between Mars/Neptune. The Sun and Moon form a well-balanced trine in air signs on Monday, October 14. The Aquarius Moon increases your ability to be inventive and to inspire others with your ideas, while the Libra Sun gives you the ability to charm your way through anything. Because air signs are also very sociable, this is a great week for any type of community get-togethers. The Full Moon in Aries on Friday, October 18, marks the time of the year to find a balance between doing what other people want so they will like you and doing what you want without feeling bad. In general, every Full Moon signifies that the unconscious lunar forces have reached their monthly power peak. The two weeks following the Full Moon are the best times to detox, wrap things up, or get rid of bad habits. The Aries Full Moon is special this year because it is also home to a Lunar Eclipse. Eclipses are special times when the Sun/Moon/Earth are in a unique alignment. Eclipses symbolize the opening up of a channel for change to occur. The end of this Lunar Eclipse will be visible from North and South America, Europe, Africa, and most of Asia. In general, Lunar Eclipses are weaker than Solar Eclipses, but if your birthday is today (October 18) or April 18, this one could signal a significant turning point or milestone in your life during the next six months. On Saturday, October 19, Mars has a dangerous showdown with Neptune that could mean problems with hidden or invisible enemies. Don't forget about chemicals and gases in addition to the usual suspects. With Neptune in the picture there's always the likelihood of a cover-up or that the real dangers will be denied. This showdown will have its strongest influence this week. The best way to get ready for the Mercury retrograde next week is by taking care of business this week. Get new projects up and running and sign important papers before Monday, October 21.

October 20–26

A retrograde, a sign change for the Sun, and an emotional trine are on the agenda for this week. Miscommunication and confusion are the name of the game for the next three weeks as Mercury goes retrograde for the last time this year on Monday, October 21. As with the other Mercury retrogrades, this is a reminder not to start anything new or sign important papers for the next three weeks. Although that advice may put a wrench in your immediate plans, a Mercury retrograde period also has its perks. It's a great time for looking back and reviewing your life over the last three months. This Mercury retrograde is in secretive Scorpio, which sharpens and focuses communications, though its deeply critical and unforgiving nature can also pepper words with hidden barbs or sarcasm. This retrograde will extend Mercury's trek through Scorpio into December. On Wednesday, October 23, the Sun will also dance to the same powerful Scorpio theme, so the next four weeks will be a time to dig down deep. Scorpio areas of interest encompass the darker sides of life, including crime and passion, the underworld, secret investigations, business or personal takeovers, computer hacking, and fanatic dedication to a cause. Scorpio's mode of operation is stealthy, shrewd, loyal, and extremely proud. As mentioned earlier, while Scorpio is capable of forgiving a wrong, it rarely forgets one. On the same day the watery Moon forms an easy trine with the Sun, which makes Wednesday a supersensitive and emotional day. Depending on your viewpoint, this trine could make for a big plus or a devastating minus.

October 27–November 2

This week is marked by two interesting movements, one of which is celestial and the other humanmade. The first one involves the second Mercury/Saturn meet-up (see the forecast for October 6–12). The humanmade movement is the end of Daylight Saving Time. Because Mercury is going backwards, it bumps into Saturn again for their second (of three) rendezvous on Tuesday, October 29. These Mercury/Saturn get-togethers can be downers because their focus is on hard-edged reality. And let's face it, that usually includes the most negative aspects of any situation. Even though this reality-based style of communication might not be a lot of laughs, it's wise to be grateful for this opportunity to see the glass as half full and try to keep your sense of humor. It might be easy to be tricked instead of treated this year because Halloween, on Thursday, October 31, falls during the Mercury retrograde. Since Mercury retrograde rules mix-ups, this is a clear sign for parents to be extra vigilant with their kids' Halloween treats. Daylight Saving Time ends on Saturday, November 2, so according to the tag "spring ahead, fall back," its time to go set your clocks back one hour on Saturday night at 2:00 AM Local Time. This includes every state in the U.S. except Arizona and Hawaii. Although adjusting to these arbitrary time changes is often difficult, it also means you'll get an extra hour of sleep on Sunday morning.

November 3–9

A total Solar Eclipse, followed by a Venus sign change and a change of direction for Jupiter, make up the headlines for this week. The Scorpio New Moon on Sunday, November 3, comes bearing a gift. It gives you a powerful chance to kick-start your life into a new gear by finding new ways to forgive everyone, especially yourself. Every New Moon signifies a time of the month when the nights are dark and the lunar forces are at rest. Because all seeds grow better when planted during the waxing Moon, the two weeks after the New Moon are the best times of the month to start letting go of the past so you can move on. This Scorpio New Moon is particularly powerful for two reasons. First, it is in Scorpio, and second, it is a total Solar Eclipse. This is the last eclipse of the year. Total Solar Eclipses are rare and happen only during a unique alignment between the Sun/Moon/Earth when the Moon is positioned between the Sun and the earth and casts a shadow that completely covers the Sun. This unusual and disturbing sight will be visible only on the eastern side of North and South America, southern Europe, and Africa. If your birthday falls on November 3 or May 3, there could be a significant turning point or milestone in your life sometime during the next year. Because Mercury/Saturn are also involved in this Solar Eclipse, it is important to be realistic and accountable in all situations. On Tuesday, November 5, sensuous Venus enters somber Capricorn, where it will remain for the rest of the year. If Scorpio is the sign Venus loves least, duty-bound Capricorn is definitely a close second. The reason is that Capricorn is all work and no play! The bad news is that because Venus turns retrograde next month, this uncomfortable Venus/Capricorn match-up will extend into March 2014. On the positive side, this is a time when making a commitment will seem like the only thing to do. On Thursday, November 7, Jupiter turns retrograde. This is a positive U-turn that will ensure that Jupiter remains happily in Cancer also until July of 2014. Due to Jupiter's positive nature, its retrograde period is usually just as fortunate a time as when it's direct. The only difference is that the energy is turned inward. In Cancer, Jupiter's retrograde will extend a good luck period to those with mid-Cancer birthdays. (See the forecast for December 29–31 for more information about Jupiter retrograde.)

November 10–16

With two planets turning direct this week, it looks like life is beginning to move forward. It starts off on Sunday, November 10, when Mercury retrograde comes to an end. This positive about-face means that communications are returning to normal and it's safe to take on new projects. On Wednesday, November 13, Neptune also ends its five-month retrograde and turns direct. Things are never easy with murky Neptune, and although direct motion is generally a positive, in Neptune's case it means there is an even greater tendency to sink into denial and illusion than when it went retrograde! (See the forecast for June 2–8.) On the other hand, because Neptune also symbolizes the desire to be compassionate, there is always hope that the Golden Rule of Do Unto Others will come to reign over the remainder of the year. Love, money, and other items of value may be in crisis-management mode this week when this unsmiling Venus in Capricorn gets together with muckraking Pluto on Friday, November 15. Unfortunately this aspect brings personal relationships or financial crises into focus.

November 17–23

The week before Thanksgiving features both a Full Moon and a sign change for the Sun. On Sunday, November 17, the Taurus Full Moon is a powerhouse because it's the time of the year that encourages you to find a way to balance out your inner demons. In other words, you could exorcise the demons by exercising! To paraphrase the words of Carl Jung, in order to affect a cure, it is not necessary to deal with a problem on the same level that it occurs. This is welcome news since the two weeks following the Full Moon are the best days of the month to detox, wrap things up, and get rid of bad habits. While you're busy getting all the devils under control, the Sun enters fiery Sagittarius on Thursday, November 21. This entry ushers in the time of year when we are most grateful, cheerful, positive, and adventurous. The only downside of outgoing Sagittarius energy is the tendency to lose focus and go past the point of success. When the Sun is in this fiery sign you will want to be out hunting for knowledge or excitement. It is natural to shoot so many exploratory arrows that it will be hard to keep track of all of them. God bless Sagittarius, but it is the sign of the zodiac that doesn't know the meaning of the word *moderation*. It's the one sign where too much always means not enough! One thing to be thankful for is that this carefree energy will be yours for the taking over the next four weeks.

November 24–30

There are four things to be thankful for during this Thanksgiving week. The first is on Monday, November 25, when Mercury joins together with Saturn for the third and last time. Although the depressing influence of this conjunction has been in play for the last month, it will finally breathe its last breath and reach its natural end this week. The second thing to be thankful for happens on Thanksgiving Day, Thursday, November 28. That's when the Libra Moon enters into the Uranus/Pluto firefight to form a difficult T-square. Although at first sight this might look more like a minus than a plus, T-squares also represent opportunities to resolve issues between two warring parties. The gift in this difficult T-square is the rational and diplomatic Libra Moon. What better energy could you ask for to handle the tricky negotiations between two powerful bullies like Uranus and Pluto? A sextile from the Sun to the Moon also on Thanksgiving Day will provide a major assist in "keeping your head when all around you are losing theirs," in the words of Rudyard Kipling. An opposition from Venus to Jupiter on the same day completes the picture for this Thanksgiving week. This Venus/Jupiter showdown means that even though you might overdo a few things during the holiday, at least you'll enjoy the heck out of it.

December 1–7

This week holds another Mercury sign change and a New Moon. December is the third and last month this year when Mercury will make three sign changes. On Monday, December 2, the Sagittarius New Moon opens the door to new and exciting adventures. The dual and open-handed nature of Sagittarius means that this adventure could be (a) physical, (b) mental, (c) spiritual, or (d) all three. Every New Moon signifies a time of the month when the nights are dark and the unconscious lunar forces are at rest. Because all seeds grow better when planted during the dark of the Moon, the two weeks after the New Moon are the best times of the month to start your new adventures. On Wednesday, December 4, Mercury finally completes its extended nine-week tour of Scorpio and enters Sagittarius for the next three weeks. When Mercury is in carefree and optimistic Sagittarius, it is not considered a time when we are able to make good judgments. That's because in Sagittarius communications tend to be exaggerated and details are frequently forgotten. However Sagittarius's honesty is a breath of fresh air after the last few months with Mercury in secretive Scorpio. It's refreshing to know that communications will, like Alice in Wonderland, "mean what you say and say what you mean.'"

December 8–14

An easy Grand Trine is the main feature of this week, but Mars's last sign change of the year is also an important player. The effortless Grand Trine on Monday, December 9, between the Moon, Jupiter, and Saturn is in feminine water signs that comfort and heal. Since the Pisces Moon is one of the players in this celestial gift, the shelf life of this Grand Trine is limited to one to three days, but Jupiter and Saturn will continue in trine (though not Grand Trine) up until Christmas. It's still a heck of a nice handout, because this trine is a welcome echo of the feminine healing energy that was pictured during the Grand Sextile (see the forecast for July 28–August 3). But any time Jupiter is involved (even in a trine), there is also a warning that it could produce too much of something. On the negative side this could also be a warning of flooding in different areas of the globe. The energy shifts when gutsy Mars enters rational Libra on Saturday, December 7. Mars and Libra do not make the most compatible couple on the block, mainly because it's very difficult to fight when you're trying to be nice! Although prone to fence sitting and changing its mind, Mars can be its most diplomatic and charming in Libra. Mars will remain in Libra throughout the holiday season until the end of the year. Use its virtues well.

December 15–21

The winter solstice is the headliner of this week, along with a fiery Full Moon and important changes of direction for both Uranus and Venus. The solstice is on Saturday, December 21, but things start heating up with the Gemini Full Moon on Tuesday, December 17. Every Full Moon signifies the time that the lunar forces have reached their monthly power peak. But the special gift of the Gemini Full Moon is finding a balance between getting excited about the big picture and remembering to take care of the small stuff. The next two weeks when the Moon is waning are the best times to wrap things up or to get rid of bad habits. At the Full Moon on the same day, December 17, Uranus, the planet of shock and awe, will end its retrograde and turn direct. This forward motion is a sign that revolutionary Uranus has woken from its five-month sleep. It's time to brace yourself and get ready to expect the unexpected. As the dragon awakens, so will a resurgence of sudden change that could take the form of global disruptions or earth-based eruptions. On the positive side this could also include important personal, socio-political, or ecological breakthroughs. The beat slows down when Venus retrogrades on Saturday, December 21. This U-turn extends Venus's difficult trek through Capricorn into next year. If you're looking for a good date to get married during this December, the Venus retrograde is a deal breaker and Venus in Capricorn makes it a double no-no. While the next 43 days of the Venus retrograde may not be the best time to get married, it's not all bad if you think of it as a time to reboot whatever program is running your love life. And don't be surprised if an old flame turns up during the next few weeks, as that's a frequent occurrence when Venus is making a U-turn. In the seasonal calendar, Saturday, December 21, is the shortest and darkest day of the year. This is the day when the Sun enters Capricorn. It marks the first day of winter, the last stop in the earth's seasonal journey around the Sun. Also called the winter solstice, this is the time of year when the Sun appears to stand still for a few days. This is a celestial message that it's also time for you to take a moment for a personal standstill in your busy holiday schedule. Although the winter solstice is the low point of light of the year, there is still reason to rejoice. Light follows darkness, and after the darkest day, the light of the Sun begins to increase. The journey through the four seasons—spring, summer, fall, and winter—was symbolized by the Sun's progress through the four cardinal signs of the zodiac—Aries, Cancer, Libra, and today into Capricorn. This journey marks the four stopping points in the circle of the earth's orbit around the Sun. An interesting note is that one of the oldest symbols found on Earth is a cross within a circle etched on rocks dating back thousands of years ago. These findings cause us to ask if this means it's possible that our ancestors had knowledge of the Earth's path thousands of years ago. And if so, how did they know?

December 22–28

The star forecast for Christmas week is definitely cloudy with a chance of some showers. At worst this could be a deeply troubling week; at best it will be one when rational thought and common sense become your best friends. Because this week doesn't look like it holds a whole lot of laughs, it will be especially important to remember the message of last week's solstice: that even though this is the darkest time of the year, it's also the time when the light begins to return. As this year winds down, so does Mercury as it enters Capricorn on Christmas Eve, December 24, and makes a conjunction with the Sun on Saturday, December 28. Since Capricorn is the sign of endings and conclusions, these Sun/Mercury movements seem to hit the right note for communications and life in general—reserved, solemn, and serious. Unfortunately the stars are just not cooperating very well with the holidays this year. On Christmas Day,

December 25, seven out of ten planets are completely out of alignment. This lineup includes the same T-square that was in place at Thanksgiving (see the forecast for November 24–30) between the Libra Moon and the ongoing Uranus/Pluto battle. Because this aspect is repeated, so is the advice: use the gifts of Libra, such as calm and reasoned thinking and charming diplomacy, to deal with rebellions sparked by Uranus and the powerful resistance symbolized by Pluto. Because so many tensions are in play and Libra appears to be the way out, this is the week when it is important to play fair and give everyone their due. This will apply among nations and also when dealing with friends, partners, and family members or with the government.

December 29–31

The last week of 2013 finds both Venus and Jupiter moving backwards in feminine symbols, Capricorn and Cancer. Since Venus represents personal values and Jupiter represents social codes of behavior, these two planetary motions echo the rise of watery feminine energy during this year and the healing energy of the Grand Sextile (see the forecast for July 28–August 3). Although Venus retrograde in Capricorn has a Scrooge-like quality and is a symbol that austerity measures are becoming more of a necessity than a choice, it also urges us to take responsibility for whatever predicament we find ourselves in. If this seems like a bit of cold comfort, remember that Capricorn is all about what is practical, not about being warm and fuzzy. Although Jupiter turned retrograde in November, its influence is especially felt now at year's end when we're taking stock of the pluses and minuses in our lives during the last twelve months. Jupiter retrograde asks that at the end of 2013 we look inside ourselves (and not to the outer world) to measure our success. Jupiter retrograde on New Year's Eve tells us that real success can be measured only by what we've become, not by what we've achieved or accumulated. It might be interesting to note that we were given the same challenge twice before, once at the beginning of 2013 as well as at the end of 2012. Maybe it's time to listen up! Hopefully this year's predominance of planets in feminine water signs and the Grand Sextile in July were the saving grace that has helped to soften the hard edges and allowed us to see the way forward. If all goes well, our collective energies will begin to move away from the solar force with its masculine power plays and towards more lunar ways of finding inner paths that will balance and heal the myriad problems afflicting the earth, our beautiful water planet.

Best wishes for a happy, holy, and healthy New Year!

About the Astrologer

Pam Ciampi is a Certified Professional Astrologer (ISAR). She has practiced astrology since 1975 and is the past President of the San Diego Astrological Society and President Emeritus of the San Diego Chapter of NCGR. Pam has written the Daily Planetary Forecasts since 2007 and is also the author of several astrological almanacs on gardening by the moon. In addition to moon cycles she is also interested in archeo-astronomy and has written about the astrological significance of the paintings at the caves of Lascaux. Pam maintains a full-time astrological counseling practice for clients all over the United States and teaches Intermediate Astrology classes in southern California. She can be contacted at www.pciampi-astrology.com or pamciampi@gmail.com.

Finding Opportunity Periods

by Jim Shawvan

There are times when the most useful things you can do are ordinary tasks such as laundry, cooking, listening to music, reading, learning, or meditating. There are other times when the universe opens the gates of opportunity. Meetings, decisions, or commitments during these "Opportunity Periods" can lead to new and positive developments in your life. Most people are unaware of these subtle changes in the energies, so they wind up doing laundry when they could be signing an important contract, or they go out to try to meet a new sweetheart when the energies for such a thing are totally blocked.

I developed the Opportunity Periods system over more than thirty years, as I tested first one hypothesis and then another in real life. In about 1998, when I studied classical astrology with Lee Lehman, the system got some added zing, including William Lilly's idea that the Moon when void-of-course in the signs of the Moon and Jupiter "performeth somewhat." The signs of the Moon and Jupiter are Taurus, Cancer, Sagittarius, and Pisces. For those who want to understand the details of the system, they are explained here. If you simply want to use the system, all the information you need is on the calendar pages (you don't need to learn the technicalities).

An Opportunity Period (OP) is a period in which the aspects of the transiting Moon to other transiting planets show no interference with the free flow of decision and action.

Opportunity Periods apply to everyone in the world all at once; although, if the astrological influences on your own chart are putting blocks in your path, you may not be able to use every OP to the fullest. Nevertheless, you are always better off taking important actions and making crucial decisions during an Opportunity Period.

Signs of the Moon and Jupiter

- Taurus: the Moon's exaltation
- Cancer: the Moon's domicile and Jupiter's exaltation
- Sagittarius: Jupiter's fiery domicile
- Pisces: Jupiter's watery domicile

Steps to Find Your Opportunity Periods

Under Sun's Beams

Step 1: Determine whether the Moon is "under Sun's beams"; that is, less than 17 degrees from the Sun. If it is, go to step 7. If not, continue to step 2.

Moon Void-of-Course

Step 2: Determine when the Moon goes void-of-course (v/c). The Moon is said to be void-of-course from the time it makes the last Ptolemaic aspect (conjunction, sextile, square, trine, or opposition) in a sign until it enters the next sign.

In eight of the twelve signs of the zodiac, Moon-void periods are NOT Opportunity Periods. In the other four signs, however, they are! According to seventeenth-century astrologer William Lilly, the Moon in the signs of the Moon and Jupiter "performeth somewhat." Lee Lehman says that she has taken this to the bank many times—and so have I.

Stressful or Easy Aspect

Step 3: Determine whether the aspect on which the Moon goes void is a stressful or an easy aspect. Every square is stressful, and every trine and every sextile is easy. Conjunctions and oppositions require judgment according to the nature of the planet the Moon is aspecting, and according to your individual ability to cope with the energies of that planet. For example, the Moon applying to a conjunction of Jupiter, Venus, or Mercury is easy, whereas, for most purposes, the Moon applying to a conjunction of Saturn, Mars, Neptune, Pluto, or Uranus is stressful. However, if you are a person for whom Uranus or Pluto is a familiar and more or less comfortable energy, you may find that the period before the Moon's conjunction to that planet is an Opportunity Period for you. (Since this is true for relatively few people, such periods are not marked as OPs in this book.)

Oppositions can work if the Moon is applying to an opposition of Jupiter, Venus, Mercury, or the Sun (just before the Full Moon). The Moon applying to a conjunction with the Sun (New Moon) presents a whole set of issues on its own. See step 7.

Easy Equals Opportunity

Step 4: If the aspect on which the Moon goes void is an easy aspect, there is an Opportunity Period before the void period. If the aspect on which the Moon goes void is a stressful aspect, there is no Opportunity Period preceding the void period in that sign. To determine the beginning of the Opportunity Period, find the last stressful aspect the Moon makes in the sign. The Opportunity Period runs from the last stressful aspect to the last aspect (assuming that the last aspect is an easy one). If the Moon makes no stressful aspects at all while in the sign, then the Opportunity Period begins as soon as the Moon enters the sign, and ends at the last aspect.

When Is an Aspect Over?

Step 5: When is an aspect over? There are three different answers to this question, and I recommend observation to decide. I also recommend caution.

- An aspect is over (in electional astrology) as soon as it is no longer exact. For example, if the Moon's last stressful aspect in a sign is a square to Saturn at 1:51 P.M., the Opportunity Period (if there is one) would be considered to begin immediately. This is the way the Opportunity Periods are shown in this book.
- Lee Lehman says an aspect is effective (for electional purposes) until it is no longer partile. An aspect is said to be partile if the two planets are in the same degree numerically. For example, a planet at 0° Aries 00' 00" is in partile trine to a planet at 0° Leo 59' 59", but it is not in partile conjunction to a planet at 29° Pisces 59' 59", even though the orb of the conjunction is only one second of arc (1⁄3,600) of a degree.
- An aspect is effective until the Moon has separated from the exact aspect by a full degree, which takes about two hours. This is the most cautious viewpoint. If you have doubts about the wisdom of signing a major contract while the Moon is still within one degree of a nasty aspect, then for your own peace of mind you should give it two hours, to get the one-degree separating orb.

Translating Light and Translating Darkness

Step 6: One should avoid starting important matters when the Moon is translating light from a stressful aspect with a malefic planet to an ostensibly easy aspect with another malefic planet—or even a series of such aspects uninterrupted by any aspects to benefic planets. I refer to this as "translating darkness." Translation of light is a concept used primarily in horary astrology, and it is discussed in great detail in books and on Web sites on that subject. For example, the Moon's last difficult aspect is a square to Saturn, and there is an apparent Opportunity Period because the Moon's next aspect is a trine to Mars, on which the Moon goes void-of-course. The problem is this: the Moon is translating light from one malefic to another, and this vitiates what would otherwise be an Opportunity Period. The same would be true if the sequence were, for example, Moon square Saturn, then Moon trine Mars, then Moon sextile Neptune—an unbroken series of malefics.

For the purpose of this system, we may regard all of the following planets as malefics: Mars, Saturn, Uranus, Neptune, and Pluto. I can almost hear the howls of protest from the folks who believe there is no such thing as a malefic planet or a bad aspect. On the level of spiritual growth, that is doubtless true, but this book is meant to be used to make your everyday life easier. Anyone who urges others to suffer more than absolutely necessary in the name of spirituality is indulging in great spiritual arrogance themselves.

New Moon, Balsamic Phase, and Cazimi Notes

Step 7: Here are some notes on the period around the New Moon: waxing, waning, Balsamic, under beams, combust, and Cazimi.

As it separates from conjunction with the Sun (New Moon) and moves towards opposition (Full Moon), the Moon is said to be waxing, or increasing in light. Traditionally the period of the waxing Moon is considered favorable for electional purposes.

Then after the Full Moon, as the Moon applies to a conjunction with the Sun, the Moon is said to be waning, or decreasing in light. Traditionally this period is regarded as a poor choice for electional purposes, and the closer the Moon gets to the Sun, the worse it is said to be. In practice, I find that problems seem to occur only as the Moon gets very close to the Sun.

When the Moon is applying to a conjunction with the Sun (New Moon) and is less than 45 degrees away from the Sun, the Moon is said to be in its Balsamic phase. This phase is associated with giving things up and is considered especially unfavorable for starting things you wish to increase.

Any planet within 17 degrees of the Sun is said to be under Sun's beams. Traditionally this weakens the planet, particularly for electional and horary purposes.

Any planet within 8 degrees of the Sun is said to be combust. Traditionally this weakens the planet even more, particularly in electional and horary work.

Any planet whose center is within 17 minutes of arc of the center of the Sun in celestial longitude is said to be Cazimi. Oddly, this is considered the highest form of accidental dignity. In other words, a planet is thought to be weak when under Sun's beams, weaker still when combust, but—surprisingly—very powerful and benefic when Cazimi!

The average speed of the Moon is such that it remains Cazimi for about an hour; that is, half an hour before and half an hour after the exact conjunction with the Sun (New Moon). Other things being equal, you can use the Cazimi Moon to start something if you really want it to succeed.

However, please do not attempt to use the Cazimi Moon at the time of a Solar Eclipse, nor if the Moon is moving from the Cazimi into a stressful aspect. Cazimi is powerful, but it cannot override the difficulties shown by a Solar Eclipse, nor those shown by, say, the Moon's application to a square of Saturn.

If you really need to start something around the time of the New Moon, and you cannot use the Cazimi, it is a good idea to wait until the first Opportunity Period after the Moon has begun waxing. Even if the Moon is still under Sun's beams at that time, it is better than starting the new project while the Moon is still waning. However, if you can reasonably do so, it is best to wait for the first Opportunity Period after the Moon is no longer under Sun's beams;

that is, after the Moon has separated from the Sun by at least 17 degrees. For the principles to use at that time, see step 2.

About the Astrologer

Jim Shawvan developed the system of Opportunity Periods over a period of three decades, out of his interest in electional astrology —the art of picking times for important actions such as getting married, opening a business, or incorporating a company (or even matters of only medium importance). Jim began the study of astrology in 1969; he teaches classes in predictive astrology and has lectured numerous times to the San Diego Astrological Society and other astrological groups and conferences.

Jim's articles have appeared in the *Mountain Astrologer* and other publications, a number of which are linked at his Web site, www.jshawvan.homestead.com. He predicted the delay in the results of the U.S. presidential election of 2000; and in early 2001, he predicted that, in response to anti-American terrorism, the U.S. would be at war in Afghanistan in the first two years of George W. Bush's presidency.

Jim studied cultural anthropology and structural linguistics at Cornell University, and later became a computer programmer and systems analyst. From 1989 to 1997, he was the technical astrologer at Neil Michelsen's Astro Communications Services, handling the most difficult questions and orders. He holds the Certified Astrological Professional certificate issued by the International Society for Astrological Research (ISAR).

Jim offers consultations in the areas of electional, horary, karmic, natal, predictive, relationship, relocation, and travel astrology. Consultations are done by phone or in person, and are taped. The client receives both the cassette and the charts.

Contact Jim Shawvan and Right Place Consulting at jshawvan@yahoo.com or www.jshawvan.homestead.com.

Business Guide

Collections

Try to make collections on days when your Sun is well aspected. Avoid days when Mars or Saturn are aspected. If possible, the Moon should be in a cardinal sign: Aries, Cancer, Libra, or Capricorn. It is more difficult to collect when the Moon is in Taurus or Scorpio.

Employment, Promotion

Choose a day when your Sun is favorably aspected or the Moon is in your tenth house. Good aspects of Venus or Jupiter are beneficial.

Loans

Moon in the first and second quarters favors the lender; in the third and fourth it favors the borrower. Good aspects of Jupiter or Venus to the Moon are favorable to both, as is Moon in Leo, Sagittarius, Aquarius, or Pisces.

New Ventures

Things usually get off to a better start during the increase of the Moon. If there is impatience, anxiety, or deadlock, it can often be broken at the Full Moon. Agreements can be reached then.

Partnerships

Agreements and partnerships should be made on a day that is favorable to both parties. Mars, Neptune, Pluto, and Saturn should not be square or opposite the Moon. It is best to make an agreement or partnership when the Moon is in a mutable sign, especially Gemini or Virgo. The other signs are not favorable, with the possible exception of Leo or Capricorn. Begin partnerships when the Moon is increasing in light, as this is a favorable time for starting new ventures.

Public Relations

The Moon rules the public, so this must be well aspected, particularly by the Sun, Mercury, Uranus, or Neptune.

Selling

Selling is favored by good aspects of Venus, Jupiter, or Mercury to the Moon. Avoid aspects to Saturn. Try to get the planetary ruler of your product well aspected by Venus, Jupiter, or the Moon.

Signing Important Papers

Sign contracts or agreements when the Moon is increasing in a fruitful sign. Avoid days when Mars, Saturn, Neptune, or Pluto are afflicting the Moon. Don't sign anything if your Sun is badly afflicted.

Calendar Pages

How to Use Your Daily Planetary Guide

Both Eastern and Pacific times are given in the datebook. The Eastern times are listed in the left-hand column. The Pacific times are in the right-hand column in bold typeface. Note that adjustments have been made for Daylight Saving Time. The void-of-course Moon is listed to the right of the daily aspect at the exact time it occurs. It is indicated by "☽ v/c." On days when it occurs for only one time zone and not the other, it is indicated next to the appropriate column and then repeated on the next day for the other time zone. Note that the monthly ephemerides in the back of the book are shown for midnight, Greenwich Mean Time (GMT). Opportunity Periods are designated by the letters "OP." See page 75 for a detailed discussion on how to use Opportunity Periods.

Symbol Key

Planets/ Asteroids	☉	Sun	♃	Jupiter
	☽	Moon	♄	Saturn
	☿	Mercury	♅	Uranus
	♀	Venus	♆	Neptune
	♂	Mars	♇	Pluto
	⚷	Chiron		
Signs	♈	Aries	♎	Libra
	♉	Taurus	♏	Scorpio
	♊	Gemini	♐	Sagittarius
	♋	Cancer	♑	Capricorn
	♌	Leo	♒	Aquarius
	♍	Virgo	♓	Pisces
Aspects	☌	Conjunction (0°)	△	Trine (120°)
	⚹	Sextile (60°)	⚻	Quincunx (150°)
	□	Square (90°)	☍	Opposition (180°)
Motion	℞	Retrograde	D	Direct
Moon Phase	●	New Moon	◐	Second Quarter
	○	Full Moon	◑	Fourth Quarter

DECEMBER 2012 • JANUARY 2013

31 MON
3rd ♌
NEW YEAR'S EVE

☿ enters ♑	9:03 am	**6:03 am**
☽♌ △ ♀♐	4:52 pm	**1:52 pm** ☽ v/c
♂♒ ⚹ ♅♈	9:31 pm	**6:31 pm**
☿♑ ⚹ ♆♓		**10:50 pm**

1 TUE
3rd ♌
NEW YEAR'S DAY
KWANZAA ENDS

☿♑ ⚹ ♆♓	1:50 am	
☽ enters ♍	12:35 pm	**9:35 am**
☽♍ ☍ ♆♓	2:39 pm	**11:39 am**
☽♍ △ ☿♑	4:24 pm	**1:24 pm**
☽♍ ⚻ ♅♈	9:36 pm	**6:36 pm**
☽♍ ⚻ ♂♒	11:09 pm	**8:09 pm**
☽♍ ☍ ⚷♓		**9:04 pm**
☽♍ □ ♃♊		**11:59 pm**

2 WED
3rd ♍

☽♍ ☍ ⚷♓	12:04 am	
☽♍ □ ♃♊	2:59 am	
☽♍ △ ♇♑	6:13 am	**3:13 am**
☽♍ ⚹ ♄♏	6:45 am	**3:45 am**
☽♍ △ ☉♑	11:59 am	**8:59 am**

3 THU
3rd ♍

☽♍ □ ♀♐	7:15 am	**4:15 am** ☽ v/c
☿♑ □ ♅♈	11:30 am	**8:30 am**
☽ enters ♎	8:11 pm	**5:11 pm**
☽♎ ⚻ ♆♓	10:16 pm	**7:16 pm**

☽♎☍ ♅♈	4:52 am	**1:52 am**
☽♎□ ☿♑	7:08 am	**4:08 am**
☽♎⚻ ⚷♓	7:20 am	**4:20 am**
♂♒△ ♃♊	7:46 am	**4:46 am**
☿♑⚹ ⚷♓	8:54 am	**5:54 am**
☽♎△ ♃♊	9:35 am	**6:35 am**
☽♎△ ♂♒	9:43 am	**6:43 am**
☽♎□ ♇♑	1:10 pm	**10:10 am**
☽♎□ ☉♑	10:58 pm	**7:58 pm**

FRI 4

3rd ♎

◑ 14 ♎ 58

OP: After Moon squares Sun today until v/c Moon on Saturday. Good time for friendship and love.

☿♑⚻ ♃♊	3:09 am	**12:09 am**
☽♎⚹ ♀♐	6:13 pm	**3:13 pm** ☽ v/c
☽ enters ♏		**10:09 pm**

SAT 5

4th ♎

☽ enters ♏	1:09 am	
☽♏△ ♆♓	3:15 am	**12:15 am**
☽♏⚻ ♅♈	9:28 am	**6:28 am**
☿♑☌ ♇♑	11:43 am	**8:43 am**
☽♏△ ⚷♓	11:55 am	**8:55 am**
☽♏⚻ ♃♊	1:35 pm	**10:35 am**
☽♏□ ♂♒	5:04 pm	**2:04 pm**
☽♏⚹ ♇♑	5:24 pm	**2:24 pm**
☽♏⚹ ☿♑	6:06 pm	**3:06 pm**
☽♏☌ ♄♏	6:10 pm	**3:10 pm**
☿♑⚹ ♄♏	6:44 pm	**3:44 pm**

SUN 6

4th ♎

OP: After Moon conjoins Saturn today until v/c Moon on Monday. If you're up late, you can get a lot done now.

Eastern Time plain / **Pacific Time bold**

DECEMBER 2012

S	M	T	W	T	F	S
						1
2	3	4	5	6	7	8
9	10	11	12	13	14	15
16	17	18	19	20	21	22
23	24	25	26	27	28	29
30	31					

JANUARY

S	M	T	W	T	F	S
		1	2	3	4	5
6	7	8	9	10	11	12
13	14	15	16	17	18	19
20	21	22	23	24	25	26
27	28	29	30	31		

FEBRUARY

S	M	T	W	T	F	S
					1	2
3	4	5	6	7	8	9
10	11	12	13	14	15	16
17	18	19	20	21	22	23
24	25	26	27	28		

7 MON
4th ♏
OP: After Moon conjoins Saturn on Sunday until v/c Moon today. If you're up early, you can get a lot done now.

☽♏ ✶ ☉♑	6:31 am	**3:31 am** ☽ v/c
♂♒ □ ♄♏	2:33 pm	**11:33 am**

8 TUE
4th ♏
OP: After Moon squares Neptune today until Moon enters Capricorn on Thursday. Sagittarius is one of four signs in which the v/c Moon is a good thing. (See page 75.) Try to get important things done before the Moon becomes Balsamic late Wednesday evening.

☽ enters ♐	3:28 am	**12:28 am**
☽♐ □ ♆♓	5:34 am	**2:34 am**
☽♐ △ ♅♈	11:29 am	**8:29 am**
☽♐ □ ⚷♓	1:55 pm	**10:55 am**
☽♐ ☍ ♃♊	3:05 pm	**12:05 pm**
☽♐ ✶ ♂♒	9:28 pm	**6:28 pm** ☽ v/c
♀ enters ♑	11:11 pm	**8:11 pm**

9 WED
4th ♐

♀♑ ✶ ♆♓		**9:45 pm**

10 THU
4th ♐

♀♑ ✶ ♆♓	12:45 am	
☽ enters ♑	3:54 am	**12:54 am**
☽♑ ✶ ♆♓	6:03 am	**3:03 am**
☽♑ ☌ ♀♑	6:31 am	**3:31 am**
☽♑ □ ♅♈	11:49 am	**8:49 am**
☽♑ ✶ ⚷♓	2:17 pm	**11:17 am**
☽♑ ⚻ ♃♊	3:04 pm	**12:04 pm**
☽♑ ☌ ♇♑	7:22 pm	**4:22 pm**
☽♑ ✶ ♄♏	8:18 pm	**5:18 pm**

☽♑ ☌ ☿♑ 7:25 am **4:25 am**
☽♑ ☌ ☉♑ 2:44 pm **11:44 am** ☽ v/c

FRI 11
4th ♑
● New Moon 21 ♑ 46

OP: This Cazimi Moon is usable ½ hour before and ½ hour after the Sun-Moon conjunction. If you have something important to start around now, this is a great time to do it.

☽ enters ♒ 4:01 am **1:01 am**
☽♒ ⚹ ♅♈ 12:09 pm **9:09 am**
☽♒ △ ♃♊ 3:11 pm **12:11 pm**
☽♒ □ ♄♏ 8:58 pm **5:58 pm**
♀♑ □ ♅♈ 11:13 pm **8:13 pm**

SAT 12
1st ♑

☽♒ ☌ ♂♒ 3:37 am **12:37 am** ☽ v/c

SUN 13
1st ♒

Eastern Time plain / **Pacific Time bold**

DECEMBER 2012

S	M	T	W	T	F	S
						1
2	3	4	5	6	7	8
9	10	11	12	13	14	15
16	17	18	19	20	21	22
23	24	25	26	27	28	29
30	31					

JANUARY

S	M	T	W	T	F	S
		1	2	3	4	5
6	7	8	9	10	11	12
13	14	15	16	17	18	19
20	21	22	23	24	25	26
27	28	29	30	31		

FEBRUARY

S	M	T	W	T	F	S
					1	2
3	4	5	6	7	8	9
10	11	12	13	14	15	16
17	18	19	20	21	22	23
24	25	26	27	28		

January

14 Mon

1st ♒

OP: After Moon squares Jupiter today until Moon enters Aries on Wednesday. Pisces is another of the four signs in which the v/c Moon is a good thing. (See page 75.) This is a good time for the arts, meditation, and helping others.

☽ enters ♓	5:49 am	**2:49 am**
♀♑ ⚹ ⚷♓	7:09 am	**4:09 am**
☽♓ ☌ ♆♓	8:20 am	**5:20 am**
♀♑ ⚻ ♃♊	8:36 am	**5:36 am**
☽♓ ☌ ⚷♓	5:23 pm	**2:23 pm**
☽♓ □ ♃♊	5:26 pm	**2:26 pm**
☽♓ ⚹ ♀♑	6:21 pm	**3:21 pm**
☽♓ ⚹ ♇♑	10:49 pm	**7:49 pm**
☽♓ △ ♄♏		**9:01 pm**
♃♊ □ ⚷♓		**10:09 pm**

15 Tue

1st ♓

☽♓ △ ♄♏	12:01 am	
♃♊ □ ⚷♓	1:09 am	
☽♓ ⚹ ☿♑		**10:54 pm**

16 Wed

1st ♓

☽♓ ⚹ ☿♑	1:54 am	
☽♓ ⚹ ☉♑	4:32 am	**1:32 am** ☽ v/c
☽ enters ♈	11:07 am	**8:07 am**
♀♑ ☌ ♇♑	8:29 pm	**5:29 pm**
☽♈ ☌ ♅♈	8:38 pm	**5:38 pm**
☽♈ ⚹ ♃♊	11:28 pm	**8:28 pm**

17 Thu

1st ♈

☽♈ □ ♇♑	5:38 am	**2:38 am**
☽♈ □ ♀♑	6:37 am	**3:37 am**
☽♈ ⚻ ♄♏	7:02 am	**4:02 am**
♀♑ ⚹ ♄♏	11:02 am	**8:02 am**
☽♈ ⚹ ♂♒	9:27 pm	**6:27 pm**

FRI 18
1st ♈
◐ 29 ♈ 04

☉♑☌ ☿♑ 3:56 am **12:56 am**
☽♈□ ☉♑ 6:45 pm **3:45 pm**
☽♈□ ☿♑ 7:40 pm **4:40 pm** ☽ v/c
☽ enters ♉ 8:36 pm **5:36 pm**
☽♉ ⚹ ♆♓ 11:49 pm **8:49 pm**
☿ enters ♒ **11:25 pm**

SAT 19
2nd ♉
SUN ENTERS AQUARIUS

☿ enters ♒ 2:25 am
☽♉ ⚹ ⚷♓ 10:27 am **7:27 am**
☽♉ △ ♇♑ 4:30 pm **1:30 pm**
☉ enters ♒ 4:52 pm **1:52 pm**
☽♉ ☍ ♄♏ 6:05 pm **3:05 pm**
☽♉ △ ♀♑ **9:17 pm**

SUN 20
2nd ♉
INAUGURATION DAY

☽♉ △ ♀♑ 12:17 am
☽♉ □ ♂♒ 1:16 pm **10:16 am** ☽ v/c

OP: After Moon squares Mars today until Moon enters Gemini on Monday. Taurus is another of the four signs in which the v/c Moon is a good thing. (See page 75.) Enjoy a pleasant dinner and socializing with friends and family.

Eastern Time plain / **Pacific Time bold**

DECEMBER 2012

S	M	T	W	T	F	S
						1
2	3	4	5	6	7	8
9	10	11	12	13	14	15
16	17	18	19	20	21	22
23	24	25	26	27	28	29
30	31					

JANUARY

S	M	T	W	T	F	S
		1	2	3	4	5
6	7	8	9	10	11	12
13	14	15	16	17	18	19
20	21	22	23	24	25	26
27	28	29	30	31		

FEBRUARY

S	M	T	W	T	F	S
					1	2
3	4	5	6	7	8	9
10	11	12	13	14	15	16
17	18	19	20	21	22	23
24	25	26	27	28		

21 Mon
2nd ♉

Birthday of Martin Luther King, Jr. (observed)

OP: After Moon squares Mars on Sunday until Moon enters Gemini today.

OP: After Moon squares Neptune today until v/c Moon on Wednesday. A very good time to accomplish a lot.

☽ enters ♊	9:04 am	**6:04 am**
☽♊ □ ♆♓	12:33 pm	**9:33 am**
☽♊ △ ☉♒	12:53 pm	**9:53 am**
☽♊ △ ☿♒	6:13 pm	**3:13 pm**
☽♊ ⚹ ♅♈	7:49 pm	**4:49 pm**
☽♊ ☌ ♃♊	10:13 pm	**7:13 pm**
☽♊ □ ⚷♓	11:32 pm	**8:32 pm**

22 Tue
2nd ♊

☿♒ ⚹ ♅♈	5:28 am	**2:28 am**
☽♊ ⊼ ♇♑	5:36 am	**2:36 am**
☽♊ ⊼ ♄♏	7:16 am	**4:16 am**
☽♊ ⊼ ♀♑	8:32 pm	**5:32 pm**
☿♒ △ ♃♊	9:26 pm	**6:26 pm**

23 Wed
2nd ♊

☽♊ △ ♂♒	6:42 am	**3:42 am** ☽ v/c
☽ enters ♋	10:00 pm	**7:00 pm**
☽♋ △ ♆♓		**10:36 pm**

24 Thu
2nd ♋

☽♋ △ ♆♓	1:36 am	
☽♋ ⊼ ☉♒	7:24 am	**4:24 am**
☽♋ □ ♅♈	8:45 am	**5:45 am**
☽♋ △ ⚷♓	12:31 pm	**9:31 am**
☽♋ ⊼ ☿♒	5:07 pm	**2:07 pm**
☽♋ ☍ ♇♑	6:19 pm	**3:19 pm**
☽♋ △ ♄♏	8:00 pm	**5:00 pm**
☉♒ ⚹ ♅♈	11:46 pm	**8:46 pm**

☿≈ □ ♄♏ 1:42 pm **10:42 am**
☽♋ ☍ ♀♑ 3:35 pm **12:35 pm** ☽ v/c
☽♋ ⚻ ♂≈ 10:40 pm **7:40 pm**
☉≈ △ ♃♊ 10:56 pm **7:56 pm**

FRI 25
2nd ♋

OP: After Moon trines Saturn on Thursday until Moon enters Leo on Saturday. (See "Translating Darkness" on page 78.) Cancer is another of the four signs in which the v/c Moon is a good thing. (See page 75.) Great for social contacts and sales.

☽ enters ♌ 9:20 am **6:20 am**
☽♌ ⚻ ♆♓ 12:59 pm **9:59 am**
☽♌ △ ♅♈ 7:52 pm **4:52 pm**
☽♌ ⚹ ♃♊ 9:36 pm **6:36 pm**
☽♌ ⚻ ⚷♓ 11:36 pm **8:36 pm**
☽♌ ☍ ☉≈ 11:38 pm **8:38 pm**

SAT 26
2nd ♋
○ Full Moon 7 ♌ 24

☽♌ ⚻ ♇♑ 5:04 am **2:04 am**
☽♌ □ ♄♏ 6:43 am **3:43 am**
☽♌ ☍ ☿≈ 1:09 pm **10:09 am**

SUN 27
3rd ♌

Eastern Time plain / **Pacific Time bold**

DECEMBER 2012

S	M	T	W	T	F	S
						1
2	3	4	5	6	7	8
9	10	11	12	13	14	15
16	17	18	19	20	21	22
23	24	25	26	27	28	29
30	31					

JANUARY

S	M	T	W	T	F	S
		1	2	3	4	5
6	7	8	9	10	11	12
13	14	15	16	17	18	19
20	21	22	23	24	25	26
27	28	29	30	31		

FEBRUARY

S	M	T	W	T	F	S
					1	2
3	4	5	6	7	8	9
10	11	12	13	14	15	16
17	18	19	20	21	22	23
24	25	26	27	28		

28 Mon
3rd ♌

☽♌ ⚻ ♀♑	7:41 am	**4:41 am**
☽♌ ☍ ♂♒	11:59 am	**8:59 am** ☽ v/c
☽ enters ♍	6:27 pm	**3:27 pm**
☽♍ ☍ ♆♓	10:07 pm	**7:07 pm**

29 Tue
3rd ♍

OP: After Moon squares Jupiter today until v/c Moon on Wednesday. Good for socializing and sales.

☽♍ ⚻ ♅♈	4:45 am	**1:45 am**
☽♍ □ ♃♊	6:14 am	**3:14 am**
☽♍ ☍ ⚷♓	8:27 am	**5:27 am**
☽♍ ⚻ ☉♒	1:02 pm	**10:02 am**
☽♍ △ ♇♑	1:36 pm	**10:36 am**
☽♍ ⚹ ♄♏	3:13 pm	**12:13 pm**

30 Wed
3rd ♍

☽♍ ⚻ ☿♒	5:57 am	**2:57 am**
♃♊ D	6:37 am	**3:37 am**
☉♒ □ ♄♏	5:49 pm	**2:49 pm**
☽♍ △ ♀♑	8:59 pm	**5:59 pm** ☽ v/c
☽♍ ⚻ ♂♒	10:51 pm	**7:51 pm**
☽ enters ♎		**10:36 pm**

31 Thu
3rd ♍

☽ enters ♎	1:36 am	
☽♎ ⚻ ♆♓	5:17 am	**2:17 am**
☽♎ ☍ ♅♈	11:43 am	**8:43 am**
☽♎ △ ♃♊	1:00 pm	**10:00 am**
☽♎ ⚻ ⚷♓	3:23 pm	**12:23 pm**
☽♎ □ ♇♑	8:16 pm	**5:16 pm**
☽♎ △ ☉♒		**9:04 pm**

☽♎△☉♒ 12:04 am
☽♎△☿♒ 8:03 pm **5:03 pm** ☽ v/c
♂ enters ♓ 8:54 pm **5:54 pm**
♀ enters ♒ 9:47 pm **6:47 pm**

Fri 1
3rd ♎

OP: After Moon squares Pluto on Thursday until v/c Moon today. We can accomplish a great deal now.

☽ enters ♏ 7:02 am **4:02 am**
☽♏△♂♓ 7:39 am **4:39 am**
☽♏□♀♒ 7:57 am **4:57 am**
☽♏△♆♓ 10:45 am **7:45 am**
☽♏⚻♅♈ 5:00 pm **2:00 pm**
☽♏⚻♃♊ 6:07 pm **3:07 pm**
☽♏△⚷♓ 8:38 pm **5:38 pm**
☽♏⚹♇♑ **10:14 pm**
☽♏☌♄♏ **11:45 pm**

Sat 2
3rd ♎
Groundhog Day
Imbolc

☽♏⚹♇♑ 1:14 am
☽♏☌♄♏ 2:45 am
☽♏□☉♒ 8:56 am **5:56 am**

Sun 3
3rd ♏
◑ 14 ♏ 54

Eastern Time plain / **Pacific Time bold**

JANUARY

S	M	T	W	T	F	S
		1	2	3	4	5
6	7	8	9	10	11	12
13	14	15	16	17	18	19
20	21	22	23	24	25	26
27	28	29	30	31		

FEBRUARY

S	M	T	W	T	F	S
					1	2
3	4	5	6	7	8	9
10	11	12	13	14	15	16
17	18	19	20	21	22	23
24	25	26	27	28		

MARCH

S	M	T	W	T	F	S
					1	2
3	4	5	6	7	8	9
10	11	12	13	14	15	16
17	18	19	20	21	22	23
24	25	26	27	28	29	30
31						

February

4 Mon
4th ♏

OP: After Moon squares Neptune today until Moon enters Capricorn on Wednesday. Although things can threaten to get out of hand now, as Mars conjoins Neptune, you can use this time productively and wisely.

☽♏ □ ☿♒	7:31 am	**4:31 am** ☽ v/c
☽ enters ♐	10:45 am	**7:45 am**
☽♐ □ ♂♓	2:25 pm	**11:25 am**
☽♐ □ ♆♓	2:29 pm	**11:29 am**
♂♓ ☌ ♆♓	3:56 pm	**12:56 pm**
☽♐ ⚹ ♀♒	4:40 pm	**1:40 pm**
☽♐ △ ♅♈	8:33 pm	**5:33 pm**
☽♐ ☍ ♃♊	9:32 pm	**6:32 pm**
☽♐ □ ⚷♓		**9:08 pm**

5 Tue
4th ♐

☽♐ □ ⚷♓	12:08 am	
☿ enters ♓	9:55 am	**6:55 am**
☽♐ ⚹ ☉♒	3:42 pm	**12:42 pm** ☽ v/c

6 Wed
4th ♐

☽ enters ♑	12:55 pm	**9:55 am**
♀♒ ⚹ ♅♈	2:08 pm	**11:08 am**
☽♑ ⚹ ☿♓	4:31 pm	**1:31 pm**
☽♑ ⚹ ♆♓	4:41 pm	**1:41 pm**
☿♓ ☌ ♆♓	6:00 pm	**3:00 pm**
☽♑ ⚹ ♂♓	7:21 pm	**4:21 pm**
☽♑ □ ♅♈	10:37 pm	**7:37 pm**
☽♑ ⚻ ♃♊	11:31 pm	**8:31 pm**
♀♒ △ ♃♊		**9:57 pm**
☽♑ ⚹ ⚷♓		**11:11 pm**

7 Thu
4th ♑

♀♒ △ ♃♊	12:57 am	
☽♑ ⚹ ⚷♓	2:11 am	
☽♑ ☌ ♇♑	6:20 am	**3:20 am**
☽♑ ⚹ ♄♏	7:44 am	**4:44 am** ☽ v/c

Fri 8
4th ♑

☿♓ ☌ ♂♓ 12:57 pm **9:57 am**
☽ enters ♒ 2:16 pm **11:16 am**
☽♒ ⚹ ♅♈ **9:07 pm**
☽♒ △ ♃♊ **9:59 pm**

Sat 9
4th ♒

☽♒ ⚹ ♅♈ 12:07 am
☽♒ △ ♃♊ 12:59 am
☽♒ ☌ ♀♒ 5:25 am **2:25 am**
☿♓ □ ♃♊ 7:08 am **4:08 am**
☽♒ □ ♄♏ 9:12 am **6:12 am**
☽♒ ☌ ☉♒ **11:20 pm** ☽ v/c

OP: This Cazimi Moon is usable ½ hour before and ½ hour after the Sun-Moon conjunction. Good for night owls.

Sun 10
4th ♒

● New Moon 21 ♒ 43

Chinese New Year (snake)

☽♒ ☌ ☉♒ 2:20 am ☽ v/c
♂♓ □ ♃♊ 3:12 am **12:12 am**
☿♓ ☌ ⚷♓ 9:53 am **6:53 am**
☽ enters ♓ 4:20 pm **1:20 pm**
☽♓ ☌ ♆♓ 8:29 pm **5:29 pm**
♀♒ □ ♄♏ **10:42 pm**

Eastern Time plain / **Pacific Time bold**

January

S	M	T	W	T	F	S
		1	2	3	4	5
6	7	8	9	10	11	12
13	14	15	16	17	18	19
20	21	22	23	24	25	26
27	28	29	30	31		

February

S	M	T	W	T	F	S
					1	2
3	4	5	6	7	8	9
10	11	12	13	14	15	16
17	18	19	20	21	22	23
24	25	26	27	28		

March

S	M	T	W	T	F	S
					1	2
3	4	5	6	7	8	9
10	11	12	13	14	15	16
17	18	19	20	21	22	23
24	25	26	27	28	29	30
31						

February

11 Mon

1st ♓

OP: After Moon conjoins Mars today until Moon enters Aries on Tuesday. Good for artistic matters, meditation, and helping others.

♀♒ □ ♄♏	1:42 am	
☽♓ □ ♃♊	3:33 am	**12:33 am**
☽♓ ☌ ♂♓	4:57 am	**1:57 am**
☽♓ ☌ ⚷♓	6:34 am	**3:34 am**
☽♓ ☌ ☿♓	9:00 am	**6:00 am**
☽♓ ⚹ ♇♑	10:40 am	**7:40 am**
☽♓ △ ♄♏	12:03 pm	**9:03 am** ☽ v/c
☿♓ ⚹ ♇♑		**10:00 pm**

12 Tue

1st ♓

Mardi Gras (Fat Tuesday)

☿♓ ⚹ ♇♑	1:00 am	
♂♓ ☌ ⚷♓	11:52 am	**8:52 am**
☿♓ △ ♄♏	2:15 pm	**11:15 am**
☽ enters ♈	8:51 pm	**5:51 pm**

13 Wed

1st ♈

Ash Wednesday

OP: After Moon squares Pluto today until v/c Moon on Thursday. Matters go smoothly now. Write down your plans before Mercury enters its Storm on February 19.

☽♈ ☌ ♅♈	8:06 am	**5:06 am**
☽♈ ⚹ ♃♊	9:01 am	**6:01 am**
☽♈ □ ♇♑	4:34 pm	**1:34 pm**
☽♈ ⚻ ♄♏	5:58 pm	**2:58 pm**
☽♈ ⚹ ♀♒		**9:51 pm**

14 Thu

1st ♈

Valentine's Day

☽♈ ⚹ ♀♒	12:51 am	
☽♈ ⚹ ☉♒	10:35 pm	**7:35 pm** ☽ v/c

Fri 15
1st ♈

☽ enters ♉	5:08 am	**2:08 am**
☽♉ ⚹ ♆♓	10:13 am	**7:13 am**
♂♓ ⚹ ♇♑	1:17 pm	**10:17 am**
☽♉ ⚹ ⚷♓	9:59 pm	**6:59 pm**
☽♉ △ ♇♑		**11:21 pm**

Sat 16
1st ♉

☽♉ △ ♇♑	2:21 am	
☽♉ ⚹ ♂♓	3:13 am	**12:13 am**
☽♉ ☍ ♄♏	3:44 am	**12:44 am**
♂♓ △ ♄♏	11:14 am	**8:14 am**
☽♉ ⚹ ☿♓	1:21 pm	**10:21 am**
☽♉ □ ♀♒	5:48 pm	**2:48 pm**

Sun 17
1st ♉
◐ 29 ♉ 21

☽♉ □ ☉♒	3:31 pm	**12:31 pm**	☽ v/c
☽ enters ♊	4:50 pm	**1:50 pm**	
☽♊ □ ♆♓	10:19 pm	**7:19 pm**	

Eastern Time plain / **Pacific Time bold**

JANUARY

S	M	T	W	T	F	S
		1	2	3	4	5
6	7	8	9	10	11	12
13	14	15	16	17	18	19
20	21	22	23	24	25	26
27	28	29	30	31		

FEBRUARY

S	M	T	W	T	F	S
					1	2
3	4	5	6	7	8	9
10	11	12	13	14	15	16
17	18	19	20	21	22	23
24	25	26	27	28		

MARCH

S	M	T	W	T	F	S
					1	2
3	4	5	6	7	8	9
10	11	12	13	14	15	16
17	18	19	20	21	22	23
24	25	26	27	28	29	30
31						

February

Mercury Note: Mercury enters its Storm (moving less than 40 minutes of arc per day) on Tuesday, as it slows down before going retrograde. The Storm acts like the retrograde. Don't start any new projects now—just follow through with the items that are already on your plate. Write down new ideas with date and time they occurred.

18 Mon

2nd ♊

Presidents' Day (observed)

Sun enters Pisces

☽♊ ✶ ♅♈	5:49 am	**2:49 am**
☽♊ ☌ ♃♊	6:54 am	**3:54 am**
☉ enters ♓	7:02 am	**4:02 am**
☽♊ □ ⚷♓	10:39 am	**7:39 am**
♄♏℞	12:02 pm	**9:02 am**
☽♊ ⚻ ♇♑	2:56 pm	**11:56 am**
☽♊ ⚻ ♄♏	4:15 pm	**1:15 pm**
☽♊ □ ♂♓	8:02 pm	**5:02 pm**

19 Tue

2nd ♊

OP: After Moon squares Mercury until v/c Moon. A pleasant time.

☽♊ □ ☿♓	6:39 am	**3:39 am**
☽♊ △ ♀♒	1:48 pm	**10:48 am** ☽ v/c

20 Wed

2nd ♊

☽ enters ♋	5:45 am	**2:45 am**
☽♋ △ ☉♓	10:04 am	**7:04 am**
☽♋ △ ♆♓	11:24 am	**8:24 am**
☽♋ □ ♅♈	6:52 pm	**3:52 pm**
☽♋ △ ⚷♓	11:42 pm	**8:42 pm**
☉♓ ☌ ♆♓		**11:19 pm**

21 Thu

2nd ♋

OP: After Moon trines Mars today until Moon enters Leo on Friday. (See "Translating Darkness" on page 78.) We can be highly productive as long as we're following through on projects begun before February 18.

☉♓ ☌ ♆♓	2:19 am	
☽♋ ☍ ♇♑	3:43 am	**12:43 am**
☽♋ △ ♄♏	4:52 am	**1:52 am**
☽♋ △ ♂♓	12:47 pm	**9:47 am**
☽♋ △ ☿♓	9:08 pm	**6:08 pm** ☽ v/c

Mercury Note: Mercury goes retrograde on Saturday and remains so until March 17, after which it will still be in its Storm until March 26. Projects begun during this entire period may not work out as planned. It's best to use this time for review, editing, escrows, and so forth.

FRI 22

2nd ♋

☽♋ ⚻ ♀♒	8:39 am	**5:39 am**
☽ enters ♌	5:12 pm	**2:12 pm**
☽♌ ⚻ ♆♓	10:48 pm	**7:48 pm**
☽♌ ⚻ ☉♓		**11:33 pm**

OP: After Moon trines Mars on Thursday until Moon enters Leo today. (See "Translating Darkness" on page 78.) We can be highly productive as long as we're following through on projects begun before February 18.

SAT 23

2nd ♌

☽♌ ⚻ ☉♓	2:33 am	
☿♓ ℞	4:41 am	**1:41 am**
☽♌ △ ♅♈	6:00 am	**3:00 am**
☽♌ ⚹ ♃♊	7:14 am	**4:14 am**
☽♌ ⚻ ⚷♓	10:41 am	**7:41 am**
☽♌ ⚻ ♇♑	2:19 pm	**11:19 am**
☽♌ □ ♄♏	3:16 pm	**12:16 pm**
☽♌ ⚻ ♂♓		**11:40 pm**

OP: After Moon squares Saturn today until v/c Moon on Sunday. A wonderful time for dealing with people.

SUN 24

2nd ♌

PURIM

☽♌ ⚻ ♂♓	2:40 am		
☽♌ ⚻ ☿♓	6:53 am	**3:53 am**	
☽♌ ☍ ♀♒	11:50 pm	**8:50 pm**	☽ v/c
☽ enters ♍		**10:52 pm**	

Eastern Time plain / **Pacific Time bold**

JANUARY

S	M	T	W	T	F	S
		1	2	3	4	5
6	7	8	9	10	11	12
13	14	15	16	17	18	19
20	21	22	23	24	25	26
27	28	29	30	31		

FEBRUARY

S	M	T	W	T	F	S
					1	2
3	4	5	6	7	8	9
10	11	12	13	14	15	16
17	18	19	20	21	22	23
24	25	26	27	28		

MARCH

S	M	T	W	T	F	S
					1	2
3	4	5	6	7	8	9
10	11	12	13	14	15	16
17	18	19	20	21	22	23
24	25	26	27	28	29	30
31						

February

25 Mon
2nd ♌
○ Full Moon 7 ♍ 24

☽ enters ♍	1:52 am		
☽♍ ☍ ♆♓	7:22 am	**4:22 am**	
☽♍ ⚻ ♅♈	2:16 pm	**11:16 am**	
☽♍ ☍ ☉♓	3:26 pm	**12:26 pm**	
☽♍ □ ♃♊	3:34 pm	**12:34 pm**	
☉♓ □ ♃♊	5:26 pm	**2:26 pm**	
☽♍ ☍ ⚷♓	6:47 pm	**3:47 pm**	
♀ enters ♓	9:03 pm	**6:03 pm**	
☽♍ △ ♇♑	10:05 pm	**7:05 pm**	
☽♍ ⚹ ♄♏	10:51 pm	**7:51 pm**	

26 Tue
3rd ♍

☿♓ ☌ ♂♓	4:09 am	**1:09 am**	
☽♍ ☍ ☿♓	12:22 pm	**9:22 am**	
☽♍ ☍ ♂♓	1:13 pm	**10:13 am**	☽ v/c

27 Wed
3rd ♍

☽ enters ♎	8:02 am	**5:02 am**	
☽♎ ⚻ ♀♓	11:35 am	**8:35 am**	
☽♎ ⚻ ♆♓	1:28 pm	**10:28 am**	
☉♓ ☌ ⚷♓	2:17 pm	**11:17 am**	
☽♎ ☍ ♅♈	8:11 pm	**5:11 pm**	
☽♎ △ ♃♊	9:35 pm	**6:35 pm**	
☽♎ ⚻ ⚷♓		**9:36 pm**	
☽♎ ⚻ ☉♓		**10:22 pm**	

28 Thu
3rd ♎

☽♎ ⚻ ⚷♓	12:36 am		
☽♎ ⚻ ☉♓	1:22 am		
☽♎ □ ♇♑	3:37 am	**12:37 am**	☽ v/c
♀♓ ☌ ♆♓	8:37 am	**5:37 am**	
☽♎ ⚻ ☿♓	2:57 pm	**11:57 am**	
☽♎ ⚻ ♂♓	9:25 pm	**6:25 pm**	

March

Fri 1
3rd ♎

☉♓✶ ♇♑	8:38 am	**5:38 am**
☽ enters ♏	12:33 pm	**9:33 am**
☉♓△ ♄♏	3:31 pm	**12:31 pm**
☽♏△ ♆♓	6:01 pm	**3:01 pm**
☽♏△ ♀♓	9:13 pm	**6:13 pm**
☽♏⚻ ♅♈		**9:39 pm**
☽♏⚻ ♃♊		**11:11 pm**

Sat 2
3rd ♏

☽♏⚻ ♅♈	12:39 am	
☽♏⚻ ♃♊	2:11 am	
☽♏△ ⚷♓	5:02 am	**2:02 am**
☽♏✶ ♇♑	7:50 am	**4:50 am**
☽♏☌ ♄♏	8:16 am	**5:16 am**
☽♏△ ☉♓	9:35 am	**6:35 am**
☽♏△ ☿♓	3:48 pm	**12:48 pm**

OP: After Moon conjoins Saturn today until v/c Moon on Sunday. Focus on projects you had already begun, and get a lot done.

Sun 3
3rd ♏

☽♏△ ♂♓	4:19 am	**1:19 am** ☽ v/c
☽ enters ♐	4:11 pm	**1:11 pm**
☽♐□ ♆♓	9:42 pm	**6:42 pm**

Eastern Time plain / **Pacific Time bold**

FEBRUARY

S	M	T	W	T	F	S
					1	2
3	4	5	6	7	8	9
10	11	12	13	14	15	16
17	18	19	20	21	22	23
24	25	26	27	28		

MARCH

S	M	T	W	T	F	S
					1	2
3	4	5	6	7	8	9
10	11	12	13	14	15	16
17	18	19	20	21	22	23
24	25	26	27	28	29	30
31						

APRIL

S	M	T	W	T	F	S
	1	2	3	4	5	6
7	8	9	10	11	12	13
14	15	16	17	18	19	20
21	22	23	24	25	26	27
28	29	30				

March

4 Mon

3rd ♐
◑ 14 ♐ 29

☽♐ △ ♅♈	4:19 am	**1:19 am**
☽♐ □ ♀♓	5:45 am	**2:45 am**
☽♐ ☍ ♃♊	6:00 am	**3:00 am**
☉♓ ☌ ☿♓	7:58 am	**4:58 am**
☽♐ □ ⚷♓	8:41 am	**5:41 am**
♀♓ □ ♃♊	8:52 am	**5:52 am**
☽♐ □ ☿♓	3:41 pm	**12:41 pm**
☽♐ □ ☉♓	4:53 pm	**1:53 pm**

5 Tue

4th ♐

☽♐ □ ♂♓	10:28 am	**7:28 am** ☽ v/c
♀♓ ☌ ⚷♓	4:28 pm	**1:28 pm**
☽ enters ♑	7:14 pm	**4:14 pm**
☽♑ ⚹ ♆♓		**9:50 pm**

6 Wed

4th ♑

OP: After Moon sextiles Saturn today until v/c Moon on Thursday. This is yet another chance to work toward the goals you had already set for yourself.

☽♑ ⚹ ♆♓	12:50 am	
☽♑ □ ♅♈	7:28 am	**4:28 am**
☽♑ ⊼ ♃♊	9:20 am	**6:20 am**
☽♑ ⚹ ⚷♓	11:50 am	**8:50 am**
☽♑ ⚹ ♀♓	1:36 pm	**10:36 am**
☽♑ ☌ ♇♑	2:15 pm	**11:15 am**
☽♑ ⚹ ♄♏	2:22 pm	**11:22 am**
☽♑ ⚹ ☿♓	3:08 pm	**12:08 pm**
♀♓ ⚹ ♇♑	9:03 pm	**6:03 pm**
♀♓ △ ♄♏	10:07 pm	**7:07 pm**
☽♑ ⚹ ☉♓	11:37 pm	**8:37 pm**
☿♓ ☌ ♀♓	11:54 pm	**8:54 pm**
☿♓ △ ♄♏		**11:17 pm**

7 Thu

4th ♑

☿♓ △ ♄♏	2:17 am	
☿♓ ⚹ ♇♑	3:24 am	**12:24 am**
☽♑ ⚹ ♂♓	4:14 pm	**1:14 pm** ☽ v/c
☽ enters ♒	10:01 pm	**7:01 pm**
♄♏ ⚹ ♇♑		**11:06 pm**

Fri 8
4th ♒

♄♏ ⚹ ♇♑ 2:06 am
☽♒ ⚹ ♅♈ 10:29 am **7:29 am**
☿♓ ☌ ⚷♓ 12:32 pm **9:32 am**
☽♒ △ ♃♊ 12:34 pm **9:34 am**
☽♒ □ ♄♏ 5:08 pm **2:08 pm** ☽ v/c

Sat 9
4th ♒

☿♓ □ ♃♊ 10:38 pm **7:38 pm**
☽ enters ♓ **10:19 pm**

Sun 10
4th ♒
Daylight Saving Time begins at 2:00 am

☽ enters ♓ 1:19 am
☽♓ ☌ ♆♓ 8:20 am **5:20 am**
☽♓ ☌ ☿♓ 4:33 pm **1:33 pm**
☽♓ □ ♃♊ 5:39 pm **2:39 pm**
☽♓ ☌ ⚷♓ 7:51 pm **4:51 pm**
☽♓ △ ♄♏ 9:46 pm **6:46 pm**
☽♓ ⚹ ♇♑ 10:01 pm **7:01 pm**

Eastern Time plain / **Pacific Time bold**

FEBRUARY

S	M	T	W	T	F	S
					1	2
3	4	5	6	7	8	9
10	11	12	13	14	15	16
17	18	19	20	21	22	23
24	25	26	27	28		

MARCH

S	M	T	W	T	F	S
					1	2
3	4	5	6	7	8	9
10	11	12	13	14	15	16
17	18	19	20	21	22	23
24	25	26	27	28	29	30
31						

APRIL

S	M	T	W	T	F	S
	1	2	3	4	5	6
7	8	9	10	11	12	13
14	15	16	17	18	19	20
21	22	23	24	25	26	27
28	29	30				

March

11 Mon

4th ♓

● New Moon 21 ♓ 24

OP: This Cazimi Moon is usable ½ hour before and ½ hour after the Sun-Moon conjunction. Since Mercury is retrograde, use this time to start something that contributes to a project already underway.

☽♓ ☌ ♀♓	7:33 am	**4:33 am**	
☽♓ ☌ ☉♓	3:51 pm	**12:51 pm**	☽ v/c
♂ enters ♈		**11:26 pm**	

12 Tue

1st ♓

♂ enters ♈	2:26 am	
☽ enters ♈	7:17 am	**4:17 am**
☽♈ ☌ ♂♈	7:35 am	**4:35 am**
☽♈ ☌ ♅♈	9:06 pm	**6:06 pm**
☽♈ ⚹ ♃♊	11:52 pm	**8:52 pm**

13 Wed

1st ♈

☽♈ ⚻ ♄♏	3:34 am	**12:34 am**	
☽♈ □ ♇♑	4:02 am	**1:02 am**	☽ v/c

14 Thu

1st ♈

☽ enters ♉	3:08 pm	**12:08 pm**
☽♉ ⚹ ♆♓	10:08 pm	**7:08 pm**
☽♉ ⚹ ☿♓		**11:39 pm**

Mercury Note: Mercury goes direct on Sunday but remains in its Storm, moving slowly until March 26. Until then, it is not yet time for new ideas to be workable.

Fri 15

1st ♉

☽♉ ⚹ ☿♓ 2:39 am
☽♉ ⚹ ⚷♓ 11:13 am **8:13 am**
☽♉ ☍ ♄♏ 12:27 pm **9:27 am**
☽♉ △ ♇♑ 1:12 pm **10:12 am**

OP: After Moon trines Pluto today until Moon enters Gemini on Saturday/Sunday. Enjoy a delicious meal as you socialize with friends and family.

Sat 16

1st ♉

☽♉ ⚹ ♀♓ 12:35 pm **9:35 am**
☽♉ ⚹ ☉♓ 7:11 pm **4:11 pm** ☽ v/c
☽ enters ♊ **11:09 pm**

Sun 17

1st ♉

St. Patrick's Day

☽ enters ♊ 2:09 am
☽♊ □ ♆♓ 9:39 am **6:39 am**
☽♊ ⚹ ♂♈ 10:29 am **7:29 am**
☽♊ □ ☿♓ 1:30 pm **10:30 am**
☿♓ D 4:03 pm **1:03 pm**
☽♊ ⚹ ♅♈ 5:59 pm **2:59 pm**
☽♊ ☌ ♃♊ 9:48 pm **6:48 pm**
☽♊ □ ⚷♓ 11:24 pm **8:24 pm**
☽♊ ⚻ ♄♏ **9:09 pm**
☽♊ ⚻ ♇♑ **10:12 pm**

Eastern Time plain / **Pacific Time bold**

FEBRUARY

S	M	T	W	T	F	S
					1	2
3	4	5	6	7	8	9
10	11	12	13	14	15	16
17	18	19	20	21	22	23
24	25	26	27	28		

MARCH

S	M	T	W	T	F	S
					1	2
3	4	5	6	7	8	9
10	11	12	13	14	15	16
17	18	19	20	21	22	23
24	25	26	27	28	29	30
31						

APRIL

S	M	T	W	T	F	S
	1	2	3	4	5	6
7	8	9	10	11	12	13
14	15	16	17	18	19	20
21	22	23	24	25	26	27
28	29	30				

18 Mon
1st ♊

☽♊ ⚻ ♄♏	12:09 am	
☽♊ ⚻ ♇♑	1:12 am	

19 Tue
1st ♊
◐ 29 ♊ 16

☽♊ □ ♀♓	8:18 am	**5:18 am**
☽♊ □ ☉♓	1:27 pm	**10:27 am** ☽ v/c
☽ enters ♋	2:55 pm	**11:55 am**
☽♋ △ ♆♓	10:39 pm	**7:39 pm**
☽♋ △ ☿♓		**11:54 pm**

20 Wed
2nd ♋
Spring Equinox
Ostara
International Astrology Day
Sun enters Aries

OP: After Moon opposes Pluto today until Moon enters Leo on Thursday/Friday. If you stick to projects you began before February 18, you can accomplish a lot.

☽♋ △ ☿♓	2:54 am	
☽♋ □ ♂♈	3:32 am	**12:32 am**
☉ enters ♈	7:02 am	**4:02 am**
☽♋ □ ♅♈	7:05 am	**4:05 am**
☽♋ △ ⚷♓	12:30 pm	**9:30 am**
☽♋ △ ♄♏	12:41 pm	**9:41 am**
☽♋ ☍ ♇♑	2:02 pm	**11:02 am** ☽ v/c

21 Thu
2nd ♋

♄♏ △ ⚷♓	7:42 am	**4:42 am**
♀ enters ♈	11:15 pm	**8:15 pm**
☽ enters ♌		**11:50 pm**

Fri 22
2nd ♋

☽ enters ♌	2:50 am	
☽♌ △ ♀♈	3:14 am	**12:14 am**
☽♌ △ ☉♈	6:40 am	**3:40 am**
☽♌ ⚻ ♆♓	10:26 am	**7:26 am**
♂♈☌ ♅♈	2:17 pm	**11:17 am**
☽♌ ⚻ ☿♓	4:02 pm	**1:02 pm**
☽♌ △ ♅♈	6:38 pm	**3:38 pm**
☽♌ △ ♂♈	6:54 pm	**3:54 pm**
☽♌ ⚹ ♃♊	11:05 pm	**8:05 pm**
☽♌ □ ♄♏	11:28 pm	**8:28 pm** ☽ v/c
☽♌ ⚻ ⚷♓	11:49 pm	**8:49 pm**
☽♌ ⚻ ♇♑		**10:02 pm**

Sat 23
2nd ♌

☽♌ ⚻ ♇♑	1:02 am	
♃♊ ⚻ ♄♏	10:51 pm	**7:51 pm**

Sun 24
2nd ♌
Palm Sunday

☽ enters ♍	11:49 am	**8:49 am**
☽♍ ⚻ ♀♈	6:11 pm	**3:11 pm**
☽♍ ☍ ♆♓	7:08 pm	**4:08 pm**
☽♍ ⚻ ☉♈	8:05 pm	**5:05 pm**
☽♍ ☍ ☿♓		**11:38 pm**
☽♍ ⚻ ♅♈		**11:56 pm**

Eastern Time plain / **Pacific Time bold**

FEBRUARY

S	M	T	W	T	F	S
					1	2
3	4	5	6	7	8	9
10	11	12	13	14	15	16
17	18	19	20	21	22	23
24	25	26	27	28		

MARCH

S	M	T	W	T	F	S
					1	2
3	4	5	6	7	8	9
10	11	12	13	14	15	16
17	18	19	20	21	22	23
24	25	26	27	28	29	30
31						

APRIL

S	M	T	W	T	F	S
	1	2	3	4	5	6
7	8	9	10	11	12	13
14	15	16	17	18	19	20
21	22	23	24	25	26	27
28	29	30				

March

25 Mon
2nd ♍

☽♍ ☍ ☿♓	2:38 am	
☽♍ ⚻ ♅♈	2:56 am	
☽♍ ⚻ ♂♈	6:24 am	**3:24 am**
☽♍ ⚹ ♄♏	7:01 am	**4:01 am**
☽♍ □ ♃♊	7:31 am	**4:31 am**
☽♍ ☍ ⚷♓	7:50 am	**4:50 am**
☽♍ △ ♇♑	8:46 am	**5:46 am** ☽ v/c
♂♈ ⚻ ♄♏	4:32 pm	**1:32 pm**

26 Tue
2nd ♍

Passover begins

♂♈ ⚹ ♃♊	6:26 am	**3:26 am**
☽ enters ♎	5:32 pm	**2:32 pm**
♂♈ □ ♇♑	11:47 pm	**8:47 pm**
☽♎ ⚻ ♆♓		**9:35 pm**
♃♊ □ ⚷♓		**11:46 pm**

27 Wed
2nd ♎

○ Full Moon 6 ♎ 52

☽♎ ⚻ ♆♓	12:35 am	
♃♊ □ ⚷♓	2:46 am	
☽♎ ☍ ♀♈	4:49 am	**1:49 am**
☽♎ ☍ ☉♈	5:27 am	**2:27 am**
☽♎ ☍ ♅♈	8:05 am	**5:05 am**
☽♎ ⚻ ☿♓	10:23 am	**7:23 am**
☽♎ ⚻ ⚷♓	12:46 pm	**9:46 am**
☽♎ △ ♃♊	12:50 pm	**9:50 am**
☽♎ □ ♇♑	1:27 pm	**10:27 am**
☽♎ ☍ ♂♈	2:14 pm	**11:14 am** ☽ v/c

28 Thu
3rd ♎

☿♓ △ ♄♏	5:48 am	**2:48 am**
☉♈ ☌ ♀♈	1:05 pm	**10:05 am**
♀♈ ☌ ♅♈	7:01 pm	**4:01 pm**
☉♈ ☌ ♅♈	8:38 pm	**5:38 pm**
☽ enters ♏	8:53 pm	**5:53 pm**

☽♏△♆♓	3:51 am	**12:51 am**			
☿♓☌⚷♓	5:52 am	**2:52 am**			
☽♏⚻♅♈	11:14 am	**8:14 am**			
☽♏⚻☉♈	12:16 pm	**9:16 am**			
☽♏⚻♀♈	12:43 pm	**9:43 am**			
☿♓□♃♊	12:56 pm	**9:56 am**			
☽♏☌♄♏	2:13 pm	**11:13 am**			
☿♓⚹♇♑	2:34 pm	**11:34 am**			
☽♏△⚷♓	3:48 pm	**12:48 pm**			
☽♏⚻♃♊	4:14 pm	**1:14 pm**			
☽♏⚹♇♑	4:18 pm	**1:18 pm**	☽♏⚻♂♈	7:55 pm	**4:55 pm**
☽♏△☿♓	4:25 pm	**1:25 pm** ☽ v/c	♃♊⚻♇♑	10:19 pm	**7:19 pm**

Fri 29
3rd ♏
Good Friday

♀♈⚻♄♏	5:14 am	**2:14 am**
☉♈⚻♄♏	2:58 pm	**11:58 am**
☽ enters ♐	11:13 pm	**8:13 pm**

Sat 30
3rd ♏

♀♈□♇♑	6:12 am	**3:12 am**
☽♐□♆♓	6:15 am	**3:15 am**
♀♈⚹♃♊	10:49 am	**7:49 am**
☽♐△♅♈	1:41 pm	**10:41 am**
☽♐△☉♈	6:14 pm	**3:14 pm**
☽♐□⚷♓	6:15 pm	**3:15 pm**
☽♐☍♃♊	7:03 pm	**4:03 pm**
☽♐△♀♈	7:44 pm	**4:44 pm**
☽♐□☿♓	10:13 pm	**7:13 pm**
☉♈□♇♑	11:05 pm	**8:05 pm**
☽♐△♂♈		**10:00 pm** ☽ v/c

Sun 31
3rd ♐
Easter

OP: After Moon squares Mercury today until Moon enters Capricorn on Monday/Tuesday. Look at any notes you made about new ideas that occurred to you while Mercury was retrograde and/or slow. How do those ideas look now?

Eastern Time plain / **Pacific Time bold**

FEBRUARY

S	M	T	W	T	F	S
					1	2
3	4	5	6	7	8	9
10	11	12	13	14	15	16
17	18	19	20	21	22	23
24	25	26	27	28		

MARCH

S	M	T	W	T	F	S
					1	2
3	4	5	6	7	8	9
10	11	12	13	14	15	16
17	18	19	20	21	22	23
24	25	26	27	28	29	30
31						

APRIL

S	M	T	W	T	F	S
	1	2	3	4	5	6
7	8	9	10	11	12	13
14	15	16	17	18	19	20
21	22	23	24	25	26	27
28	29	30				

April

1 Mon

3rd ♐
April Fools' Day
OP: After Moon squares Mercury on Sunday until Moon enters Capricorn today/Tuesday. Look at any notes you made about new ideas that occurred to you while Mercury was retrograde and/or slow. How do those ideas look now?

☽♐ △ ♂♈	1:00 am		☽ v/c
☉♈ ⚹ ♃♊	8:24 am	**5:24 am**	
☽ enters ♑		**10:35 pm**	

2 Tue

3rd ♐
◑ 13 ♑ 35 (Pacific)
Passover ends

☽ enters ♑	1:35 am	
☽♑ ⚹ ♆♓	8:48 am	**5:48 am**
☽♑ □ ♅♈	4:25 pm	**1:25 pm**
☽♑ ⚹ ♄♏	6:35 pm	**3:35 pm**
☽♑ ⚹ ⚷♓	9:02 pm	**6:02 pm**
☽♑ ☌ ♇♑	9:10 pm	**6:10 pm**
☽♑ ⚻ ♃♊	10:15 pm	**7:15 pm**
☽♑ □ ☉♈		**9:37 pm**

3 Wed

3rd ♑
◑ 13 ♑ 35 (Eastern)

☽♑ □ ☉♈	12:37 am		
☽♑ □ ♀♈	3:13 am	**12:13 am**	
☽♑ ⚹ ☿♓	4:57 am	**1:57 am**	
☽♑ □ ♂♈	6:35 am	**3:35 am**	☽ v/c

4 Thu

4th ♑
OP: After Moon squares Saturn today until v/c Moon on Friday.

☽ enters ♒	4:41 am	**1:41 am**
♇♑ ⚹ ⚷♓	8:53 am	**5:53 am**
☽♒ ⚹ ♅♈	8:02 pm	**5:02 pm**
☽♒ □ ♄♏	9:48 pm	**6:48 pm**
☽♒ △ ♃♊		**11:26 pm**

☽≈ △ ♃♊	2:26 am		
☽≈ ⚹ ☉♈	8:11 am	**5:11 am**	
☽≈ ⚹ ♀♈	12:00 pm	**9:00 am**	
☽≈ ⚹ ♂♈	1:22 pm	**10:22 am**	☽ v/c

FRI 5

4th ≈

OP: After Moon squares Saturn on Thursday until v/c Moon today. High energy this morning is good for accomplishing your goals.

☽ enters ♓	9:00 am	**6:00 am**	
☽♓ ☌ ♆♓	4:48 pm	**1:48 pm**	
♀♈ ☌ ♂♈		**9:58 pm**	
☽♓ △ ♄♏		**11:21 pm**	

SAT 6

4th ≈

♀♈ ☌ ♂♈	12:58 am		
☽♓ △ ♄♏	2:21 am		
☽♓ ⚹ ♇♑	5:37 am	**2:37 am**	
☽♓ ☌ ⚷♓	5:53 am	**2:53 am**	
☽♓ □ ♃♊	8:06 am	**5:06 am**	
☽♓ ☌ ☿♓		**9:10 pm**	☽ v/c

SUN 7

4th ♓

OP: After Moon squares Jupiter today until Moon enters Aries on Monday. Good for artistic matters, meditation, and helping others.

Eastern Time plain / **Pacific Time bold**

MARCH

S	M	T	W	T	F	S
					1	2
3	4	5	6	7	8	9
10	11	12	13	14	15	16
17	18	19	20	21	22	23
24	25	26	27	28	29	30
31						

APRIL

S	M	T	W	T	F	S
	1	2	3	4	5	6
7	8	9	10	11	12	13
14	15	16	17	18	19	20
21	22	23	24	25	26	27
28	29	30				

MAY

S	M	T	W	T	F	S
			1	2	3	4
5	6	7	8	9	10	11
12	13	14	15	16	17	18
19	20	21	22	23	24	25
26	27	28	29	30	31	

8 Mon

4th ♓

OP: After Moon squares Jupiter on Sunday until Moon enters Aries today. Good for artistic matters, meditation, and helping others.

☽♓ ☌ ☿♓ 12:10 am ☽ v/c
☽ enters ♈ 3:02 pm **12:02 pm**

9 Tue

4th ♈

☽♈ ☌ ♅♈ 7:56 am **4:56 am**
☽♈ ⚻ ♄♏ 8:47 am **5:47 am**
☽♈ □ ♇♑ 12:29 pm **9:29 am**
☽♈ ⚹ ♃♊ 3:50 pm **12:50 pm**

10 Wed

4th ♈

● New Moon 20 ♈ 41

OP: After Moon conjoins Mars until v/c Moon. The Moon is under Sun's beams (see page 79), but the last 1 ½ hours of this short OP are good for having a pleasant time.

☽♈ ☌ ☉♈ 5:35 am **2:35 am**
☽♈ ☌ ♂♈ 9:02 am **6:02 am**
☽♈ ☌ ♀♈ 12:25 pm **9:25 am** ☽ v/c
☽ enters ♉ 11:22 pm **8:22 pm**

11 Thu

1st ♉

OP: After Moon trines Pluto today until Moon enters Gemini on Saturday.

☽♉ ⚹ ♆♓ 8:06 am **5:06 am**
☽♉ ☍ ♄♏ 5:36 pm **2:36 pm**
☽♉ △ ♇♑ 9:48 pm **6:48 pm**
☽♉ ⚹ ⚷♓ 10:34 pm **7:34 pm**

Fri 12
1st ♉

♇ ♑ ℞	3:34 pm	**12:34 pm**
♄ ♏ ⚻ ♅ ♈	11:29 pm	**8:29 pm**

OP: After Moon trines Pluto on Thursday until Moon enters Gemini on Saturday. Today is good for either work or socializing.

Sat 13
1st ♉

☽ ♉ ⚹ ☿ ♓	8:30 am	**5:30 am** ☽ v/c
☽ enters ♊	10:13 am	**7:13 am**
☽ ♊ □ ♆ ♓	7:25 pm	**4:25 pm**
☿ enters ♈	10:37 pm	**7:37 pm**

OP: After Moon squares Neptune today until v/c Moon on Monday. A good time for last-minute tax preparation, if needed.

Sun 14
1st ♊

☽ ♊ ⚻ ♄ ♏	4:48 am	**1:48 am**
☽ ♊ ⚹ ♅ ♈	5:07 am	**2:07 am**
☽ ♊ ⚻ ♇ ♑	9:30 am	**6:30 am**
☽ ♊ □ ⚷ ♓	10:33 am	**7:33 am**
☽ ♊ ☌ ♃ ♊	2:57 pm	**11:57 am**

Eastern Time plain / **Pacific Time bold**

MARCH

S	M	T	W	T	F	S
					1	2
3	4	5	6	7	8	9
10	11	12	13	14	15	16
17	18	19	20	21	22	23
24	25	26	27	28	29	30
31						

APRIL

S	M	T	W	T	F	S
	1	2	3	4	5	6
7	8	9	10	11	12	13
14	15	16	17	18	19	20
21	22	23	24	25	26	27
28	29	30				

MAY

S	M	T	W	T	F	S
			1	2	3	4
5	6	7	8	9	10	11
12	13	14	15	16	17	18
19	20	21	22	23	24	25
26	27	28	29	30	31	

April

15 Mon

1st ♊

OP: After Moon squares Neptune on Saturday until v/c Moon today. A good time for last-minute tax preparation, if needed. Some astrologers like to mail their tax returns while the Moon is v/c in order to avoid any unwanted replies from the IRS.

♀ enters ♉	3:25 am	**12:25 am**
☽♊ ✶ ☉♈	2:36 pm	**11:36 am**
☽♊ ✶ ♂♈	3:41 pm	**12:41 pm** ☽ v/c
☽ enters ♋	10:49 pm	**7:49 pm**
☽♋ ✶ ♀♉		**10:05 pm**

16 Tue

1st ♋

☽♋ ✶ ♀♉	1:05 am	
☽♋ □ ☿♈	5:48 am	**2:48 am**
☽♋ △ ♆♓	8:18 am	**5:18 am**
☽♋ △ ♄♏	5:14 pm	**2:14 pm**
☽♋ □ ♅♈	6:12 pm	**3:12 pm**
☽♋ ☍ ♇♑	10:18 pm	**7:18 pm**
☽♋ △ ⚷♓	11:37 pm	**8:37 pm**

17 Wed

1st ♋

☉♈ ☌ ♂♈	8:20 pm	**5:20 pm**

18 Thu

1st ♋

◐ 28 ♋ 38

☽♋ □ ♂♈	8:16 am	**5:16 am**
☽♋ □ ☉♈	8:31 am	**5:31 am** ☽ v/c
☽ enters ♌	11:13 am	**8:13 am**
☽♌ □ ♀♉	8:16 pm	**5:16 pm**
☽♌ ⚻ ♆♓	8:34 pm	**5:34 pm**
♀♉ ✶ ♆♓	11:15 pm	**8:15 pm**
☽♌ △ ☿♈		**11:54 pm**

Fri 19
2nd ♌
Sun enters Taurus

☽♌ △ ☿♈	2:54 am	
☽♌ □ ♄♏	4:44 am	**1:44 am**
☽♌ △ ♅♈	6:18 am	**3:18 am**
☽♌ ⚻ ♇♑	9:58 am	**6:58 am**
☽♌ ⚻ ⚷♓	11:29 am	**8:29 am**
☿♈ ⚻ ♄♏	4:16 pm	**1:16 pm**
☽♌ ⚹ ♃♊	5:06 pm	**2:06 pm** ☽ v/c
☉ enters ♉	6:03 pm	**3:03 pm**

OP: After Moon trines Uranus until v/c Moon. An excellent day to accomplish your goals.

Sat 20
2nd ♌

☿♈ ☌ ♅♈	5:20 am	**2:20 am**
♂ enters ♉	7:48 am	**4:48 am**
☽ enters ♍	9:08 pm	**6:08 pm**
☽♍ △ ♂♉	9:58 pm	**6:58 pm**
☽♍ △ ☉♉	11:22 pm	**8:22 pm**

Sun 21
2nd ♍

☽♍ ☍ ♆♓	6:03 am	**3:03 am**
☿♈ □ ♇♑	7:46 am	**4:46 am**
☽♍ △ ♀♉	11:42 am	**8:42 am**
☽♍ ⚹ ♄♏	1:17 pm	**10:17 am**
☽♍ ⚻ ♅♈	3:19 pm	**12:19 pm**
☽♍ △ ♇♑	6:30 pm	**3:30 pm**
☽♍ ⚻ ☿♈	8:04 pm	**5:04 pm**
☽♍ ☍ ⚷♓	8:09 pm	**5:09 pm**
☽♍ □ ♃♊		**11:02 pm** ☽ v/c

Eastern Time plain / **Pacific Time bold**

MARCH

S	M	T	W	T	F	S
					1	2
3	4	5	6	7	8	9
10	11	12	13	14	15	16
17	18	19	20	21	22	23
24	25	26	27	28	29	30
31						

APRIL

S	M	T	W	T	F	S
	1	2	3	4	5	6
7	8	9	10	11	12	13
14	15	16	17	18	19	20
21	22	23	24	25	26	27
28	29	30				

MAY

S	M	T	W	T	F	S
			1	2	3	4
5	6	7	8	9	10	11
12	13	14	15	16	17	18
19	20	21	22	23	24	25
26	27	28	29	30	31	

April

22 Mon
2nd ♍
Earth Day

☽♍ □ ♃♊	2:02 am	☽ v/c
♀♉ ☍ ♄♏	3:43 am **12:43 am**	

23 Tue
2nd ♍
OP: After Moon squares Pluto today until v/c Moon on Wednesday. Good for night owls.

☽ enters ♎	3:25 am	**12:25 am**
☽♎ ⚻ ♂♉	7:18 am	**4:18 am**
☽♎ ⚻ ☉♉	9:36 am	**6:36 am**
☽♎ ⚻ ♆♓	11:50 am	**8:50 am**
☽♎ ☍ ♅♈	8:37 pm	**5:37 pm**
☽♎ ⚻ ♀♉	10:11 pm	**7:11 pm**
☽♎ □ ♇♑	11:23 pm	**8:23 pm**
☿♈ ⚹ ♃♊	11:25 pm	**8:25 pm**
☽♎ ⚻ ⚷♓		**10:07 pm**

24 Wed
2nd ♎

☽♎ ⚻ ⚷♓	1:07 am		
☽♎ △ ♃♊	7:13 am	**4:13 am**	
☽♎ ☍ ☿♈	8:12 am	**5:12 am**	☽ v/c
♀♉ △ ♇♑	11:43 am	**8:43 am**	
☉♉ ⚹ ♆♓	5:58 pm	**2:58 pm**	

25 Thu
2nd ♎
○ Full Moon 5 ♏ 51 | Partial Lunar Eclipse
OP: After Moon conjoins Saturn today until v/c Moon on Friday. Short, but good for night owls.

☽ enters ♏	6:25 am	**3:25 am**
♀♉ ⚹ ⚷♓	8:42 am	**5:42 am**
☽♏ ☍ ♂♉	12:52 pm	**9:52 am**
☽♏ △ ♆♓	2:31 pm	**11:31 am**
☽♏ ☍ ☉♉	3:57 pm	**12:57 pm**
☽♏ ☌ ♄♏	8:17 pm	**5:17 pm**
☽♏ ⚻ ♅♈	11:00 pm	**8:00 pm**
☽♏ ⚹ ♇♑		**10:27 pm**

FRI 26
3rd ♏

☽♏ ⚹ ♇♑	1:27 am	
☽♏ △ ⚷♓	3:17 am	**12:17 am**
☽♏ ☍ ♀♉	4:56 am	**1:56 am** ☽ v/c
☽♏ ⚻ ♃♊	9:42 am	**6:42 am**
☽♏ ⚻ ☿♈	4:50 pm	**1:50 pm**
♂♉ ⚹ ♆♓	9:46 pm	**6:46 pm**

SAT 27
3rd ♏

☽ enters ♐	7:32 am	**4:32 am**
☽♐ □ ♆♓	3:32 pm	**12:32 pm**
☽♐ ⚻ ♂♉	4:27 pm	**1:27 pm**
☽♐ ⚻ ☉♉	8:19 pm	**5:19 pm**
☽♐ △ ♅♈		**9:01 pm**

OP: After Moon squares Neptune today until Moon enters Capricorn on Monday. The Sag Moon wants to have fun, though Sun opposing Saturn creates a feeling of seriousness. Your path is up to you.

SUN 28
3rd ♐

☽♐ △ ♅♈	12:01 am	
☽♐ □ ⚷♓	4:14 am	**1:14 am**
☉♉ ☍ ♄♏	4:27 am	**1:27 am**
☽♐ ⚻ ♀♉	10:10 am	**7:10 am**
☽♐ ☍ ♃♊	11:08 am	**8:08 am**
☽♐ △ ☿♈		**9:37 pm** ☽ v/c

Eastern Time plain / **Pacific Time bold**

MARCH

S	M	T	W	T	F	S
					1	2
3	4	5	6	7	8	9
10	11	12	13	14	15	16
17	18	19	20	21	22	23
24	25	26	27	28	29	30
31						

APRIL

S	M	T	W	T	F	S
	1	2	3	4	5	6
7	8	9	10	11	12	13
14	15	16	17	18	19	20
21	22	23	24	25	26	27
28	29	30				

MAY

S	M	T	W	T	F	S
			1	2	3	4
5	6	7	8	9	10	11
12	13	14	15	16	17	18
19	20	21	22	23	24	25
26	27	28	29	30	31	

29 Mon
3rd ♐

☽♐ △ ☿♈	12:37 am		☽ v/c
☽ enters ♑	8:21 am	**5:21 am**	
☽♑ ✶ ♆♓	4:32 pm	**1:32 pm**	
☽♑ △ ♂♉	8:01 pm	**5:01 pm**	
☽♑ ✶ ♄♏	9:39 pm	**6:39 pm**	
☽♑ △ ☉♉		**9:50 pm**	
☽♑ □ ♅♈		**10:16 pm**	

30 Tue
3rd ♑

☽♑ △ ☉♉	12:50 am	
☽♑ □ ♅♈	1:16 am	
☽♑ ☌ ♇♑	3:19 am	**12:19 am**
☽♑ ✶ ⚷♓	5:32 am	**2:32 am**
☽♑ ⚻ ♃♊	1:10 pm	**10:10 am**
☽♑ △ ♀♉	4:05 pm	**1:05 pm**
♂♉ ☍ ♄♏		**10:12 pm**

1 Wed
3rd ♑
Beltane

♂♉ ☍ ♄♏	1:12 am		
☽♑ □ ☿♈	10:07 am	**7:07 am**	☽ v/c
☽ enters ♒	10:20 am	**7:20 am**	
☿ enters ♉	11:37 am	**8:37 am**	
☉♉ △ ♇♑	1:36 pm	**10:36 am**	
☽♒ □ ♄♏	11:51 pm	**8:51 pm**	
☽♒ □ ♂♉		**10:15 pm**	

2 Thu
3rd ♒
◑ 12 ♒ 13

☽♒ □ ♂♉	1:15 am		
☽♒ ✶ ♅♈	4:04 am	**1:04 am**	
☽♒ □ ☉♉	7:14 am	**4:14 am**	
☽♒ △ ♃♊	5:05 pm	**2:05 pm**	
☽♒ □ ♀♉		**9:24 pm**	☽ v/c
☉♉ ✶ ⚷♓		**10:31 pm**	

FRI 3
4th ♒
ORTHODOX GOOD FRIDAY

☽♒ □ ♀♉	12:24 am		☽ v/c
☉♉ ✶ ⚷♓	1:31 am		
☽ enters ♓	2:25 pm	**11:25 am**	
☽♓ ✶ ☿♉	11:16 pm	**8:16 pm**	
☽♓ ☌ ♆♓	11:27 pm	**8:27 pm**	
☿♉ ✶ ♆♓		**9:31 pm**	

SAT 4
4th ♓

☿♉ ✶ ♆♓	12:31 am	
☽♓ △ ♄♏	4:18 am	**1:18 am**
☽♓ ✶ ♂♉	9:11 am	**6:11 am**
☽♓ ✶ ♇♑	11:00 am	**8:00 am**
☽♓ ☌ ⚷♓	1:48 pm	**10:48 am**
☽♓ ✶ ☉♉	4:33 pm	**1:33 pm**
☽♓ □ ♃♊	11:32 pm	**8:32 pm**

OP: After Moon squares Jupiter today until Moon enters Aries on Sunday. Good for artistic matters, meditation, and helping others.

SUN 5
4th ♓
ORTHODOX EASTER
CINCO DE MAYO

☿♉ ☍ ♄♏	7:12 am	**4:12 am**	
☽♓ ✶ ♀♉	12:00 pm	**9:00 am**	☽ v/c
♂♉ △ ♇♑	5:29 pm	**2:29 pm**	
☽ enters ♈	9:03 pm	**6:03 pm**	

Eastern Time plain / **Pacific Time bold**

APRIL

S	M	T	W	T	F	S
	1	2	3	4	5	6
7	8	9	10	11	12	13
14	15	16	17	18	19	20
21	22	23	24	25	26	27
28	29	30				

MAY

S	M	T	W	T	F	S
			1	2	3	4
5	6	7	8	9	10	11
12	13	14	15	16	17	18
19	20	21	22	23	24	25
26	27	28	29	30	31	

JUNE

S	M	T	W	T	F	S
						1
2	3	4	5	6	7	8
9	10	11	12	13	14	15
16	17	18	19	20	21	22
23	24	25	26	27	28	29
30						

May

6 Mon

4th ♈

OP: After Moon squares Pluto today until v/c Moon on Tuesday. The Last Quarter Moon suggests that the best use of our time now is to rest and sleep.

☽♈ ⚻ ♄♏	11:16 am	**8:16 am**
☽♈ ☌ ♅♈	4:57 pm	**1:57 pm**
☽♈ □ ♇♑	6:33 pm	**3:33 pm**
☿♉ △ ♇♑		**11:34 pm**

7 Tue

4th ♈

☿♉ △ ♇♑	2:34 am	
☽♈ ✶ ♃♊	8:40 am	**5:40 am** ☽ v/c
☿♉ ☌ ♂♉	8:33 pm	**5:33 pm**
☿♉ ✶ ⚷♓	9:45 pm	**6:45 pm**
♂♉ ✶ ⚷♓		**9:08 pm**

8 Wed

4th ♈

♂♉ ✶ ⚷♓	12:08 am	
☽ enters ♉	6:09 am	**3:09 am**
☽♉ ✶ ♆♓	4:09 pm	**1:09 pm**
☽♉ ☍ ♄♏	8:36 pm	**5:36 pm**

9 Thu

4th ♉

● New Moon 19 ♉ 33 | Annular Solar Eclipse

Annular Solar Eclipse (not a usable Cazimi). The eclipse will be visible in Australia, New Zealand, and the western Pacific, where it will already be Friday. Every total or annular solar eclipse becomes partial away from its path of totality.

☽♉ △ ♇♑	4:27 am	**1:27 am**
☽♉ ✶ ⚷♓	7:55 am	**4:55 am**
☽♉ ☌ ♂♉	9:52 am	**6:52 am**
♀ enters ♊	11:03 am	**8:03 am**
☽♉ ☌ ☿♉	3:06 pm	**12:06 pm**
☽♉ ☌ ☉♉	8:28 pm	**5:28 pm** ☽ v/c

Fri 10
1st ♉

☽ enters ♊ 5:21 pm **2:21 pm**
☽♊ ☌ ♀♊ 8:49 pm **5:49 pm**

Sat 11
1st ♊

☽♊ □ ♆♓ 3:44 am **12:44 am**
☽♊ ⚻ ♄♏ 7:52 am **4:52 am**
☽♊ ⚹ ♅♈ 3:07 pm **12:07 pm**
☽♊ ⚻ ♇♑ 4:14 pm **1:14 pm**
☉♉ ☌ ☿♉ 5:10 pm **2:10 pm**
☽♊ □ ⚷♓ 8:01 pm **5:01 pm**

OP: After Moon squares Neptune today until v/c Moon on Sunday. A highly productive time.

Sun 12
1st ♊
Mother's Day

☽♊ ☌ ♃♊ 9:32 am **6:32 am** ☽ v/c

Eastern Time plain / **Pacific Time bold**

APRIL

S	M	T	W	T	F	S
	1	2	3	4	5	6
7	8	9	10	11	12	13
14	15	16	17	18	19	20
21	22	23	24	25	26	27
28	29	30				

MAY

S	M	T	W	T	F	S
			1	2	3	4
5	6	7	8	9	10	11
12	13	14	15	16	17	18
19	20	21	22	23	24	25
26	27	28	29	30	31	

JUNE

S	M	T	W	T	F	S
						1
2	3	4	5	6	7	8
9	10	11	12	13	14	15
16	17	18	19	20	21	22
23	24	25	26	27	28	29
30						

May

13 Mon
1st ♊

☽ enters ♋	5:57 am	**2:57 am**
☽♋ △ ♆♓	4:32 pm	**1:32 pm**
♀♊ □ ♆♓	4:47 pm	**1:47 pm**
☽♋ △ ♄♏	8:15 pm	**5:15 pm**

14 Tue
1st ♋

OP: After Moon sextiles Mars today until Moon enters Leo on Wednesday. We can create what we want now.

☽♋ □ ♅♈	4:10 am	**1:10 am**
☽♋ ☍ ♇♑	4:58 am	**1:58 am**
☽♋ △ ⚷♓	9:01 am	**6:01 am**
☽♋ ⚹ ♂♉	6:38 pm	**3:38 pm**
♀♊ ⚻ ♄♏		**11:54 pm**

15 Wed
1st ♋

Shavuot

♀♊ ⚻ ♄♏	2:54 am	
☽♋ ⚹ ☉♉	8:14 am	**5:14 am** ☽ v/c
☿ enters ♊	4:41 pm	**1:41 pm**
☽ enters ♌	6:38 pm	**3:38 pm**
☽♌ ⚹ ☿♊	7:03 pm	**4:03 pm**

16 Thu
1st ♌

☽♌ ⚻ ♆♓	5:06 am	**2:06 am**
☽♌ □ ♄♏	8:21 am	**5:21 am**
☽♌ ⚹ ♀♊	11:52 am	**8:52 am**
☽♌ △ ♅♈	4:39 pm	**1:39 pm**
☽♌ ⚻ ♇♑	5:08 pm	**2:08 pm**
☽♌ ⚻ ⚷♓	9:18 pm	**6:18 pm**

May

☽♌ □ ♂♉	10:15 am	**7:15 am**	
☽♌ ⚹ ♃♊	12:17 pm	**9:17 am**	
☽♌ □ ☉♉		**9:35 pm**	☽ v/c

Fri 17

1st ♌

◐ 27 ♌ 25 (Pacific)

☽♌ □ ☉♉	12:35 am		☽ v/c
☿♊ □ ♆♓	3:19 am	**12:19 am**	
☽ enters ♍	5:33 am	**2:33 am**	
♀♊ ⚹ ♅♈	12:40 pm	**9:40 am**	
♀♊ ⚻ ♇♑	3:16 pm	**12:16 pm**	
☽♍ ☍ ♆♓	3:35 pm	**12:35 pm**	
☽♍ □ ☿♊	6:02 pm	**3:02 pm**	
☽♍ ⚹ ♄♏	6:18 pm	**3:18 pm**	
☿♊ ⚻ ♄♏	7:33 pm	**4:33 pm**	
☽♍ ⚻ ♅♈		**11:41 pm**	
☽♍ △ ♇♑		**11:52 pm**	

Sat 18

1st ♌

◐ 27 ♌ 25 (Eastern)

☽♍ ⚻ ♅♈	2:41 am	
☽♍ △ ♇♑	2:52 am	
☽♍ □ ♀♊	4:06 am	**1:06 am**
☽♍ ☍ ⚷♓	6:58 am	**3:58 am**
☽♍ □ ♃♊	9:55 pm	**6:55 pm**
☽♍ △ ♂♉	10:23 pm	**7:23 pm**

Sun 19

2nd ♍

OP: After Moon squares Jupiter today until v/c Moon on Monday.

Eastern Time plain / **Pacific Time bold**

APRIL

S	M	T	W	T	F	S
	1	2	3	4	5	6
7	8	9	10	11	12	13
14	15	16	17	18	19	20
21	22	23	24	25	26	27
28	29	30				

MAY

S	M	T	W	T	F	S
			1	2	3	4
5	6	7	8	9	10	11
12	13	14	15	16	17	18
19	20	21	22	23	24	25
26	27	28	29	30	31	

JUNE

S	M	T	W	T	F	S
						1
2	3	4	5	6	7	8
9	10	11	12	13	14	15
16	17	18	19	20	21	22
23	24	25	26	27	28	29
30						

May

Uranus-Pluto Note: These two slow outer planets make the third exact square of their current series on Monday. They will make seven exact squares in all from June 24, 2012, to March 16, 2015. Think of the 1930s and the 1960s all over again, with the appropriate changes. "History doesn't repeat, but it rhymes."

20 Mon

2nd ♍

Sun enters Gemini

OP: After Moon squares Jupiter on Sunday until v/c Moon today. Much can be accomplished early today.

♀♊ □ ⚷♓	10:50 am	**7:50 am**
☽♍ △ ☉♉	12:48 pm	**9:48 am** ☽ v/c
☽ enters ♎	1:07 pm	**10:07 am**
☉ enters ♊	5:09 pm	**2:09 pm**
♅♈ □ ♇♑	7:02 pm	**4:02 pm**
☽♎ ⚻ ♆♓	10:31 pm	**7:31 pm**
☿♊ ⚻ ♇♑	11:38 pm	**8:38 pm**
☿♊ ⚹ ♅♈	11:46 pm	**8:46 pm**

21 Tue

2nd ♎

OP: After Moon opposes Uranus today until v/c Moon on Wednesday. A great time to start any new project.

☽♎ □ ♇♑	8:55 am	**5:55 am**
☽♎ ☍ ♅♈	8:59 am	**5:59 am**
☽♎ △ ☿♊	10:33 am	**7:33 am**
☽♎ ⚻ ⚷♓	12:55 pm	**9:55 am**
☽♎ △ ♀♊	3:24 pm	**12:24 pm**
☿♊ □ ⚷♓		**11:49 pm**

22 Wed

2nd ♎

☿♊ □ ⚷♓	2:49 am	
☽♎ △ ♃♊	3:35 am	**12:35 am** ☽ v/c
☽♎ ⚻ ♂♉	6:01 am	**3:01 am**
☽ enters ♏	4:55 pm	**1:55 pm**
☽♏ ⚻ ☉♊	8:20 pm	**5:20 pm**
☽♏ △ ♆♓		**10:45 pm**

23 Thu

2nd ♏

☽♏ △ ♆♓	1:45 am	
☽♏ ☌ ♄♏	3:34 am	**12:34 am**
☽♏ ⚹ ♇♑	11:25 am	**8:25 am**
☽♏ ⚻ ♅♈	11:41 am	**8:41 am**
☽♏ △ ⚷♓	3:19 pm	**12:19 pm**
☽♏ ⚻ ☿♊	8:55 pm	**5:55 pm**
☽♏ ⚻ ♀♊	10:07 pm	**7:07 pm**

Fri 24
2nd ♏

☽♏ ⚻ ♃♊ 5:52 am **2:52 am**
☽♏ ☍ ♂♉ 9:55 am **6:55 am** ☽ v/c
☽ enters ♐ 5:49 pm **2:49 pm**
☿♊ ☌ ♀♊ 7:54 pm **4:54 pm**
☽♐ ☍ ☉♊ **9:25 pm**
☽♐ □ ♆♓ **11:19 pm**

Penumbral Lunar Eclipse | ○ Full Moon 3 ♐ 58 (Pacific)

Sat 25
2nd ♐

☽♐ ☍ ☉♊ 12:25 am
☽♐ □ ♆♓ 2:19 am
☽♐ △ ♅♈ 12:01 pm **9:01 am**
☽♐ □ ⚷♓ 3:29 pm **12:29 pm**
☽♐ ☍ ♀♊ **11:16 pm**

Penumbral Lunar Eclipse | ○ Full Moon 3 ♐ 58 (Eastern)

OP: After Moon trines Uranus today until Moon enters Capricorn on Sunday. Good for either work or play.

Sun 26
3rd ♐

☽♐ ☍ ♀♊ 2:16 am
☽♐ ☍ ☿♊ 3:46 am **12:46 am**
☽♐ ☍ ♃♊ 6:22 am **3:22 am** ☽ v/c
☉♊ □ ♆♓ 6:26 am **3:26 am**
☽♐ ⚻ ♂♉ 12:02 pm **9:02 am**
☽ enters ♑ 5:28 pm **2:28 pm**
☽♑ ⚹ ♆♓ **10:58 pm**

Eastern Time plain / **Pacific Time bold**

APRIL

S	M	T	W	T	F	S
	1	2	3	4	5	6
7	8	9	10	11	12	13
14	15	16	17	18	19	20
21	22	23	24	25	26	27
28	29	30				

MAY

S	M	T	W	T	F	S
			1	2	3	4
5	6	7	8	9	10	11
12	13	14	15	16	17	18
19	20	21	22	23	24	25
26	27	28	29	30	31	

JUNE

S	M	T	W	T	F	S
						1
2	3	4	5	6	7	8
9	10	11	12	13	14	15
16	17	18	19	20	21	22
23	24	25	26	27	28	29
30						

May

27 Mon

3rd ♑

Memorial Day (observed)

OP: After Moon squares Uranus today until v/c Moon on Tuesday. You can be highly productive now, or just enjoy life.

☽♑ ⚹ ♆♓	1:58 am	
☉♊ ⚻ ♄♏	3:16 am	**12:16 am**
☽♑ ⚹ ♄♏	3:18 am	**12:18 am**
☽♑ ⚻ ☉♊	3:18 am	**12:18 am**
☿♊ ☌ ♃♊	3:56 am	**12:56 am**
☽♑ ☌ ♇♑	11:12 am	**8:12 am**
☽♑ □ ♅♈	11:50 am	**8:50 am**
☽♑ ⚹ ⚷♓	3:17 pm	**12:17 pm**

28 Tue

3rd ♑

☽♑ ⚻ ♀♊	6:30 am	**3:30 am**
☽♑ ⚻ ♃♊	7:07 am	**4:07 am**
☽♑ ⚻ ☿♊	10:22 am	**7:22 am**
☽♑ △ ♂♉	2:40 pm	**11:40 am** ☽ v/c
♀♊ ☌ ♃♊	3:29 pm	**12:29 pm**
☽ enters ♒	5:48 pm	**2:48 pm**

29 Wed

3rd ♒

☽♒ □ ♄♏	3:47 am	**12:47 am**
☽♒ △ ☉♊	7:28 am	**4:28 am**
☽♒ ⚹ ♅♈	1:01 pm	**10:01 am**

30 Thu

3rd ♒

☽♒ △ ♃♊	10:01 am	**7:01 am**
☽♒ △ ♀♊	1:21 pm	**10:21 am**
☽♒ △ ☿♊	7:37 pm	**4:37 pm**
☽♒ □ ♂♉	7:57 pm	**4:57 pm** ☽ v/c
☽ enters ♓	8:30 pm	**5:30 pm**

Fri 31
3rd ♓
◑ 10 ♓ 28

☿ enters ♋ 3:07 am **12:07 am**
☽♓ ☌ ♆♓ 5:54 am **2:54 am**
♂ enters ♊ 6:39 am **3:39 am**
☽♓ △ ♄♏ 6:54 am **3:54 am**
☽♓ □ ☉♊ 2:58 pm **11:58 am**
☽♓ ⚹ ♇♑ 3:58 pm **12:58 pm**
☽♓ ☌ ⚷♓ 8:47 pm **5:47 pm**

Sat 1
4th ♓

☉♊ ⚻ ♇♑ 4:40 am **1:40 am**
☽♓ □ ♃♊ 4:18 pm **1:18 pm**
☉♊ ⚹ ♅♈ 9:46 pm **6:46 pm**
☽♓ □ ♀♊ **9:30 pm** ☽ v/c
☽ enters ♈ **11:33 pm**

Sun 2
4th ♓

☽♓ □ ♀♊ 12:30 am ☽ v/c
☽ enters ♈ 2:33 am
☽♈ ⚹ ♂♊ 5:08 am **2:08 am**
☽♈ □ ☿♋ 9:07 am **6:07 am**
☽♈ ⚻ ♄♏ 1:25 pm **10:25 am**
♀ enters ♋ 10:13 pm **7:13 pm**
☽♈ □ ♇♑ 11:12 pm **8:12 pm**
☽♈ ☌ ♅♈ **9:39 pm**
☽♈ ⚹ ☉♊ **11:47 pm**

OP: After Moon conjoins Uranus today/Monday until v/c Moon on Monday/Tuesday.

Eastern Time plain / **Pacific Time bold**

MAY

S	M	T	W	T	F	S
			1	2	3	4
5	6	7	8	9	10	11
12	13	14	15	16	17	18
19	20	21	22	23	24	25
26	27	28	29	30	31	

JUNE

S	M	T	W	T	F	S
						1
2	3	4	5	6	7	8
9	10	11	12	13	14	15
16	17	18	19	20	21	22
23	24	25	26	27	28	29
30						

JULY

S	M	T	W	T	F	S
	1	2	3	4	5	6
7	8	9	10	11	12	13
14	15	16	17	18	19	20
21	22	23	24	25	26	27
28	29	30	31			

JUNE

3 MON

4th ♈

OP: After Moon conjoins Uranus on Sunday/today until v/c Moon today/Tuesday. Good for following through on matters already begun.

☽♈ ☌ ♅♈	12:39 am		
☽♈ ✶ ☉♊	2:47 am		
☿♋ △ ♆♓	3:17 pm	**12:17 pm**	
☿♋ △ ♄♏	9:22 pm	**6:22 pm**	
☉♊ □ ⚷♓		**10:26 pm**	
☽♈ ✶ ♃♊		**11:09 pm**	☽ v/c

4 TUE

4th ♈

OP: After Moon opposes Saturn today until Moon enters Gemini on Thursday. The Moon is almost Balsamic; okay for follow-through, but not for innovation.

☉♊ □ ⚷♓	1:26 am		
☽♈ ✶ ♃♊	2:09 am		☽ v/c
☽ enters ♉	11:53 am	**8:53 am**	
☽♉ ✶ ♀♋	4:04 pm	**1:04 pm**	
☽♉ ✶ ♆♓	10:26 pm	**7:26 pm**	
☽♉ ☍ ♄♏	11:03 pm	**8:03 pm**	
☽♉ ✶ ☿♋		**11:30 pm**	

5 WED

4th ♉

☽♉ ✶ ☿♋	2:30 am		
☽♉ △ ♇♑	9:25 am	**6:25 am**	☽ v/c
☽♉ ✶ ⚷♓	3:05 pm	**12:05 pm**	

6 THU

4th ♉

☽ enters ♊	11:32 pm	**8:32 pm**	

♆♓℞	4:24 am	**1:24 am**	
♀♋△♆♓	7:46 am	**4:46 am**	
☽♊☌♂♊	9:45 am	**6:45 am**	
☽♊□♆♓	10:22 am	**7:22 am**	
☽♊⚻♄♏	10:44 am	**7:44 am**	
♀♋△♄♏	11:23 am	**8:23 am**	
☿♋☍♇♑	6:03 pm	**3:03 pm**	
♂♊□♆♓	7:57 pm	**4:57 pm**	
☽♊⚻♇♑	9:29 pm	**6:29 pm**	
☽♊✶♅♈	11:33 pm	**8:33 pm**	
♂♊⚻♄♏		**10:18 pm**	

Fri 7
4th ♊

♂♊⚻♄♏	1:18 am		
☽♊□⚷♓	3:25 am	**12:25 am**	
☽♊☌☉♊	11:56 am	**8:56 am**	
☿♋□♅♈	2:47 pm	**11:47 am**	

Sat 8
4th ♊

● New Moon 18 ♊ 01

OP: This Cazimi Moon is usable ½ hour before and ½ hour after the Sun-Moon conjunction. If you need to start something important around now, this is the time to do it.

☽♊☌♃♊	4:29 am	**1:29 am**	☽ v/c
☽ enters ♋	12:16 pm	**9:16 am**	
☽♋△♆♓	11:10 pm	**8:10 pm**	
☽♋△♄♏	11:19 pm	**8:19 pm**	

Sun 9
1st ♊

Eastern Time plain / **Pacific Time bold**

MAY

S	M	T	W	T	F	S
			1	2	3	4
5	6	7	8	9	10	11
12	13	14	15	16	17	18
19	20	21	22	23	24	25
26	27	28	29	30	31	

JUNE

S	M	T	W	T	F	S
						1
2	3	4	5	6	7	8
9	10	11	12	13	14	15
16	17	18	19	20	21	22
23	24	25	26	27	28	29
30						

JULY

S	M	T	W	T	F	S
	1	2	3	4	5	6
7	8	9	10	11	12	13
14	15	16	17	18	19	20
21	22	23	24	25	26	27
28	29	30	31			

June

10 Mon

1st ♋

OP: After Moon squares Uranus today until Moon enters Leo on Tuesday/Wednesday. We have the wind at our backs now.

☽♋ ☌ ♀♋ 6:28 am **3:28 am**
☿♋ △ ⚷♓ 6:48 am **3:48 am**
☽♋ ☍ ♇♑ 10:12 am **7:12 am**
☽♋ □ ♅♈ 12:34 pm **9:34 am**
☽♋ △ ⚷♓ 4:18 pm **1:18 pm**
☽♋ ☌ ☿♋ 5:15 pm **2:15 pm** ☽ v/c

11 Tue

1st ♋

♀♋ ☍ ♇♑ 6:08 pm **3:08 pm**
♄♏ △ ♆♓ 7:26 pm **4:26 pm**
☽ enters ♌ **9:58 pm**

12 Wed

1st ♋

☽ enters ♌ 12:58 am
☽♌ □ ♄♏ 11:41 am **8:41 am**
☽♌ ⚻ ♆♓ 11:44 am **8:44 am**
☽♌ ⚹ ♂♊ 6:44 pm **3:44 pm**
♀♋ □ ♅♈ 6:49 pm **3:49 pm**
☽♌ ⚻ ♇♑ 10:30 pm **7:30 pm**
☽♌ △ ♅♈ **10:04 pm**

13 Thu

1st ♌

OP: After Moon trines Uranus on Wednesday/today until v/c Moon on Friday. Today is excellent for whatever you want to do. Write down your plans before Mercury enters its Storm on June 17.

☽♌ △ ♅♈ 1:04 am
☽♌ ⚻ ⚷♓ 4:37 am **1:37 am**
☽♌ ⚹ ☉♊ 11:13 pm **8:13 pm**

♀♋ △ ⚷♓	6:07 am	**3:07 am**	
☽♌ ⚹ ♃♊	7:14 am	**4:14 am**	☽ v/c
☽ enters ♍	12:26 pm	**9:26 am**	
☽♍ ⚹ ♄♏	10:36 pm	**7:36 pm**	
☽♍ ☍ ♆♓	10:49 pm	**7:49 pm**	

Fri 14
1st ♌
Flag Day

OP: Last of the OP that began on Wednesday/Thursday.

☽♍ □ ♂♊	9:04 am	**6:04 am**	
☽♍ △ ♇♑	9:05 am	**6:05 am**	
♂♊ ⚻ ♇♑	9:19 am	**6:19 am**	
☽♍ ⚻ ♅♈	11:46 am	**8:46 am**	
☽♍ ☍ ⚷♓	3:03 pm	**12:03 pm**	
☽♍ ⚹ ♀♋	6:34 pm	**3:34 pm**	
☽♍ ⚹ ☿♋		**10:06 pm**	

Sat 15
1st ♍

☽♍ ⚹ ☿♋	1:06 am		
⚷♓ ℞	5:17 am	**2:17 am**	
☽♍ □ ☉♊	1:24 pm	**10:24 am**	
☽♍ □ ♃♊	5:26 pm	**2:26 pm**	☽ v/c
☽ enters ♎	9:19 pm	**6:19 pm**	

Sun 16
1st ♍
◐ 25 ♍ 43
Father's Day

Eastern Time plain / **Pacific Time bold**

MAY

S	M	T	W	T	F	S
			1	2	3	4
5	6	7	8	9	10	11
12	13	14	15	16	17	18
19	20	21	22	23	24	25
26	27	28	29	30	31	

JUNE

S	M	T	W	T	F	S
						1
2	3	4	5	6	7	8
9	10	11	12	13	14	15
16	17	18	19	20	21	22
23	24	25	26	27	28	29
30						

JULY

S	M	T	W	T	F	S
	1	2	3	4	5	6
7	8	9	10	11	12	13
14	15	16	17	18	19	20
21	22	23	24	25	26	27
28	29	30	31			

June

Mercury Note: Mercury enters its Storm (moving less than 40 minutes of arc per day) on Monday, as it slows down before going retrograde. The Storm acts like the retrograde. Don't start any new projects now—just follow through with the items that are already on your plate. Write down new ideas with date and time they occurred.

17 Mon
2nd ♎

☽♎ ⚻ ♆♓	7:05 am	**4:05 am**
♂♊ ⚹ ♅♈	11:20 am	**8:20 am**
☽♎ □ ♇♑	4:39 pm	**1:39 pm**
☽♎ ☍ ♅♈	7:23 pm	**4:23 pm**
☽♎ △ ♂♊	7:49 pm	**4:49 pm**
☽♎ ⚻ ⚷♓	10:22 pm	**7:22 pm**

18 Tue
2nd ♎

OP: After Moon squares Mercury until v/c Moon. Great for following through on matters begun before Monday.

☽♎ □ ♀♋	7:05 am	**4:05 am**
☽♎ □ ☿♋	10:34 am	**7:34 am**
☽♎ △ ☉♊	11:14 pm	**8:14 pm**
☽♎ △ ♃♊	11:55 pm	**8:55 pm** ☽ v/c
☽ enters ♏		**11:38 pm**

19 Wed
2nd ♎

OP: After Moon sextiles Pluto today until v/c Moon on Thursday. We can be very productive now—just avoid beginning new projects.

☽ enters ♏	2:38 am	
☽♏ ☌ ♄♏	11:20 am	**8:20 am**
☽♏ △ ♆♓	11:44 am	**8:44 am**
☉♊ ☌ ♃♊	12:11 pm	**9:11 am**
☽♏ ⚹ ♇♑	8:36 pm	**5:36 pm**
♂♊ □ ⚷♓	8:42 pm	**5:42 pm**
☽♏ ⚻ ♅♈	11:19 pm	**8:19 pm**
☽♏ △ ⚷♓		**11:00 pm**
☽♏ ⚻ ♂♊		**11:17 pm**

20 Thu
2nd ♏

Summer Solstice (Pacific)
Litha
Sun enters Cancer (Pacific)

☽♏ △ ⚷♓	2:00 am	
☽♏ ⚻ ♂♊	2:17 am	
☽♏ △ ♀♋	2:49 pm	**11:49 am**
☽♏ △ ☿♋	3:16 pm	**12:16 pm** ☽ v/c
☿♋ ☌ ♀♋	10:57 pm	**7:57 pm**
☉ enters ♋		**10:04 pm**
☽♏ ⚻ ♃♊		**11:44 pm**

Fri 21

2nd ♏

Summer Solstice (Eastern)

Litha

Sun enters Cancer (Eastern)

☉ enters ♋	1:04 am	
☽♏ ⚻ ♃♊	2:44 am	
☽ enters ♐	4:31 am	**1:31 am**
☽♐ ⚻ ☉♋	4:45 am	**1:45 am**
☽♐ □ ♆♓	1:04 pm	**10:04 am**
☽♐ △ ♅♈		**9:09 pm**
☽♐ □ ⚷♓		**11:37 pm**

Sat 22

2nd ♐

OP: After Moon opposes Mars today until Moon enters Capricorn on Sunday. All day today is great for having fun.

☽♐ △ ♅♈	12:09 am	
☽♐ □ ⚷♓	2:37 am	
☽♐ ☍ ♂♊	5:14 am	**2:14 am**
☽♐ ⚻ ☿♋	4:29 pm	**1:29 pm**
☽♐ ⚻ ♀♋	7:04 pm	**4:04 pm**

Sun 23

2nd ♐

○ Full Moon 2 ♑ 10

OP: After Moon squares Uranus today until v/c Moon on Monday.

☽♐ ☍ ♃♊	3:08 am	**12:08 am**	☽ v/c
☽ enters ♑	4:08 am	**1:08 am**	
☽♑ ☍ ☉♋	7:32 am	**4:32 am**	
☽♑ ⚹ ♄♏	11:58 am	**8:58 am**	
☽♑ ⚹ ♆♓	12:28 pm	**9:28 am**	
☽♑ ☌ ♇♑	8:37 pm	**5:37 pm**	
☽♑ □ ♅♈	11:27 pm	**8:27 pm**	
☽♑ ⚹ ⚷♓		**10:49 pm**	

Eastern Time plain / **Pacific Time bold**

MAY

S	M	T	W	T	F	S
			1	2	3	4
5	6	7	8	9	10	11
12	13	14	15	16	17	18
19	20	21	22	23	24	25
26	27	28	29	30	31	

JUNE

S	M	T	W	T	F	S
						1
2	3	4	5	6	7	8
9	10	11	12	13	14	15
16	17	18	19	20	21	22
23	24	25	26	27	28	29
30						

JULY

S	M	T	W	T	F	S
	1	2	3	4	5	6
7	8	9	10	11	12	13
14	15	16	17	18	19	20
21	22	23	24	25	26	27
28	29	30	31			

June

Mercury Note: Mercury goes retrograde on Wednesday and remains so until July 20, after which it will still be in its Storm until July 27. Projects begun during this entire period may not work out as planned. It's best to use this time for review, editing, escrows, and so forth.

24 Mon

3rd ♑

OP: After Moon squares Uranus on Sunday until v/c Moon today. Today is excellent for communication and sales.

☽♑ ⚹ ⚷♓	1:49 am	
☽♑ ⚻ ♂♊	6:41 am	**3:41 am**
☽♑ ☍ ☿♋	4:20 pm	**1:20 pm**
☽♑ ☍ ♀♋	10:24 pm	**7:24 pm** ☽ v/c

25 Tue

3rd ♑

☽♑ ⚻ ♃♊	3:10 am	**12:10 am**
☽ enters ♒	3:27 am	**12:27 am**
☽♒ ⚻ ☉♋	10:07 am	**7:07 am**
☽♒ □ ♄♏	11:22 am	**8:22 am**
♃ enters ♋	9:40 pm	**6:40 pm**
☽♒ ⚹ ♅♈	11:18 pm	**8:18 pm**

26 Wed

3rd ♒

☉♋ △ ♄♏	5:12 am	**2:12 am**
☿♋ ℞	9:08 am	**6:08 am**
☽♒ △ ♂♊	9:08 am	**6:08 am** ☽ v/c
☉♋ △ ♆♓	1:48 pm	**10:48 am**
☽♒ ⚻ ☿♋	5:00 pm	**2:00 pm**

27 Thu

3rd ♒

☽♒ ⚻ ♀♋	3:44 am	**12:44 am**
☽ enters ♓	4:32 am	**1:32 am**
☽♓ △ ♃♋	5:02 am	**2:02 am**
☽♓ △ ♄♏	12:52 pm	**9:52 am**
♀ enters ♌	1:03 pm	**10:03 am**
☽♓ ☌ ♆♓	1:28 pm	**10:28 am**
☽♓ △ ☉♋	3:13 pm	**12:13 pm**
☽♓ ⚹ ♇♑	10:17 pm	**7:17 pm**

FRI 28
3rd ♓

☽♓ ☌ ⚷♓ 4:10 am **1:10 am**
☽♓ □ ♂♊ 2:58 pm **11:58 am**
☽♓ △ ☿♋ 8:16 pm **5:16 pm** ☽ v/c

OP: After Moon squares Mars today until Moon enters Aries on Saturday. Good for artistic matters, meditation, and helping others.

SAT 29
3rd ♓
◑ 8 ♈ 35 (Pacific)

☽ enters ♈ 9:07 am **6:07 am**
☽♈ □ ♃♋ 10:35 am **7:35 am**
☽♈ △ ♀♌ 1:36 pm **10:36 am**
☽♈ ⚻ ♄♏ 6:02 pm **3:02 pm**
☽♈ □ ☉♋ **9:54 pm**

SUN 30
3rd ♈
◑ 8 ♈ 35 (Eastern)

☽♈ □ ☉♋ 12:54 am
☽♈ □ ♇♑ 4:10 am **1:10 am**
☽♈ ☌ ♅♈ 8:03 am **5:03 am**
☽♈ ⚹ ♂♊ **10:27 pm**
☽♈ □ ☿♋ **11:48 pm** ☽ v/c

Eastern Time plain / **Pacific Time bold**

MAY

S	M	T	W	T	F	S
			1	2	3	4
5	6	7	8	9	10	11
12	13	14	15	16	17	18
19	20	21	22	23	24	25
26	27	28	29	30	31	

JUNE

S	M	T	W	T	F	S
						1
2	3	4	5	6	7	8
9	10	11	12	13	14	15
16	17	18	19	20	21	22
23	24	25	26	27	28	29
30						

JULY

S	M	T	W	T	F	S
	1	2	3	4	5	6
7	8	9	10	11	12	13
14	15	16	17	18	19	20
21	22	23	24	25	26	27
28	29	30	31			

July

1 Mon

4th ♈

☽♈ ✶ ♂♊	1:27 am		
☽♈ □ ☿♋	2:48 am		☽ v/c
♀♌ □ ♄♏	1:03 pm	**10:03 am**	
☽ enters ♉	5:43 pm	**2:43 pm**	
☉♋ ☍ ♇♑	8:06 pm	**5:06 pm**	
♀♌ ⚻ ♆♓	8:12 pm	**5:12 pm**	
☽♉ ✶ ♃♋	8:21 pm	**5:21 pm**	

2 Tue

4th ♉

OP: After Moon squares Venus today until Moon enters Gemini on Thursday. The Last Quarter Moon and Mercury Retrograde warn us not to start anything important now, but we can still follow through on matters already begun.

☽♉ ☍ ♄♏	3:11 am	**12:11 am**
☽♉ ✶ ♆♓	3:54 am	**12:54 am**
☽♉ □ ♀♌	4:45 am	**1:45 am**
☽♉ △ ♇♑	1:53 pm	**10:53 am**
☽♉ ✶ ☉♋	3:26 pm	**12:26 pm**
☽♉ ✶ ⚷♓	8:42 pm	**5:42 pm**

3 Wed

4th ♉

☽♉ ✶ ☿♋	11:51 am	**8:51 am**	☽ v/c
☉♋ □ ♅♈		**11:22 pm**	

4 Thu

4th ♉

Independence Day

☉♋ □ ♅♈	2:22 am	
☽ enters ♊	5:21 am	**2:21 am**
☽♊ ⚻ ♄♏	3:07 pm	**12:07 pm**
☽♊ □ ♆♓	3:49 pm	**12:49 pm**
☽♊ ✶ ♀♌	11:37 pm	**8:37 pm**
☽♊ ⚻ ♇♑		**11:02 pm**

FRI 5
4th ♊

☽♊ ⚻ ♇♑ 2:02 am
☽♊ ⚹ ♅♈ 6:36 am **3:36 am**
☉♋ △ ⚷♓ 9:01 am **6:01 am**
☽♊ □ ⚷♓ 9:03 am **6:03 am**
♀♌ ⚻ ♇♑ 10:43 pm **7:43 pm**

SAT 6
4th ♊

☽♊ ☌ ♂♊ 8:30 am **5:30 am** ☽ v/c
☽ enters ♋ 6:14 pm **3:14 pm**
☽♋ ☌ ♃♋ 11:21 pm **8:21 pm**

SUN 7
4th ♋

☽♋ △ ♄♏ 4:00 am **1:00 am**
☽♋ △ ♆♓ 4:39 am **1:39 am**
☽♋ ☍ ♇♑ 2:48 pm **11:48 am**
☽♋ □ ♅♈ 7:32 pm **4:32 pm**
♀♌ △ ♅♈ 8:14 pm **5:14 pm**
☽♋ △ ⚷♓ 9:50 pm **6:50 pm**
♄♏ D **10:12 pm**

Eastern Time plain / **Pacific Time bold**

JUNE

S	M	T	W	T	F	S
						1
2	3	4	5	6	7	8
9	10	11	12	13	14	15
16	17	18	19	20	21	22
23	24	25	26	27	28	29
30						

JULY

S	M	T	W	T	F	S
	1	2	3	4	5	6
7	8	9	10	11	12	13
14	15	16	17	18	19	20
21	22	23	24	25	26	27
28	29	30	31			

AUGUST

S	M	T	W	T	F	S
				1	2	3
4	5	6	7	8	9	10
11	12	13	14	15	16	17
18	19	20	21	22	23	24
25	26	27	28	29	30	31

8 Mon

4th ♋

● New Moon 16 ♋ 18

OP: This Cazimi Moon is usable ½ hour before and ½ hour after the Sun-Moon conjunction. Mercury Retrograde is not good for new beginnings, but if you have something really important that's just part of a large project already underway, you could conceivably take advantage of this Cazimi.

♄♏ D	1:12 am	
☽♋ ☌ ☉♋	3:14 am	**12:14 am**
☽♋ ☌ ☿♋	7:44 am	**4:44 am** ☽ v/c
♀♌ ⚻ ⚷♓	6:26 pm	**3:26 pm**

9 Tue

1st ♋

Ramadan begins

OP: After Moon squares Saturn today until v/c Moon on Thursday. Follow through on matters you began before June 17.

☽ enters ♌	6:48 am	**3:48 am**
☉♋ ☌ ☿♋	2:41 pm	**11:41 am**
☽♌ □ ♄♏	4:27 pm	**1:27 pm**
☽♌ ⚻ ♆♓	5:00 pm	**2:00 pm**
☽♌ ⚻ ♇♑		**11:56 pm**

10 Wed

1st ♌

☽♌ ⚻ ♇♑	2:56 am	
☽♌ △ ♅♈	7:44 am	**4:44 am**
☽♌ ⚻ ⚷♓	9:51 am	**6:51 am**
☽♌ ☌ ♀♌	2:18 pm	**11:18 am**

11 Thu

1st ♌

OP: After Moon squares Saturn on Tuesday until v/c Moon today. Follow through on matters begun before June 17.

☽♌ ⚹ ♂♊	3:54 pm	**12:54 pm** ☽ v/c
☽ enters ♍	6:12 pm	**3:12 pm**
☽♍ ⚹ ♃♋		**10:20 pm**

FRI 12
1st ♍

☽♍ ⚹ ♃♋ 1:20 am
☽♍ ⚹ ♄♏ 3:36 am **12:36 am**
☽♍ ☍ ♆♓ 4:03 am **1:03 am**
☽♍ △ ♇♑ 1:39 pm **10:39 am**
☽♍ ⚻ ♅♈ 6:27 pm **3:27 pm**
☽♍ ☍ ⚷♓ 8:22 pm **5:22 pm**
☽♍ ⚹ ☿♋ **9:30 pm**

OP: After Moon opposes Neptune today until v/c Moon on Saturday. Follow through on matters begun before June 17.

SAT 13
1st ♍

☽♍ ⚹ ☿♋ 12:30 am
♂ enters ♋ 9:22 am **6:22 am**
☽♍ ⚹ ☉♋ 11:26 am **8:26 am** ☽ v/c

SUN 14
1st ♍

☽ enters ♎ 3:41 am **12:41 am**
☽♎ □ ♂♋ 4:42 am **1:42 am**
☽♎ □ ♃♋ 11:32 am **8:32 am**
☽♎ ⚻ ♆♓ 1:02 pm **10:02 am**
☽♎ □ ♇♑ 10:12 pm **7:12 pm**
☽♎ ☍ ♅♈ **11:54 pm**

Eastern Time plain / **Pacific Time bold**

JUNE

S	M	T	W	T	F	S
						1
2	3	4	5	6	7	8
9	10	11	12	13	14	15
16	17	18	19	20	21	22
23	24	25	26	27	28	29
30						

JULY

S	M	T	W	T	F	S
	1	2	3	4	5	6
7	8	9	10	11	12	13
14	15	16	17	18	19	20
21	22	23	24	25	26	27
28	29	30	31			

AUGUST

S	M	T	W	T	F	S
				1	2	3
4	5	6	7	8	9	10
11	12	13	14	15	16	17
18	19	20	21	22	23	24
25	26	27	28	29	30	31

July

15 Mon
1st ♎
◐ 23 ♎ 46

☽♎☍ ♅♈	2:54 am	
☽♎⚻ ⚷♓	4:36 am	**1:36 am**
☽♎□ ☿♋	6:38 am	**3:38 am**
☽♎⚹ ♀♌	8:24 pm	**5:24 pm**
☽♎□ ☉♋	11:18 pm	**8:18 pm** ☽ v/c

16 Tue
2nd ♎

☽ enters ♏	10:24 am	**7:24 am**
☽♏△ ♂♋	2:14 pm	**11:14 am**
☽♏△ ♃♋	6:43 pm	**3:43 pm**
☽♏☌ ♄♏	7:00 pm	**4:00 pm**
☽♏△ ♆♓	7:10 pm	**4:10 pm**

17 Wed
2nd ♏

☽♏⚹ ♇♑	3:46 am	**12:46 am**
☽♏⚻ ♅♈	8:17 am	**5:17 am**
☽♏△ ⚷♓	9:48 am	**6:48 am**
☽♏△ ☿♋	10:30 am	**7:30 am**
♅♈℞	1:20 pm	**10:20 am**
♃♋ △ ♄♏	1:31 pm	**10:31 am**
♃♋ △ ♆♓	8:14 pm	**5:14 pm**

18 Thu
2nd ♏

☽♏□ ♀♌	5:35 am	**2:35 am**
☽♏△ ☉♋	7:12 am	**4:12 am** ☽ v/c
☽ enters ♐	1:54 pm	**10:54 am**
☽♐⚻ ♂♋	8:00 pm	**5:00 pm**
☽♐□ ♆♓	10:05 pm	**7:05 pm**
☽♐⚻ ♃♋	10:31 pm	**7:31 pm**

Mercury Note: Mercury goes direct on Saturday but remains in its Storm, moving slowly until July 27. Until then, it is not yet time for new ideas to be workable.

Fri 19
2nd ♐

♄♏△♆♓ 9:20 am **6:20 am**
☽♐△♅♈ 10:31 am **7:31 am**
☽♐□⚷♓ 11:51 am **8:51 am**
☽♐⚻☿♋ 11:58 am **8:58 am**

OP: After Moon trines Uranus today until Moon enters Capricorn on Saturday. Keep on following up on matters begun before June 17.

Sat 20
2nd ♐

☽♐△♀♌ 11:00 am **8:00 am** ☽ v/c
☽♐⚻☉♋ 11:35 am **8:35 am**
☿♋ D 2:22 pm **11:22 am**
☽ enters ♑ 2:39 pm **11:39 am**
♂♋△♆♓ 3:42 pm **12:42 pm**
♂♋△♄♏ 5:34 pm **2:34 pm**
☽♑✶♆♓ 10:25 pm **7:25 pm**
☽♑✶♄♏ 10:31 pm **7:31 pm**
☽♑☍♂♋ 10:45 pm **7:45 pm**
☽♑☍♃♋ 11:37 pm **8:37 pm**

Sun 21
2nd ♑

☽♑☌♇♑ 6:13 am **3:13 am**
☽♑□♅♈ 10:30 am **7:30 am**
☽♑✶⚷♓ 11:42 am **8:42 am**
☽♑☍☿♋ 11:53 am **8:53 am** ☽ v/c

Eastern Time plain / **Pacific Time bold**

JUNE

S	M	T	W	T	F	S
						1
2	3	4	5	6	7	8
9	10	11	12	13	14	15
16	17	18	19	20	21	22
23	24	25	26	27	28	29
30						

JULY

S	M	T	W	T	F	S
	1	2	3	4	5	6
7	8	9	10	11	12	13
14	15	16	17	18	19	20
21	22	23	24	25	26	27
28	29	30	31			

AUGUST

S	M	T	W	T	F	S
				1	2	3
4	5	6	7	8	9	10
11	12	13	14	15	16	17
18	19	20	21	22	23	24
25	26	27	28	29	30	31

July

22 Mon

2nd ♑
○ Full Moon 0 ♒ 06
Sun enters Leo

♂♋ ☌ ♃♋	3:35 am	**12:35 am**
♀ enters ♍	8:41 am	**5:41 am**
☉ enters ♌	11:56 am	**8:56 am**
☽ enters ♒	2:07 pm	**11:07 am**
☽♒ ☍ ☉♌	2:16 pm	**11:16 am**
☽♒ ⚻ ♀♍	2:35 pm	**11:35 am**
☽♒ □ ♄♏	10:02 pm	**7:02 pm**
☽♒ ⚻ ♃♋	11:46 pm	**8:46 pm**
☽♒ ⚻ ♂♋		**9:24 pm**

23 Tue

3rd ♒

☽♒ ⚻ ♂♋	12:24 am	
☽♒ ⚹ ♅♈	10:01 am	**7:01 am** ☽ v/c
☽♒ ⚻ ☿♋	12:01 pm	**9:01 am**

24 Wed

3rd ♒

☽ enters ♓	2:22 pm	**11:22 am**
☽♓ ⚻ ☉♌	5:55 pm	**2:55 pm**
☽♓ ☍ ♀♍	7:12 pm	**4:12 pm**
☽♓ ☌ ♆♓	10:19 pm	**7:19 pm**
☽♓ △ ♄♏	10:44 pm	**7:44 pm**
☽♓ △ ♃♋		**10:12 pm**

25 Thu

3rd ♓

OP: After Moon trines Saturn on Wednesday until Moon enters Aries on Friday. Good for artistic matters, meditation, and helping others.

☽♓ △ ♃♋	1:12 am	
☽♓ △ ♂♋	3:29 am	**12:29 am**
☽♓ ⚹ ♇♑	6:32 am	**3:32 am**
☽♓ ☌ ⚷♓	12:19 pm	**9:19 am**
☽♓ △ ☿♋	2:43 pm	**11:43 am** ☽ v/c

Fri 26
3rd ♓

♀♍ ☍ ♆♓	8:08 am	**5:08 am**
♀♍ ⚹ ♄♏	2:36 pm	**11:36 am**
☽ enters ♈	5:29 pm	**2:29 pm**
☽♈ △ ☉♌		**10:13 pm**
☽♈ ⚻ ♄♏		**11:36 pm**

OP: After Moon trines Saturn on Wednesday until Moon enters Aries today. Good for artistic matters, meditation, and helping others.

Sat 27
3rd ♈

☽♈ △ ☉♌	1:13 am	
☽♈ ⚻ ♄♏	2:36 am	
☽♈ ⚻ ♀♍	3:45 am	**12:45 am**
☽♈ □ ♃♋	6:00 am	**3:00 am**
☽♈ □ ♂♋	10:23 am	**7:23 am**
☽♈ □ ♇♑	10:49 am	**7:49 am**
☉♌ ⚻ ♆♓	11:20 am	**8:20 am**
☽♈ ☌ ♅♈	3:56 pm	**12:56 pm**
♂♋ ☍ ♇♑	6:51 pm	**3:51 pm**
☉♌ □ ♄♏	9:05 pm	**6:05 pm**
☽♈ □ ☿♋	10:19 pm	**7:19 pm** ☽ v/c

Sun 28
3rd ♈

♀♍ ⚹ ♃♋	9:42 am	**6:42 am**
☽ enters ♉		**9:43 pm**

Eastern Time plain / **Pacific Time bold**

JUNE

S	M	T	W	T	F	S
						1
2	3	4	5	6	7	8
9	10	11	12	13	14	15
16	17	18	19	20	21	22
23	24	25	26	27	28	29
30						

JULY

S	M	T	W	T	F	S
	1	2	3	4	5	6
7	8	9	10	11	12	13
14	15	16	17	18	19	20
21	22	23	24	25	26	27
28	29	30	31			

AUGUST

S	M	T	W	T	F	S
				1	2	3
4	5	6	7	8	9	10
11	12	13	14	15	16	17
18	19	20	21	22	23	24
25	26	27	28	29	30	31

29 Mon
3rd ♈
◑ 6 ♉ 45

OP: After Moon squares Sun today until Moon enters Gemini on Wednesday. Look over your list of new ideas from the Mercury Retrograde and slow periods, and see what they look like now.

☽ enters ♉	12:43 am	
☽♉ ⚹ ♆♓	9:45 am	**6:45 am**
☽♉ ☍ ♄♏	10:41 am	**7:41 am**
☽♉ □ ☉♌	1:43 pm	**10:43 am**
☽♉ ⚹ ♃♋	3:12 pm	**12:12 pm**
☽♉ △ ♀♍	5:48 pm	**2:48 pm**
☽♉ △ ♇♑	7:17 pm	**4:17 pm**
☽♉ ⚹ ♂♋	10:09 pm	**7:09 pm**
☽♉ ⚹ ⚷♓		**10:53 pm**

30 Tue
4th ♉

☽♉ ⚹ ⚷♓	1:53 am	
♀♍ △ ♇♑	8:52 am	**5:52 am**
☽♉ ⚹ ☿♋	11:58 am	**8:58 am** ☽ v/c

31 Wed
4th ♉

☽ enters ♊	11:42 am	**8:42 am**
☽♊ □ ♆♓	9:03 pm	**6:03 pm**
☽♊ ⚻ ♄♏	10:20 pm	**7:20 pm**
♂♋ □ ♅♈	11:08 pm	**8:08 pm**

1 Thu
4th ♊
Lammas

☽♊ ⚹ ☉♌	6:33 am	**3:33 am**
☽♊ ⚻ ♇♑	7:00 am	**4:00 am**
☉♌ ⚻ ♇♑	12:06 pm	**9:06 am**
☽♊ □ ♀♍	12:17 pm	**9:17 am**
☽♊ ⚹ ♅♈	12:48 pm	**9:48 am** ☽ v/c
☽♊ □ ⚷♓	1:46 pm	**10:46 am**
♂♋ △ ⚷♓	3:48 pm	**12:48 pm**
♀♍ ⚻ ♅♈	5:28 pm	**2:28 pm**
♀♍ ☍ ⚷♓		**11:32 pm**

FRI 2
4th ♊

♀♍ ☍ ⚷♓ 2:32 am
♀♍ ⚹ ♂♋ 4:35 pm **1:35 pm**
☽ enters ♋ **9:29 pm**

SAT 3
4th ♊

☽ enters ♋ 12:29 am
☽♋ △ ♆♓ 9:48 am **6:48 am**
☽♋ △ ♄♏ 11:25 am **8:25 am**
☽♋ ☌ ♃♋ 5:55 pm **2:55 pm**
☽♋ ☍ ♇♑ 7:47 pm **4:47 pm**
☽♋ □ ♅♈ **10:37 pm**
☽♋ △ ⚷♓ **11:26 pm**

SUN 4
4th ♋

☽♋ □ ♅♈ 1:37 am
☽♋ △ ⚷♓ 2:26 am
☽♋ ☌ ♂♋ 6:05 am **3:05 am**
☽♋ ⚹ ♀♍ 7:58 am **4:58 am**
☉♌ △ ♅♈ 11:05 am **8:05 am**
☉♌ ⚻ ⚷♓ 8:38 pm **5:38 pm**
☽♋ ☌ ☿♋ **11:49 pm** ☽ v/c

OP: After Moon conjoins Mars today until Moon enters Leo on Monday. Good for following through, before the Moon goes Balsamic on Monday.

Eastern Time plain / **Pacific Time bold**

JULY

S	M	T	W	T	F	S
	1	2	3	4	5	6
7	8	9	10	11	12	13
14	15	16	17	18	19	20
21	22	23	24	25	26	27
28	29	30	31			

AUGUST

S	M	T	W	T	F	S
				1	2	3
4	5	6	7	8	9	10
11	12	13	14	15	16	17
18	19	20	21	22	23	24
25	26	27	28	29	30	31

SEPTEMBER

S	M	T	W	T	F	S
1	2	3	4	5	6	7
8	9	10	11	12	13	14
15	16	17	18	19	20	21
22	23	24	25	26	27	28
29	30					

August

5 Mon

4th ♋

☽♋ ☌ ☿♋	2:49 am	☽ v/c
☽ enters ♌	12:58 pm	**9:58 am**
☽♌ ⚻ ♆♓	9:58 pm	**6:58 pm**
☽♌ □ ♄♏	11:54 pm	**8:54 pm**

6 Tue

4th ♌

● New Moon 14 ♌ 35

OP: This Cazimi Moon is usable ½ hour before and ½ hour after the Sun-Moon conjunction. An excellent time to start something important.

☽♌ ⚻ ♇♑	7:45 am	**4:45 am**
☽♌ △ ♅♈	1:29 pm	**10:29 am**
☽♌ ⚻ ⚷♓	2:09 pm	**11:09 am**
☽♌ ☌ ☉♌	5:51 pm	**2:51 pm** ☽ v/c

7 Wed

1st ♌

Ramadan ends

♃♋ ☍ ♇♑	7:46 pm	**4:46 pm**
☽ enters ♍	11:57 pm	**8:57 pm**

8 Thu

1st ♍

OP: After Moon trines Pluto today until v/c Moon on Friday. Excellent for sales and socializing.

☿ enters ♌	8:13 am	**5:13 am**
☽♍ ☍ ♆♓	8:34 am	**5:34 am**
☽♍ ⚹ ♄♏	10:47 am	**7:47 am**
☽♍ △ ♇♑	6:06 pm	**3:06 pm**
☽♍ ⚹ ♃♋	6:30 pm	**3:30 pm**
☽♍ ⚻ ♅♈	11:40 pm	**8:40 pm**
☽♍ ☍ ⚷♓		**9:12 pm**

Fri 9
1st ♍

☽♍ ☍ ⚷♓ 12:12 am
☽♍ ⚹ ♂♋ 10:32 am **7:32 am**
☽♍ ☌ ♀♍ 6:05 pm **3:05 pm** ☽ v/c

Sat 10
1st ♍

☽ enters ♎ 9:08 am **6:08 am**
☽♎ ⚹ ☿♌ 4:53 pm **1:53 pm**
☽♎ ⚻ ♆♓ 5:22 pm **2:22 pm**
☿♌ ⚻ ♆♓ 8:10 pm **5:10 pm**
☽♎ □ ♇♑ **11:36 pm**

Sun 11
1st ♎

☽♎ □ ♇♑ 2:36 am
☽♎ □ ♃♋ 3:58 am **12:58 am**
☽♎ ☍ ♅♈ 7:59 am **4:59 am**
☽♎ ⚻ ⚷♓ 8:24 am **5:24 am**
☿♌ □ ♄♏ 2:05 pm **11:05 am**
☽♎ ⚹ ☉♌ 9:16 pm **6:16 pm**
☽♎ □ ♂♋ 9:29 pm **6:29 pm** ☽ v/c

Eastern Time plain / **Pacific Time bold**

JULY

S	M	T	W	T	F	S
	1	2	3	4	5	6
7	8	9	10	11	12	13
14	15	16	17	18	19	20
21	22	23	24	25	26	27
28	29	30	31			

AUGUST

S	M	T	W	T	F	S
				1	2	3
4	5	6	7	8	9	10
11	12	13	14	15	16	17
18	19	20	21	22	23	24
25	26	27	28	29	30	31

SEPTEMBER

S	M	T	W	T	F	S
1	2	3	4	5	6	7
8	9	10	11	12	13	14
15	16	17	18	19	20	21
22	23	24	25	26	27	28
29	30					

August

12 Mon
1st ♎

☽ enters ♏	4:18 pm	**1:18 pm**
☽♏ △ ♆♓		**9:05 pm**
☽♏ ☌ ♄♏		**11:48 pm**

13 Tue
1st ♏

☽♏ △ ♆♓	12:05 am	
☽♏ ☌ ♄♏	2:48 am	
☽♏ □ ☿♌	8:39 am	**5:39 am**
☽♏ ⚹ ♇♑	8:59 am	**5:59 am**
☿♌ ⚻ ♇♑	10:58 am	**7:58 am**
☽♏ △ ♃♋	11:11 am	**8:11 am**
☽♏ ⚻ ♅♈	2:07 pm	**11:07 am**
☽♏ △ ⚷♓	2:26 pm	**11:26 am**

14 Wed
1st ♏

◐ 21 ♏ 49

OP: After Moon squares Sun until v/c Moon. The First Quarter Moon can put a gentle wind in our sails.

☽♏ △ ♂♋	5:47 am	**2:47 am**
☽♏ □ ☉♌	6:56 am	**3:56 am**
☽♏ ⚹ ♀♍	5:30 pm	**2:30 pm** ☽ v/c
☽ enters ♐	9:04 pm	**6:04 pm**
☿♌ △ ♅♈	10:11 pm	**7:11 pm**
☿♌ ⚻ ⚷♓	11:56 pm	**8:56 pm**

15 Thu
2nd ♐

OP: After Moon trines Uranus today until Moon enters Capricorn on Friday. Lots of energy to direct as we wish.

☽♐ □ ♆♓	4:24 am	**1:24 am**
☽♐ ⚻ ♃♋	3:48 pm	**12:48 pm**
☽♐ △ ♅♈	5:48 pm	**2:48 pm**
☽♐ □ ⚷♓	6:01 pm	**3:01 pm**
☽♐ △ ☿♌	9:00 pm	**6:00 pm**

FRI 16
2nd ♐

☽♐ ⊼ ♂♋ 11:13 am **8:13 am**
♀ enters ♎ 11:37 am **8:37 am**
☽♐ △ ☉♌ 1:32 pm **10:32 am** ☽ v/c
☽ enters ♑ 11:25 pm **8:25 pm**
☽♑ □ ♀♎ **9:28 pm**

OP: After Moon trines Uranus on Thursday until Moon enters Capricorn today. Lots of energy to direct as we wish.

SAT 17
2nd ♑

☽♑ □ ♀♎ 12:28 am
☽♑ ⚹ ♆♓ 6:21 am **3:21 am**
☽♑ ⚹ ♄♏ 9:26 am **6:26 am**
☽♑ ☌ ♇♑ 2:34 pm **11:34 am**
☽♑ ☍ ♃♋ 6:04 pm **3:04 pm**
☽♑ □ ♅♈ 7:15 pm **4:15 pm**
☽♑ ⚹ ⚷♓ 7:23 pm **4:23 pm**

SUN 18
2nd ♑

☽♑ ⊼ ☿♌ 6:11 am **3:11 am**
☽♑ ☍ ♂♋ 2:26 pm **11:26 am** ☽ v/c
☽♑ ⊼ ☉♌ 5:50 pm **2:50 pm**
☽ enters ♒ **9:07 pm**

Eastern Time plain / **Pacific Time bold**

JULY

S	M	T	W	T	F	S
	1	2	3	4	5	6
7	8	9	10	11	12	13
14	15	16	17	18	19	20
21	22	23	24	25	26	27
28	29	30	31			

AUGUST

S	M	T	W	T	F	S
				1	2	3
4	5	6	7	8	9	10
11	12	13	14	15	16	17
18	19	20	21	22	23	24
25	26	27	28	29	30	31

SEPTEMBER

S	M	T	W	T	F	S
1	2	3	4	5	6	7
8	9	10	11	12	13	14
15	16	17	18	19	20	21
22	23	24	25	26	27	28
29	30					

August

19 Mon
2nd ♑
OP: After Moon sextiles Uranus today until v/c Moon on Tuesday. Good for getting a lot done.

☽ enters ♒	12:07 am	
☽♒ △ ♀♎	5:20 am	**2:20 am**
☽♒ □ ♄♏	10:10 am	**7:10 am**
☽♒ ⚻ ♃♋	7:08 pm	**4:08 pm**
☽♒ ⚹ ♅♈	7:36 pm	**4:36 pm**
♀♎ ⚻ ♆♓	11:53 pm	**8:53 pm**

20 Tue
2nd ♒
○ Full Moon 28 ♒ 11

☽♒ ☍ ☿♌	2:17 pm	**11:17 am**
☽♒ ⚻ ♂♋	5:08 pm	**2:08 pm**
☽♒ ☍ ☉♌	9:45 pm	**6:45 pm** ☽ v/c
☽ enters ♓		**9:43 pm**

21 Wed
3rd ♒
OP: After Moon sextiles Pluto today until Moon enters Aries on Friday. Good for artistic matters, meditation, and helping others.

☽ enters ♓	12:43 am	
♃♋ □ ♅♈	3:15 am	**12:15 am**
♃♋ △ ⚷♓	4:55 am	**1:55 am**
☽♓ ☌ ♆♓	7:30 am	**4:30 am**
☽♓ ⚻ ♀♎	10:22 am	**7:22 am**
☽♓ △ ♄♏	11:14 am	**8:14 am**
☽♓ ⚹ ♇♑	3:56 pm	**12:56 pm**
☽♓ ☌ ⚷♓	8:39 pm	**5:39 pm**
☽♓ △ ♃♋	8:55 pm	**5:55 pm**

22 Thu
3rd ♓
Sun enters Virgo

☉ enters ♍	7:02 pm	**4:02 pm**
☽♓ △ ♂♋	9:38 pm	**6:38 pm** ☽ v/c
☽♓ ⚻ ☿♌		**9:38 pm**

FRI 23
3rd ♓

Last of the OP that began on Wednesday.

☽♓ ⚻ ☿♌	12:38 am	
☽ enters ♈	3:13 am	**12:13 am**
☽♈ ⚻ ☉♍	3:50 am	**12:50 am**
☽♈ ⚻ ♄♏	2:38 pm	**11:38 am**
☽♈ ☍ ♀♎	6:17 pm	**3:17 pm**
☿ enters ♍	6:36 pm	**3:36 pm**
☽♈ □ ♇♑	7:19 pm	**4:19 pm**
☽♈ ☌ ♅♈		**9:18 pm**
☽♈ □ ♃♋		**10:25 pm**

SAT 24
3rd ♈

☽♈ ☌ ♅♈	12:18 am	
☽♈ □ ♃♋	1:25 am	
♀♎ □ ♇♑	6:01 am	**3:01 am**
☉♍ ☌ ☿♍	4:56 pm	**1:56 pm**

SUN 25
3rd ♈

☽♈ □ ♂♋	6:02 am	**3:02 am** ☽ v/c
☽ enters ♉	9:13 am	**6:13 am**
☽♉ △ ☉♍	2:17 pm	**11:17 am**
☽♉ △ ☿♍	4:16 pm	**1:16 pm**
☽♉ ⚹ ♆♓	4:43 pm	**1:43 pm**
☿♍ ☍ ♆♓	7:12 pm	**4:12 pm**
☽♉ ☍ ♄♏	9:49 pm	**6:49 pm**
☽♉ △ ♇♑		**11:30 pm**

Eastern Time plain / **Pacific Time bold**

JULY

S	M	T	W	T	F	S
	1	2	3	4	5	6
7	8	9	10	11	12	13
14	15	16	17	18	19	20
21	22	23	24	25	26	27
28	29	30	31			

AUGUST

S	M	T	W	T	F	S
				1	2	3
4	5	6	7	8	9	10
11	12	13	14	15	16	17
18	19	20	21	22	23	24
25	26	27	28	29	30	31

SEPTEMBER

S	M	T	W	T	F	S
1	2	3	4	5	6	7
8	9	10	11	12	13	14
15	16	17	18	19	20	21
22	23	24	25	26	27	28
29	30					

August

26 Mon
3rd ♉

OP: After Moon trines Pluto Sunday/today until Moon enters Gemini on Tuesday. Nervous energy and spaciness do not keep us from getting things done.

Aspect	Eastern	Pacific	
☽♉ △ ♇♑	2:30 am		
☽♉ ⚻ ♀♎	7:09 am	**4:09 am**	
☽♉ ⚹ ⚷♓	7:38 am	**4:38 am**	
☽♉ ⚹ ♃♋	9:57 am	**6:57 am**	
♀♎ ⚻ ⚷♓	12:13 pm	**9:13 am**	
♀♎ ☍ ♅♈	1:56 pm	**10:56 am**	
☉♍ ☍ ♆♓	9:43 pm	**6:43 pm**	

27 Tue
3rd ♉

Aspect	Eastern	Pacific	
☿♍ ⚹ ♄♏	5:44 am	**2:44 am**	
♀♎ □ ♃♋	5:53 pm	**2:53 pm**	
☽♉ ⚹ ♂♋	6:58 pm	**3:58 pm**	☽ v/c
☽ enters ♊	7:08 pm	**4:08 pm**	
♂ enters ♌	10:05 pm	**7:05 pm**	
☽♊ □ ♆♓		**11:57 pm**	

28 Wed
3rd ♊

◑ 5 ♊ 15

OP: After Moon squares Mercury today until v/c Moon today/Thursday. A busy day and a very pleasant, social evening.

Aspect	Eastern	Pacific	
☽♊ □ ♆♓	2:57 am		
☽♊ □ ☉♍	5:35 am	**2:35 am**	
☽♊ ⚻ ♄♏	8:51 am	**5:51 am**	
☿♍ △ ♇♑	10:52 am	**7:52 am**	
☽♊ ⚻ ♇♑	1:20 pm	**10:20 am**	
☽♊ □ ☿♍	1:49 pm	**10:49 am**	
☽♊ □ ⚷♓	6:34 pm	**3:34 pm**	
☽♊ ⚹ ♅♈	6:49 pm	**3:49 pm**	
☽♊ △ ♀♎		**9:44 pm**	☽ v/c

29 Thu
4th ♊

Aspect	Eastern	Pacific	
☽♊ △ ♀♎	12:44 am		☽ v/c
☿♍ ☍ ⚷♓	7:12 pm	**4:12 pm**	
☿♍ ⚻ ♅♈	9:00 pm	**6:00 pm**	
☉♍ ⚹ ♄♏		**10:18 pm**	

FRI 30
4th ♊

☉♍ ✶ ♄♏ 1:18 am
☽ enters ♋ 7:33 am **4:33 am**
☽♋ △ ♆♓ 3:23 pm **12:23 pm**
☽♋ △ ♄♏ 9:53 pm **6:53 pm**
☿♍ ✶ ♃♋ 11:10 pm **8:10 pm**
☽♋ ✶ ☉♍ 11:34 pm **8:34 pm**
☽♋ ☍ ♇♑ **10:58 pm**

SAT 31
4th ♋

☽♋ ☍ ♇♑ 1:58 am
☽♋ △ ⚷♓ 7:03 am **4:03 am**
☽♋ □ ♅♈ 7:23 am **4:23 am**
☽♋ ☌ ♃♋ 11:46 am **8:46 am**
☽♋ ✶ ☿♍ 1:53 pm **10:53 am**
☽♋ □ ♀♎ 8:06 pm **5:06 pm** ☽ v/c

OP: After Moon squares Venus today until Moon enters Leo on Sunday. The Last-Quarter Moon warns us to take it easy now.

SUN 1
4th ♋

☉♍ △ ♇♑ 4:46 am **1:46 am**
☽ enters ♌ 8:01 pm **5:01 pm**
☽♌ ☌ ♂♌ **11:36 pm**

Eastern Time plain / **Pacific Time bold**

AUGUST

S	M	T	W	T	F	S
				1	2	3
4	5	6	7	8	9	10
11	12	13	14	15	16	17
18	19	20	21	22	23	24
25	26	27	28	29	30	31

SEPTEMBER

S	M	T	W	T	F	S
1	2	3	4	5	6	7
8	9	10	11	12	13	14
15	16	17	18	19	20	21
22	23	24	25	26	27	28
29	30					

OCTOBER

S	M	T	W	T	F	S
		1	2	3	4	5
6	7	8	9	10	11	12
13	14	15	16	17	18	19
20	21	22	23	24	25	26
27	28	29	30	31		

September

2 Mon

4th ♌︎

Labor Day

OP: After Moon trines Uranus today until v/c Moon on Tuesday. Early on Tuesday is good for following up on contacts and sales.

☽♌︎ ☌ ♂♌︎	2:36 am	
☽♌︎ ⚻ ♆♓︎	3:33 am	**12:33 am**
☽♌︎ □ ♄♏︎	10:27 am	**7:27 am**
☽♌︎ ⚻ ♇♑︎	1:59 pm	**10:59 am**
☽♌︎ ⚻ ⚷♓︎	6:45 pm	**3:45 pm**
☽♌︎ △ ♅♈︎	7:09 pm	**4:09 pm**
♂♌︎ ⚻ ♆♓︎	8:00 pm	**5:00 pm**

3 Tue

4th ♌︎

☽♌︎ ✶ ♀♎︎	1:52 pm	**10:52 am** ☽ v/c
☉♍︎ ☍ ⚷♓︎	3:14 pm	**12:14 pm**
☉♍︎ ⚻ ♅♈︎	8:28 pm	**5:28 pm**

4 Wed

4th ♌︎

☽ enters ♍︎	6:43 am	**3:43 am**
☽♍︎ ☍ ♆♓︎	1:52 pm	**10:52 am**
☽♍︎ ✶ ♄♏︎	9:01 pm	**6:01 pm**
☽♍︎ △ ♇♑︎	11:59 pm	**8:59 pm**

5 Thu

4th ♍︎

● New Moon 13 ♍︎ 04

Rosh Hashanah

OP: This Cazimi Moon is usable ½ hour before and ½ hour after the Sun-Moon conjunction. An excellent time to begin something important.

☽♍︎ ☍ ⚷♓︎	4:23 am	**1:23 am**
☽♍︎ ⚻ ♅♈︎	4:50 am	**1:50 am**
☽♍︎ ☌ ☉♍︎	7:36 am	**4:36 am**
☽♍︎ ✶ ♃♋︎	10:49 am	**7:49 am**

FRI 6
1st ♍

☽♍ ☌ ☿♍ 6:10 am **3:10 am** ☽ v/c
☽ enters ♎ 3:12 pm **12:12 pm**
☽♎ ⚻ ♆♓ 9:58 pm **6:58 pm**

SAT 7
1st ♎

☽♎ ⚹ ♂♌ 3:11 am **12:11 am**
☽♎ □ ♇♑ 7:49 am **4:49 am**
☉♍ ⚹ ♃♋ 9:46 am **6:46 am**
☽♎ ⚻ ⚷♓ 11:53 am **8:53 am**
☽♎ ☍ ♅♈ 12:22 pm **9:22 am**
☽♎ □ ♃♋ 6:59 pm **3:59 pm**

OP: After Moon squares Jupiter today until v/c Moon on Sunday. If you're hoping to meet a new lover, you couldn't do better than this evening. Wait two hours after the square before you arrive on the scene.

SUN 8
1st ♎

☽♎ ☌ ♀♎ 4:46 pm **1:46 pm** ☽ v/c
☽ enters ♏ 9:44 pm **6:44 pm**

Eastern Time plain / **Pacific Time bold**

AUGUST

S	M	T	W	T	F	S
				1	2	3
4	5	6	7	8	9	10
11	12	13	14	15	16	17
18	19	20	21	22	23	24
25	26	27	28	29	30	31

SEPTEMBER

S	M	T	W	T	F	S
1	2	3	4	5	6	7
8	9	10	11	12	13	14
15	16	17	18	19	20	21
22	23	24	25	26	27	28
29	30					

OCTOBER

S	M	T	W	T	F	S
		1	2	3	4	5
6	7	8	9	10	11	12
13	14	15	16	17	18	19
20	21	22	23	24	25	26
27	28	29	30	31		

9 Mon
1st ♏

OP: After Moon sextiles Pluto today until v/c Moon on Tuesday. This afternoon is great for whatever you need to accomplish.

☿ enters ♎	3:07 am	**12:07 am**
☽♏ △ ♆♓	4:10 am	**1:10 am**
♂♌ □ ♄♏	7:06 am	**4:06 am**
☽♏ ☌ ♄♏	11:47 am	**8:47 am**
☽♏ □ ♂♌	11:59 am	**8:59 am**
☽♏ ⚹ ♇♑	1:48 pm	**10:48 am**
☽♏ △ ⚷♓	5:34 pm	**2:34 pm**
☽♏ ⚻ ♅♈	6:06 pm	**3:06 pm**
☽♏ △ ♃♋		**10:17 pm**

10 Tue
1st ♏

☽♏ △ ♃♋	1:17 am	
☽♏ ⚹ ☉♍	5:21 am	**2:21 am** ☽ v/c
♀ enters ♏		**11:16 pm**
☽ enters ♐		**11:36 pm**
♂♌ ⚻ ♇♑		**11:39 pm**

11 Wed
1st ♏

♀ enters ♏	2:16 am	
☽ enters ♐	2:36 am	
♂♌ ⚻ ♇♑	2:39 am	
☿♎ ⚻ ♆♓	6:43 am	**3:43 am**
☽♐ □ ♆♓	8:44 am	**5:44 am**
☽♐ ⚹ ☿♎	9:01 am	**6:01 am**
☽♐ △ ♂♌	6:54 pm	**3:54 pm**
☽♐ □ ⚷♓	9:40 pm	**6:40 pm**
☽♐ △ ♅♈	10:13 pm	**7:13 pm**

12 Thu
1st ♐

◐ 20 ♐ 06

OP: After Moon squares Sun today until Moon enters Capricorn on Friday. Good for any activity you want.

☽♐ ⚻ ♃♋	5:55 am	**2:55 am**
☽♐ □ ☉♍	1:08 pm	**10:08 am** ☽ v/c

Fri 13 — 2nd ♐

Aspect	Eastern	Pacific
☽ enters ♑	5:56 am	**2:56 am**
☽♑ ⚹ ♀♏	10:29 am	**7:29 am**
☽♑ ⚹ ♆♓	11:49 am	**8:49 am**
☽♑ □ ☿♎	6:40 pm	**3:40 pm**
☽♑ ⚹ ♄♏	7:52 pm	**4:52 pm**
☽♑ ☌ ♇♑	9:04 pm	**6:04 pm**
☽♑ ⚻ ♂♌		**9:08 pm**
☽♑ ⚹ ⚷♓		**9:20 pm**
☽♑ □ ♅♈		**9:55 pm**
♀♏ △ ♆♓		**11:33 pm**

Sat 14 — 2nd ♑ — Yom Kippur

Aspect	Eastern	Pacific
☽♑ ⚻ ♂♌	12:08 am	
☽♑ ⚹ ⚷♓	12:20 am	
☽♑ □ ♅♈	12:55 am	
♀♏ △ ♆♓	2:33 am	
♂♌ ⚻ ⚷♓	4:31 am	**1:31 am**
☽♑ ☍ ♃♋	9:05 am	**6:05 am**
☿♎ □ ♇♑	4:29 pm	**1:29 pm**
♂♌ △ ♅♈	4:57 pm	**1:57 pm**
☽♑ △ ☉♍	7:17 pm	**4:17 pm** ☽ v/c

OP: After Moon squares Uranus on Friday/today until v/c Moon. Mostly smooth sailing.

Sun 15 — 2nd ♑

Aspect	Eastern	Pacific
☽ enters ♒	8:05 am	**5:05 am**
☽♒ □ ♀♏	4:55 pm	**1:55 pm**
☿♎ ⚻ ⚷♓	9:15 pm	**6:15 pm**
☽♒ □ ♄♏	10:10 pm	**7:10 pm**
☿♎ ☍ ♅♈		**11:41 pm**
☽♒ ⚹ ♅♈		**11:42 pm**
☽♒ △ ☿♎		**11:42 pm**

Eastern Time plain / **Pacific Time bold**

AUGUST

S	M	T	W	T	F	S
				1	2	3
4	5	6	7	8	9	10
11	12	13	14	15	16	17
18	19	20	21	22	23	24
25	26	27	28	29	30	31

SEPTEMBER

S	M	T	W	T	F	S
1	2	3	4	5	6	7
8	9	10	11	12	13	14
15	16	17	18	19	20	21
22	23	24	25	26	27	28
29	30					

OCTOBER

S	M	T	W	T	F	S
		1	2	3	4	5
6	7	8	9	10	11	12
13	14	15	16	17	18	19
20	21	22	23	24	25	26
27	28	29	30	31		

September

16 Mon
2nd ♒

☿♎ ☍ ♅♈	2:41 am	
☽♒ ⚹ ♅♈	2:42 am	
☽♒ △ ☿♎	2:42 am	
☽♒ ☍ ♂♌	4:19 am	**1:19 am** ☽ v/c
☽♒ ⚻ ♃♋	11:28 am	**8:28 am**
☽♒ ⚻ ☉♍		**9:44 pm**

17 Tue
2nd ♒

OP: After Moon conjoins Neptune today until Moon enters Aries on Thursday. Good for artistic matters, meditation, and helping others.

☽♒ ⚻ ☉♍	12:44 am	
☿♎ ⚹ ♂♌	3:17 am	**12:17 am**
☽ enters ♓	9:58 am	**6:58 am**
☽♓ ☌ ♆♓	3:38 pm	**12:38 pm**
☽♓ △ ♀♏	11:15 pm	**8:15 pm**
☽♓ △ ♄♏		**9:33 pm**
☽♓ ⚹ ♇♑		**10:04 pm**

18 Wed
2nd ♓
Sukkot begins

☽♓ △ ♄♏	12:33 am	
☽♓ ⚹ ♇♑	1:04 am	
☽♓ ☌ ⚷♓	4:03 am	**1:03 am**
☽♓ ⚻ ♂♌	8:46 am	**5:46 am**
☽♓ ⚻ ☿♎	10:51 am	**7:51 am**
☽♓ △ ♃♋	2:16 pm	**11:16 am**
♀♏ ☌ ♄♏	4:54 pm	**1:54 pm**
♀♏ ⚹ ♇♑	9:51 pm	**6:51 pm**

19 Thu
2nd ♓
○ Full Moon 26 ♓ 41

☽♓ ☍ ☉♍	7:13 am	**4:13 am** ☽ v/c
☽ enters ♈	12:58 pm	**9:58 am**
☿♎ □ ♃♋	10:20 pm	**7:20 pm**

☽♈ ⚻ ♄♏	4:32 am	**1:32 am**	
☽♈ □ ♇♑	4:41 am	**1:41 am**	
☽♈ ⚻ ♀♏	7:31 am	**4:31 am**	
☽♈ ☌ ♅♈	8:20 am	**5:20 am**	
♀♏ △ ⚷♓	8:57 am	**5:57 am**	
♇♑ D	11:29 am	**8:29 am**	
☽♈ △ ♂♌	3:18 pm	**12:18 pm**	
♀♏ ⚻ ♅♈	4:53 pm	**1:53 pm**	
☽♈ □ ♃♋	7:06 pm	**4:06 pm**	
☽♈ ☍ ☿♎	9:25 pm	**6:25 pm**	☽ v/c
♄♏ ✶ ♇♑		**10:45 pm**	

Fri 20
3rd ♈

♄♏ ✶ ♇♑	1:45 am	
☽♈ ⚻ ☉♍	4:45 pm	1:45 pm
☽ enters ♉	6:33 pm	**3:33 pm**
☽♉ ✶ ♆♓		**9:37 pm**

Sat 21
3rd ♈

☽♉ ✶ ♆♓	12:37 am	
☽♉ △ ♇♑	11:16 am	**8:16 am**
☽♉ ☍ ♄♏	11:32 am	**8:32 am**
☽♉ ✶ ⚷♓	2:14 pm	**11:14 am**
☉ enters ♎	4:44 pm	**1:44 pm**
☽♉ ☍ ♀♏	7:41 pm	**4:41 pm**
☽♉ □ ♂♌		**10:25 pm**

Sun 22
3rd ♉
Fall Equinox
Mabon
Sun enters Libra

Eastern Time plain / **Pacific Time bold**

August

S	M	T	W	T	F	S
				1	2	3
4	5	6	7	8	9	10
11	12	13	14	15	16	17
18	19	20	21	22	23	24
25	26	27	28	29	30	31

September

S	M	T	W	T	F	S
1	2	3	4	5	6	7
8	9	10	11	12	13	14
15	16	17	18	19	20	21
22	23	24	25	26	27	28
29	30					

October

S	M	T	W	T	F	S
		1	2	3	4	5
6	7	8	9	10	11	12
13	14	15	16	17	18	19
20	21	22	23	24	25	26
27	28	29	30	31		

23 MON
3rd ♉

OP: After Moon squares Mars on Sunday/today until Moon enters Gemini on Tuesday. Practical accomplishments beckon.

☽♉ □ ♂♌ 1:25 am
☽♉ ✶ ♃♋ 3:13 am **12:13 am** ☽ v/c
☽♉ ⊼ ☿♎ 12:19 pm **9:19 am**

24 TUE
3rd ♉

☽ enters ♊ 3:34 am **12:34 am**
☽♊ △ ☉♎ 6:36 am **3:36 am**
☽♊ □ ♆♓ 9:53 am **6:53 am**
☽♊ ⊼ ♇♑ 9:17 pm **6:17 pm**
☽♊ ⊼ ♄♏ 10:03 pm **7:03 pm**
☽♊ □ ⚷♓ **9:12 pm**
☽♊ ✶ ♅♈ **10:00 pm**

25 WED
3rd ♊

SUKKOT ENDS

OP: After Moon sextiles Mars today until v/c Moon on Thursday. Good for communication.

☽♊ □ ⚷♓ 12:12 am
☽♊ ✶ ♅♈ 1:00 am
☽♊ ⊼ ♀♏ 12:14 pm **9:14 am**
☽♊ ✶ ♂♌ 3:22 pm **12:22 pm**
☉♎ ⊼ ♆♓ 10:51 pm **7:51 pm**

26 THU
3rd ♊

◑ 4 ♋ 13

☽♊ △ ☿♎ 7:21 am **4:21 am** ☽ v/c
☽ enters ♋ 3:24 pm **12:24 pm**
♀♏ △ ♃♋ 5:01 pm **2:01 pm**
☽♋ △ ♆♓ 9:48 pm **6:48 pm**
☽♋ □ ☉♎ 11:55 pm **8:55 pm**

Fri 27
4th ♋

☽♋ ☍ ♇♑ 9:37 am **6:37 am**
☽♋ △ ♄♏ 10:55 am **7:55 am**
☽♋ △ ⚷♓ 12:21 pm **9:21 am**
☽♋ □ ♅♈ 1:11 pm **10:11 am**

Sat 28
4th ♋

☽♋ ☌ ♃♋ 3:52 am **12:52 am**
☽♋ △ ♀♏ 7:08 am **4:08 am**
♀♏ □ ♂♌ 9:32 am **6:32 am**

Sun 29
4th ♋

☽♋ □ ☿♎ 3:30 am **12:30 am** ☽ v/c
☽ enters ♌ 3:57 am **12:57 am**
☿ enters ♏ 7:38 am **4:38 am**
☽♌ ⚻ ♆♓ 10:10 am **7:10 am**
☽♌ ⚹ ☉♎ 5:43 pm **2:43 pm**
☽♌ ⚻ ♇♑ 9:54 pm **6:54 pm**
☽♌ □ ♄♏ 11:42 pm **8:42 pm**
☽♌ ⚻ ⚷♓ **9:21 pm**
☽♌ △ ♅♈ **10:11 pm**

Eastern Time plain / **Pacific Time bold**

AUGUST

S	M	T	W	T	F	S
				1	2	3
4	5	6	7	8	9	10
11	12	13	14	15	16	17
18	19	20	21	22	23	24
25	26	27	28	29	30	31

SEPTEMBER

S	M	T	W	T	F	S
1	2	3	4	5	6	7
8	9	10	11	12	13	14
15	16	17	18	19	20	21
22	23	24	25	26	27	28
29	30					

OCTOBER

S	M	T	W	T	F	S
		1	2	3	4	5
6	7	8	9	10	11	12
13	14	15	16	17	18	19
20	21	22	23	24	25	26
27	28	29	30	31		

September • October

30 Mon
4th ♌

☽♌ ⚻ ⚷♓	12:21 am		
☽♌ △ ♅♈	1:11 am		
☽♌ ☌ ♂♌	10:03 pm	**7:03 pm**	
☽♌ □ ♀♏		**9:48 pm**	☽ v/c

1 Tue
4th ♌

OP: After Moon opposes Neptune today until v/c Moon on Thursday. Take care of routine matters.

☽♌ □ ♀♏	12:48 am		☽ v/c
☽ enters ♍	2:52 pm	**11:52 am**	
☿♏ △ ♆♓	5:46 pm	**2:46 pm**	
☽♍ ☍ ♆♓	8:43 pm	**5:43 pm**	
☽♍ ⚹ ☿♏	9:03 pm	**6:03 pm**	
☉♎ □ ♇♑	9:28 pm	**6:28 pm**	

2 Wed
4th ♍

♄♏ △ ⚷♓	5:37 am	**2:37 am**
☽♍ △ ♇♑	8:03 am	**5:03 am**
☽♍ ☍ ⚷♓	10:11 am	**7:11 am**
☽♍ ⚹ ♄♏	10:14 am	**7:14 am**
☽♍ ⚻ ♅♈	10:58 am	**7:58 am**
☉♎ ⚻ ⚷♓		**9:24 pm**
☽♍ ⚹ ♃♋		**10:58 pm**

3 Thu
4th ♍

☉♎ ⚻ ⚷♓	12:24 am		
☽♍ ⚹ ♃♋	1:58 am		
☉♎ ☍ ♅♈	10:12 am	**7:12 am**	
☽♍ ⚹ ♀♏	2:57 pm	**11:57 am**	☽ v/c
☽ enters ♎	10:59 pm	**7:59 pm**	

FRI 4
4th ♎
● New Moon 11 ♎ 56

☽♎⚻ ♆♓ 4:28 am **1:28 am**
☽♎□ ♇♑ 3:22 pm **12:22 pm**
☽♎⚻ ⚷♓ 5:12 pm **2:12 pm**
☽♎☍ ♅♈ 5:57 pm **2:57 pm**
☽♎☌ ☉♎ 8:35 pm **5:35 pm**
♄♏⚻ ♅♈ **9:45 pm**

SAT 5
1st ♎

♄♏⚻ ♅♈ 12:45 am
☽♎□ ♃♋ 8:50 am **5:50 am**

☽♎⚹ ♂♌ 6:28 pm **3:28 pm** ☽ v/c

OP: After Moon squares Jupiter until v/c Moon. A pleasant time to play, or even work if you want to.

SUN 6
1st ♎

☽ enters ♏ 4:33 am **1:33 am**
☽♏△ ♆♓ 9:44 am **6:44 am**
☽♏☌ ☿♏ 8:12 pm **5:12 pm**
☽♏⚹ ♇♑ 8:20 pm **5:20 pm**
☽♏△ ⚷♓ 9:56 pm **6:56 pm**
☿♏⚹ ♇♑ 9:57 pm **6:57 pm**
☽♏⚻ ♅♈ 10:38 pm **7:38 pm**
☽♏☌ ♄♏ 11:08 pm **8:08 pm**

Eastern Time plain / **Pacific Time bold**

SEPTEMBER

S	M	T	W	T	F	S
1	2	3	4	5	6	7
8	9	10	11	12	13	14
15	16	17	18	19	20	21
22	23	24	25	26	27	28
29	30					

OCTOBER

S	M	T	W	T	F	S
		1	2	3	4	5
6	7	8	9	10	11	12
13	14	15	16	17	18	19
20	21	22	23	24	25	26
27	28	29	30	31		

NOVEMBER

S	M	T	W	T	F	S
					1	2
3	4	5	6	7	8	9
10	11	12	13	14	15	16
17	18	19	20	21	22	23
24	25	26	27	28	29	30

OCTOBER

7 MON
1st ♏

☽♏△♃♋	1:33 pm	**10:33 am**
♀ enters ♐	1:54 pm	**10:54 am**
☿♏△⚷♓	6:06 pm	**3:06 pm**
☽♏□♂♌		**9:54 pm** ☽ v/c

8 TUE
1st ♏

☽♏□♂♌	12:54 am	☽ v/c
☿♏⚻♅♈	3:11 am	**12:11 am**
☽ enters ♐	8:21 am	**5:21 am**
☽♐☌♀♐	9:56 am	**6:56 am**
☽♐□♆♓	1:21 pm	**10:21 am**
☿♏☌♄♏	3:39 pm	**12:39 pm**
☽♐□⚷♓		**10:14 pm**
☽♐△♅♈		**10:55 pm**

9 WED
1st ♐

OP: After Moon trines Uranus on Tuesday/today until Moon enters Capricorn on Thursday. Write down your plans now, before Mercury enters its Storm on October 15.

☽♐□⚷♓	1:14 am	
☽♐△♅♈	1:55 am	
☽♐⚹☉♎	12:30 pm	**9:30 am**
☽♐⚻♃♋	5:03 pm	**2:03 pm**

10 THU
1st ♐

♀♐□♆♓	5:05 am	**2:05 am**
☽♐△♂♌	6:10 am	**3:10 am** ☽ v/c
☽ enters ♑	11:17 am	**8:17 am**
☽♑⚹♆♓	4:10 pm	**1:10 pm**
☽♑☌♇♑		**11:40 pm**

Fri 11

1st ♑
◐ 18 ♑ 47

☽♑ ☌ ♇♑ 2:40 am
☽♑ ⚹ ⚷♓ 3:54 am **12:54 am**
☽♑ □ ♅♈ 4:33 am **1:33 am**
☽♑ ⚹ ♄♏ 6:09 am **3:09 am**
☽♑ ⚹ ☿♏ 10:03 am **7:03 am**
☽♑ □ ☉♎ 7:02 pm **4:02 pm**
☽♑ ☍ ♃♋ 8:04 pm **5:04 pm** ☽ v/c

Sat 12

2nd ♑

☽♑ ⚻ ♂♌ 11:08 am **8:08 am**
☉♎ □ ♃♋ 11:09 am **8:09 am**
☽ enters ♒ 2:00 pm **11:00 am**
☽♒ ⚹ ♀♐ **9:04 pm**

Sun 13

2nd ♒

☽♒ ⚹ ♀♐ 12:04 am
☽♒ ⚹ ♅♈ 7:11 am **4:11 am**
☽♒ □ ♄♏ 9:21 am **6:21 am**
☽♒ □ ☿♏ 3:57 pm **12:57 pm**
☽♒ ⚻ ♃♋ 11:15 pm **8:15 pm**
☽♒ △ ☉♎ **10:46 pm**

Eastern Time plain / **Pacific Time bold**

SEPTEMBER

S	M	T	W	T	F	S
1	2	3	4	5	6	7
8	9	10	11	12	13	14
15	16	17	18	19	20	21
22	23	24	25	26	27	28
29	30					

OCTOBER

S	M	T	W	T	F	S
		1	2	3	4	5
6	7	8	9	10	11	12
13	14	15	16	17	18	19
20	21	22	23	24	25	26
27	28	29	30	31		

NOVEMBER

S	M	T	W	T	F	S
					1	2
3	4	5	6	7	8	9
10	11	12	13	14	15	16
17	18	19	20	21	22	23
24	25	26	27	28	29	30

October

Mercury Note: Mercury enters its Storm (moving less than 40 minutes of arc per day) on Tuesday, as it slows down before going retrograde. The Storm acts like the retrograde. Don't start any new projects now—just follow through with the items that are already on your plate. Write down new ideas with date and time they occurred.

14 Mon

2nd ♒
Columbus Day (observed)

☽♒ △ ☉♎	1:46 am		
☽♒ ☍ ♂♌	4:28 pm	**1:28 pm**	☽ v/c
☽ enters ♓	5:06 pm	**2:06 pm**	
☽♓ ☌ ♆♓	9:56 pm	**6:56 pm**	

15 Tue

2nd ♓

OP: After Moon squares Venus today until Moon enters Aries on Wednesday. Good for artistic matters, meditation, and helping others.

♂ enters ♍	7:05 am	**4:05 am**
☽♓ □ ♀♐	7:39 am	**4:39 am**
☽♓ ⚹ ♇♑	8:51 am	**5:51 am**
☽♓ ☌ ⚷♓	9:48 am	**6:48 am**
☽♓ △ ♄♏	1:12 pm	**10:12 am**
☽♓ △ ☿♏	10:04 pm	**7:04 pm**

16 Wed

2nd ♓

☽♓ △ ♃♋	3:15 am	**12:15 am**	☽ v/c
☽♓ ⚻ ☉♎	9:35 am	**6:35 am**	
♀♐ □ ⚷♓	10:29 am	**7:29 am**	
♀♐ △ ♅♈	6:04 pm	**3:04 pm**	
☽ enters ♈	9:18 pm	**6:18 pm**	
☽♈ ⚻ ♂♍	11:03 pm	**8:03 pm**	

17 Thu

2nd ♈

☽♈ □ ♇♑	1:37 pm	**10:37 am**
☽♈ ☌ ♅♈	3:01 pm	**12:01 pm**
☽♈ △ ♀♐	4:55 pm	**1:55 pm**
☽♈ ⚻ ♄♏	6:31 pm	**3:31 pm**

Fri 18
2nd ♈
Penumbral Lunar Eclipse | ○ Full Moon 25 ♈ 51

Aspect	Eastern	Pacific	
☽♈ ⚻ ☿♏	5:11 am	**2:11 am**	
☽♈ □ ♃♋	8:54 am	**5:54 am**	
☽♈ ☍ ☉♎	7:38 pm	**4:38 pm**	☽ v/c

Sat 19
3rd ♈

Aspect	Eastern	Pacific
☽ enters ♉	3:27 am	**12:27 am**
☽♉ △ ♂♍	7:53 am	**4:53 am**
☽♉ ⚹ ♆♓	8:32 am	**5:32 am**
☽♉ △ ♇♑	8:35 pm	**5:35 pm**
☽♉ ⚹ ⚷♓	9:14 pm	**6:14 pm**
♂♍ ☍ ♆♓	9:53 pm	**6:53 pm**
☽♉ ☍ ♄♏		**11:10 pm**

Sun 20
3rd ♉

Aspect	Eastern	Pacific	
☽♉ ☍ ♄♏	2:10 am		
☽♉ ⚻ ♀♐	5:00 am	**2:00 am**	
☽♉ ☍ ☿♏	1:52 pm	**10:52 am**	
☽♉ ⚹ ♃♋	5:02 pm	**2:02 pm**	☽ v/c

OP: After Moon opposes Saturn on Saturday/today until Moon enters Gemini on Monday. Taurus energy is good for enjoying ourselves as well as being productive.

Eastern Time plain / **Pacific Time bold**

SEPTEMBER

S	M	T	W	T	F	S
1	2	3	4	5	6	7
8	9	10	11	12	13	14
15	16	17	18	19	20	21
22	23	24	25	26	27	28
29	30					

OCTOBER

S	M	T	W	T	F	S
		1	2	3	4	5
6	7	8	9	10	11	12
13	14	15	16	17	18	19
20	21	22	23	24	25	26
27	28	29	30	31		

NOVEMBER

S	M	T	W	T	F	S
					1	2
3	4	5	6	7	8	9
10	11	12	13	14	15	16
17	18	19	20	21	22	23
24	25	26	27	28	29	30

October

Mercury Note: Mercury goes retrograde on Monday and remains so until November 10, after which it will still be in its Storm until November 15. Projects begun during this entire period may not work out as planned. It's best to use this time for review, editing, escrows, and so forth.

21 Mon

3rd ♉

OP: After Moon opposes Saturn on Saturday/Sunday until Moon enters Gemini today. Taurus energy is good for enjoying ourselves as well as being productive.

☿♏℞	6:29 am	**3:29 am**
☽♉ ⚻ ☉♎	8:55 am	**5:55 am**
☽ enters ♊	12:14 pm	**9:14 am**
☽♊ □ ♆♓	5:32 pm	**2:32 pm**
☽♊ □ ♂♍	7:47 pm	**4:47 pm**

22 Tue

3rd ♊

Sun enters Scorpio (Pacific)

OP: After Moon sextiles Uranus until v/c Moon. Tactful and charming communication.

☽♊ ⚻ ♇♑	6:18 am	**3:18 am**
☽♊ □ ⚷♓	6:47 am	**3:47 am**
☽♊ ✶ ♅♈	7:21 am	**4:21 am**
☽♊ ⚻ ♄♏	12:39 pm	**9:39 am**
☽♊ ☍ ♀♐	8:35 pm	**5:35 pm** ☽ v/c
☽♊ ⚻ ☿♏	11:59 pm	**8:59 pm**
☉ enters ♏		**11:10 pm**

23 Wed

3rd ♊

Sun enters Scorpio (Eastern)

☉ enters ♏	2:10 am	
☽ enters ♋	11:36 pm	**8:36 pm**
☽♋ △ ☉♏		**10:33 pm**

24 Thu

3rd ♋

☽♋ △ ☉♏	1:33 am	
☽♋ △ ♆♓	5:01 am	**2:01 am**
☽♋ ✶ ♂♍	10:30 am	**7:30 am**
☽♋ ☍ ♇♑	6:20 pm	**3:20 pm**
☽♋ △ ⚷♓	6:37 pm	**3:37 pm**
☽♋ □ ♅♈	7:09 pm	**4:09 pm**
☽♋ △ ♄♏		**10:22 pm**

	ET	PT	
☽♋ △ ♄♏	1:22 am		
☽♋ △ ☿♏	10:17 am	**7:17 am**	
☽♋ ⚻ ♀♐	2:41 pm	**11:41 am**	
☽♋ ☌ ♃♋	4:31 pm	**1:31 pm**	☽ v/c
☉♏ △ ♆♓	6:40 pm	**3:40 pm**	

Fri 25

3rd ♋

OP: After Moon trines Saturn on Thursday/today until Moon enters Leo on Saturday. Excellent for following through on projects begun before October 14.

	ET	PT
☽ enters ♌	12:12 pm	**9:12 am**
♀♐ ⚻ ♃♋	12:31 pm	**9:31 am**
☽♌ ⚻ ♆♓	5:34 pm	**2:34 pm**
☽♌ □ ☉♏	7:40 pm	**4:40 pm**

Sat 26

3rd ♋

◑ 3 ♌ 43

	ET	PT
☽♌ ⚻ ♇♑	6:57 am	**3:57 am**
☽♌ ⚻ ⚷♓	7:01 am	**4:01 am**
☽♌ △ ♅♈	7:29 am	**4:29 am**
☽♌ □ ♄♏	2:24 pm	**11:24 am**
☽♌ □ ☿♏	6:56 pm	**3:56 pm**

Sun 27

4th ♌

OP: After Moon squares Mercury today until v/c Moon on Monday. Usable for night owls.

Eastern Time plain / **Pacific Time bold**

SEPTEMBER

S	M	T	W	T	F	S
1	2	3	4	5	6	7
8	9	10	11	12	13	14
15	16	17	18	19	20	21
22	23	24	25	26	27	28
29	30					

OCTOBER

S	M	T	W	T	F	S
		1	2	3	4	5
6	7	8	9	10	11	12
13	14	15	16	17	18	19
20	21	22	23	24	25	26
27	28	29	30	31		

NOVEMBER

S	M	T	W	T	F	S
					1	2
3	4	5	6	7	8	9
10	11	12	13	14	15	16
17	18	19	20	21	22	23
24	25	26	27	28	29	30

October

28 Mon

4th ♌

OP: After Moon squares Mercury on Sunday until v/c Moon today. Usable for night owls.

♇♑ ⚹ ⚷♓	6:55 am	**3:55 am**
☽♌ △ ♀♐	8:26 am	**5:26 am** ☽ v/c
☽ enters ♍	11:45 pm	**8:45 pm**

29 Tue

4th ♍

☽♍ ☍ ♆♓	4:52 am	**1:52 am**
☽♍ ⚹ ☉♏	12:06 pm	**9:06 am**
☽♍ ☌ ♂♍	4:05 pm	**1:05 pm**
☿♏ ☌ ♄♏	4:48 pm	**1:48 pm**
☽♍ ☍ ⚷♓	5:42 pm	**2:42 pm**
☽♍ △ ♇♑	5:49 pm	**2:49 pm**
☽♍ ⚻ ♅♈	6:05 pm	**3:05 pm**
☽♍ ⚹ ☿♏		**9:35 pm**
☽♍ ⚹ ♄♏		**10:24 pm**

30 Wed

4th ♍

☽♍ ⚹ ☿♏	12:35 am	
☽♍ ⚹ ♄♏	1:24 am	
☽♍ ⚹ ♃♋	2:39 pm	**11:39 am**
☽♍ □ ♀♐	10:48 pm	**7:48 pm** ☽ v/c
♂♍ ☍ ⚷♓		**11:08 pm**

31 Thu

4th ♍

Halloween

Samhain

♂♍ ☍ ⚷♓	2:08 am	
♂♍ △ ♇♑	6:49 am	**3:49 am**
☽ enters ♎	8:22 am	**5:22 am**
♂♍ ⚻ ♅♈	8:55 am	**5:55 am**
☽♎ ⚻ ♆♓	1:09 pm	**10:09 am**
☽♎ ⚻ ⚷♓		**10:10 pm**
☽♎ □ ♇♑		**10:26 pm**
☽♎ ☍ ♅♈		**10:27 pm**

NOVEMBER

Uranus-Pluto Note: These two slow outer planets make the fourth exact square of their current series on Friday. They will make seven exact squares in all from June 24, 2012, to March 16, 2015. Think of the 1930s and the 1960s all over again, with the appropriate changes. "History doesn't repeat, but it rhymes."

FRI 1

4th ♎
ALL SAINTS' DAY

☽♎⚻ ⚷♓	1:10 am	
☽♎□ ♇♑	1:26 am	
☽♎☍ ♅♈	1:27 am	
♅♈□ ♇♑	6:30 am	**3:30 am**
☿♏⚹ ♂♍	8:03 am	**5:03 am**
☉♏△ ⚷♓	9:12 am	**6:12 am**
☉♏⚻ ♅♈	12:44 pm	**9:44 am**
☉♏⚹ ♇♑	1:05 pm	**10:05 am**
☉♏☌ ☿♏	4:19 pm	**1:19 pm**
☿♏⚹ ♇♑	6:44 pm	**3:44 pm**
☿♏⚻ ♅♈	7:15 pm	**4:15 pm**
☽♎□ ♃♋	9:00 pm	**6:00 pm**
☿♏△ ⚷♓	10:00 pm	**7:00 pm**

OP: After Moon squares Jupiter today until v/c Moon on Saturday. This evening could be great for socializing.

SAT 2

4th ♎

☽♎⚹ ♀♐	8:47 am	**5:47 am** ☽ v/c
☽ enters ♏	1:35 pm	**10:35 am**
☽♏△ ♆♓	6:05 pm	**3:05 pm**
☽♏☌ ☿♏		**11:51 pm**

SUN 3

4th ♏
Total Solar Eclipse | ● New Moon 11 ♏ 16
DAYLIGHT SAVING TIME ENDS AT 2:00 AM

☽♏☌ ☿♏	1:51 am	
☉♏⚹♂♍	3:49 am	**1:49 am**
☽♏△ ⚷♓	4:24 am	**1:24 am**
☽♏⚻ ♅♈	4:37 am	**1:37 am**
☽♏⚹ ♇♑	4:48 am	**1:48 am**
☽♏⚹♂♍	7:42 am	**4:42 am**
☽♏☌ ☉♏	7:50 am	**4:50 am**
☽♏☌ ♄♏	12:18 pm	**9:18 am**
☽♏△ ♃♋	11:23 pm	**8:23 pm** ☽ v/c

Annular/Total Hybrid Solar Eclipse (not a usable Cazimi). The eclipse is visible in parts of the Americas, the Atlantic, southern Europe, and most of Africa. Every total or annular solar eclipse becomes partial away from its path of totality.

OP: After Moon conjoins Saturn until v/c Moon. The Moon is still under Sun's beams (see page 79), but we can enjoy ourselves.

Eastern Time plain / **Pacific Time bold**

OCTOBER

S	M	T	W	T	F	S
		1	2	3	4	5
6	7	8	9	10	11	12
13	14	15	16	17	18	19
20	21	22	23	24	25	26
27	28	29	30	31		

NOVEMBER

S	M	T	W	T	F	S
					1	2
3	4	5	6	7	8	9
10	11	12	13	14	15	16
17	18	19	20	21	22	23
24	25	26	27	28	29	30

DECEMBER

S	M	T	W	T	F	S
1	2	3	4	5	6	7
8	9	10	11	12	13	14
15	16	17	18	19	20	21
22	23	24	25	26	27	28
29	30	31				

November

4 Mon
1st ♏

☽ enters ♐	3:14 pm	**12:14 pm**
☽♐ □ ♆♓	7:33 pm	**4:33 pm**

5 Tue
1st ♐
Election Day (general)
Islamic New Year

♀ enters ♑	3:43 am	**12:43 am**
☽♐ □ ⚷♓	6:30 am	**3:30 am**
☽♐ △ ♅♈	6:38 am	**3:38 am**
☽♐ □ ♂♍	11:48 am	**8:48 am** ☽ v/c
☽♐ ⊼ ♃♋		**10:06 pm**

6 Wed
1st ♐

☽♐ ⊼ ♃♋	1:06 am	
☉♏ ☌ ♄♏	7:01 am	**4:01 am**
☽ enters ♑	4:44 pm	**1:44 pm**
☽♑ ☌ ♀♑	7:22 pm	**4:22 pm**
☽♑ ⚹ ♆♓	9:00 pm	**6:00 pm**
☽♑ ⚹ ☿♏	11:01 pm	**8:01 pm**
♃♋ ℞		**9:03 pm**

7 Thu
1st ♑
OP: After Moon sextiles Saturn today until v/c Moon today/Friday. A pleasant evening.

♃♋ ℞	12:03 am	
☽♑ ⚹ ⚷♓	7:53 am	**4:53 am**
☽♑ □ ♅♈	7:58 am	**4:58 am**
☽♑ ☌ ♇♑	8:31 am	**5:31 am**
☽♑ △ ♂♍	3:17 pm	**12:17 pm**
☽♑ ⚹ ♄♏	4:31 pm	**1:31 pm**
☽♑ ⚹ ☉♏	6:43 pm	**3:43 pm**
♀♑ ⚹ ♆♓	8:16 pm	**5:16 pm**
☽♑ ☍ ♃♋		**11:39 pm** ☽ v/c

Mercury Note: Mercury goes direct on Sunday but remains in its Storm, moving slowly until November 15. Until then, it is not yet time for new ideas to be workable.

FRI 8
1st ♑

☽♑ ☍ ♃♋	2:39 am		☽ v/c
☿♏ ⚹ ♀♑	7:24 am	**4:24 am**	
☽ enters ♒	6:30 pm	**3:30 pm**	
☽♒ □ ☿♏	11:09 pm	**8:09 pm**	

SAT 9
1st ♒
◐ 18 ♒ 00 (Pacific)

♂♍ ⚹ ♄♏	6:57 am	**3:57 am**	
☽♒ ⚹ ♅♈	9:57 am	**6:57 am**	
☿♏ △ ♆♓	4:35 pm	**1:35 pm**	
☽♒ □ ♄♏	7:15 pm	**4:15 pm**	
☽♒ ⚻ ♂♍	7:40 pm	**4:40 pm**	
☽♒ □ ☉♏		**9:57 pm**	☽ v/c

SUN 10
1st ♒
◐ 18 ♒ 00 (Eastern)

☽♒ □ ☉♏	12:57 am		☽ v/c
☽♒ ⚻ ♃♋	5:13 am	**2:13 am**	
☿♏ D	4:12 pm	**1:12 pm**	
☽ enters ♓	9:36 pm	**6:36 pm**	
☽♓ △ ☿♏		**10:58 pm**	
☽♓ ☌ ♆♓		**11:05 pm**	

Eastern Time plain / **Pacific Time bold**

OCTOBER

S	M	T	W	T	F	S
		1	2	3	4	5
6	7	8	9	10	11	12
13	14	15	16	17	18	19
20	21	22	23	24	25	26
27	28	29	30	31		

NOVEMBER

S	M	T	W	T	F	S
					1	2
3	4	5	6	7	8	9
10	11	12	13	14	15	16
17	18	19	20	21	22	23
24	25	26	27	28	29	30

DECEMBER

S	M	T	W	T	F	S
1	2	3	4	5	6	7
8	9	10	11	12	13	14
15	16	17	18	19	20	21
22	23	24	25	26	27	28
29	30	31				

November

11 Mon
2nd ♓
Veterans Day

☽♓ △ ☿♏	1:58 am	
☽♓ ☌ ♆♓	2:05 am	
☽♓ ⚹ ♀♑	7:47 am	**4:47 am**
☽♓ ☌ ⚷♓	1:34 pm	**10:34 am**
☽♓ ⚹ ♇♑	2:29 pm	**11:29 am**
☿♏ △ ♆♓	3:45 pm	**12:45 pm**
☽♓ △ ♄♏	11:44 pm	**8:44 pm**
☽♓ ☍ ♂♍		**10:57 pm**

12 Tue
2nd ♓

OP: After Moon opposes Mars on Monday/today until Moon enters Aries today/Wednesday. Good for artistic matters, meditation, and helping others.

☽♓ ☍ ♂♍	1:57 am	
☽♓ △ ☉♏	9:23 am	**6:23 am**
☽♓ △ ♃♋	9:34 am	**6:34 am** ☽ v/c
☉♏ △ ♃♋	11:39 am	**8:39 am**
☽ enters ♈		**11:39 pm**

13 Wed
2nd ♓

☽ enters ♈	2:39 am	
☽♈ ⊼ ☿♏	8:18 am	**5:18 am**
♆♓ D	1:42 pm	**10:42 am**
☽♈ □ ♀♑	5:12 pm	**2:12 pm**
☽♈ ☌ ♅♈	7:05 pm	**4:05 pm**
☽♈ □ ♇♑	8:18 pm	**5:18 pm**

14 Thu
2nd ♈

☽♈ ⊼ ♄♏	6:19 am	**3:19 am**
☽♈ ⊼ ♂♍	10:34 am	**7:34 am**
☽♈ □ ♃♋	3:57 pm	**12:57 pm** ☽ v/c
♀♑ □ ♅♈	8:13 pm	**5:13 pm**
☽♈ ⊼ ☉♏	8:28 pm	**5:28 pm**
♀♑ ⚹ ⚷♓	10:59 pm	**7:59 pm**

FRI 15
2nd ♈

☽ enters ♉	9:49 am	**6:49 am**
☽♉ ⚹ ♆♓	2:40 pm	**11:40 am**
♀♑ ☌ ♇♑	4:33 pm	**1:33 pm**
☽♉ ☍ ☿♏	6:34 pm	**3:34 pm**

SAT 16
2nd ♉

☽♉ ⚹ ⚷♓	3:01 am	**12:01 am**
☽♉ △ ♇♑	4:17 am	**1:17 am**
☽♉ △ ♀♑	5:07 am	**2:07 am**
☽♉ ☍ ♄♏	3:07 pm	**12:07 pm**
☽♉ △ ♂♍	9:36 pm	**6:36 pm**
☽♉ ⚹ ♃♋		**9:26 pm**

OP: After Moon trines Mars today until Moon enters Gemini on Sunday. If you have a chance to party tonight, do it.

SUN 17
2nd ♉
○ Full Moon 25 ♉ 26

☽♉ ⚹ ♃♋	12:26 am	
☽♉ ☍ ☉♏	10:16 am	**7:16 am** ☽ v/c
☽ enters ♊	7:07 pm	**4:07 pm**
☽♊ □ ♆♓		**9:09 pm**

Eastern Time plain / **Pacific Time bold**

OCTOBER

S	M	T	W	T	F	S
		1	2	3	4	5
6	7	8	9	10	11	12
13	14	15	16	17	18	19
20	21	22	23	24	25	26
27	28	29	30	31		

NOVEMBER

S	M	T	W	T	F	S
					1	2
3	4	5	6	7	8	9
10	11	12	13	14	15	16
17	18	19	20	21	22	23
24	25	26	27	28	29	30

DECEMBER

S	M	T	W	T	F	S
1	2	3	4	5	6	7
8	9	10	11	12	13	14
15	16	17	18	19	20	21
22	23	24	25	26	27	28
29	30	31				

18 Mon
3rd ♊

☽♊ □ ♆♓	12:09 am	
☽♊ ⚻ ☿♏	8:53 am	**5:53 am**
☽♊ ✶ ♅♈	12:35 pm	**9:35 am**
☽♊ □ ⚷♓	12:56 pm	**9:56 am**
☽♊ ⚻ ♇♑	2:23 pm	**11:23 am**
☽♊ ⚻ ♀♑	7:30 pm	**4:30 pm**
☽♊ ⚻ ♄♏		**11:02 pm**

19 Tue
3rd ♊

☽♊ ⚻ ♄♏	2:02 am	
⚷♓ D	8:07 am	**5:07 am**
♂♍ ✶ ♃♋	9:48 am	**6:48 am**
☽♊ □ ♂♍	10:59 am	**7:59 am** ☽ v/c
☿♏ ⚻ ♅♈		**9:50 pm**
☽♊ ⚻ ☉♏		**11:40 pm**

20 Wed
3rd ♊

☿♏ ⚻ ♅♈	12:50 am	
☽♊ ⚻ ☉♏	2:40 am	
☿♏ △ ⚷♓	5:16 am	**2:16 am**
☽ enters ♋	6:23 am	**3:23 am**
☽♋ △ ♆♓	11:35 am	**8:35 am**
☿♏ ✶ ♇♑	9:09 pm	**6:09 pm**
☽♋ □ ♅♈		**9:14 pm**
☽♋ △ ⚷♓		**9:43 pm**
☽♋ ☍ ♇♑		**11:20 pm**
☽♋ △ ☿♏		**11:55 pm**

21 Thu
3rd ♋

Sun enters Sagittarius

OP: After Moon opposes Pluto on Wednesday/today until Moon enters Leo on Friday. Check your notes from the last Mercury retrograde and Storms, and see which of your new ideas still look good, if any.

☽♋ □ ♅♈	12:14 am	
☽♋ △ ⚷♓	12:43 am	
☽♋ ☍ ♇♑	2:20 am	
☽♋ △ ☿♏	2:55 am	
☽♋ ☍ ♀♑	11:53 am	**8:53 am**
☽♋ △ ♄♏	2:44 pm	**11:44 am**
☉ enters ♐	10:48 pm	**7:48 pm**
☽♋ ☌ ♃♋	10:58 pm	**7:58 pm**
☽♋ ✶ ♂♍		**11:11 pm** ☽ v/c

☽♋ ✶ ♂♍	2:11 am		☽ v/c
☽ enters ♌	6:56 pm	**3:56 pm**	
☽♌ △ ☉♐	8:49 pm	**5:49 pm**	
☽♌ ⊼ ♆♓		**9:13 pm**	

FRI 22
3rd ♋

OP: After Moon opposes Pluto on Wednesday/Thursday until Moon enters Leo today. Check your notes from the last Mercury retrograde and Storms, and see which of your new ideas still look good, if any.

☽♌ ⊼ ♆♓	12:13 am	
☽♌ △ ♅♈	12:48 pm	**9:48 am**
☽♌ ⊼ ⚷♓	1:24 pm	**10:24 am**
♀♑ ✶ ♄♏	1:45 pm	**10:45 am**
☽♌ ⊼ ♇♑	3:09 pm	**12:09 pm**
☽♌ □ ☿♏	11:02 pm	**8:02 pm**

SAT 23
3rd ♌

☽♌ □ ♄♏	3:59 am	**12:59 am**	☽ v/c
☽♌ ⊼ ♀♑	4:48 am	**1:48 am**	
☉♐ □ ♆♓	12:52 pm	**9:52 am**	

SUN 24
3rd ♌

Eastern Time plain / **Pacific Time bold**

OCTOBER

S	M	T	W	T	F	S
		1	2	3	4	5
6	7	8	9	10	11	12
13	14	15	16	17	18	19
20	21	22	23	24	25	26
27	28	29	30	31		

NOVEMBER

S	M	T	W	T	F	S
					1	2
3	4	5	6	7	8	9
10	11	12	13	14	15	16
17	18	19	20	21	22	23
24	25	26	27	28	29	30

DECEMBER

S	M	T	W	T	F	S
1	2	3	4	5	6	7
8	9	10	11	12	13	14
15	16	17	18	19	20	21
22	23	24	25	26	27	28
29	30	31				

November

25 Mon
3rd ♌
◑ 3 ♍ 42

☽ enters ♍	7:11 am	**4:11 am**
☽♍ ☍ ♆♓	12:21 pm	**9:21 am**
☽♍ □ ☉♐	2:28 pm	**11:28 am**
☿♏ ☌ ♄♏	8:54 pm	**5:54 pm**
☽♍ ⚻ ♅♈		**9:26 pm**
☽♍ ☍ ⚷♓		**10:08 pm**
☽♍ △ ♇♑		**11:57 pm**

26 Tue
4th ♍

☽♍ ⚻ ♅♈	12:26 am	
☽♍ ☍ ⚷♓	1:08 am	
☽♍ △ ♇♑	2:57 am	
☽♍ ⚹ ♄♏	3:42 pm	**12:42 pm**
☽♍ ⚹ ☿♏	5:55 pm	**2:55 pm**
☽♍ △ ♀♑	7:39 pm	**4:39 pm**
☽♍ ⚹ ♃♋	9:50 pm	**6:50 pm**

27 Wed
4th ♍

☽♍ ☌ ♂♍	6:44 am	**3:44 am** ☽ v/c
☽ enters ♎	5:00 pm	**2:00 pm**
☿♏ ⚹ ♀♑	9:45 pm	**6:45 pm**
☽♎ ⚻ ♆♓	9:54 pm	**6:54 pm**
☿♏ △ ♃♋		**11:23 pm**

28 Thu
4th ♎
Thanksgiving Day
Hanukkah begins

☿♏ △ ♃♋	2:23 am	
☽♎ ⚹ ☉♐	4:42 am	**1:42 am**
♀♑ ☍ ♃♋	7:00 am	**4:00 am**
☽♎ ☍ ♅♈	9:09 am	**6:09 am**
☽♎ ⚻ ⚷♓	9:55 am	**6:55 am**
☽♎ □ ♇♑	11:42 am	**8:42 am**

FRI 29
4th ♎

☽♎□ ♃♋	4:56 am	**1:56 am**	
☽♎□ ♀♑	6:13 am	**3:13 am**	☽ v/c
☽ enters ♏	11:03 pm	**8:03 pm**	

SAT 30
4th ♏

☽♏△ ♆♓	3:39 am	**12:39 am**
☉♐△ ♅♈	1:25 pm	**10:25 am**
☽♏⚻ ♅♈	2:02 pm	**11:02 am**
☽♏△ ⚷♓	2:50 pm	**11:50 am**
☽♏⚹ ♇♑	4:34 pm	**1:34 pm**
☉♐□ ⚷♓		**9:40 pm**

SUN 1
4th ♏

☉♐□ ⚷♓	12:40 am		
☽♏☌ ♄♏	4:19 am	**1:19 am**	
☽♏△ ♃♋	8:15 am	**5:15 am**	
☽♏⚹ ♀♑	12:10 pm	**9:10 am**	
☽♏☌ ☿♏	5:37 pm	**2:37 pm**	
☽♏⚹ ♂♍	8:34 pm	**5:34 pm**	☽ v/c
☽ enters ♐		**10:31 pm**	

OP: After Moon conjoins Saturn until v/c Moon. The Moon is Balsamic, so it's best to just play.

Eastern Time plain / **Pacific Time bold**

NOVEMBER

S	M	T	W	T	F	S
					1	2
3	4	5	6	7	8	9
10	11	12	13	14	15	16
17	18	19	20	21	22	23
24	25	26	27	28	29	30

DECEMBER

S	M	T	W	T	F	S
1	2	3	4	5	6	7
8	9	10	11	12	13	14
15	16	17	18	19	20	21
22	23	24	25	26	27	28
29	30	31				

JANUARY 2014

S	M	T	W	T	F	S
			1	2	3	4
5	6	7	8	9	10	11
12	13	14	15	16	17	18
19	20	21	22	23	24	25
26	27	28	29	30	31	

December

2 Mon

4th ♏

● New Moon 10 ♐ 59

☽ enters ♐	1:31 am	
☽♐ □ ♆♓	5:54 am	**2:54 am**
☽♐ △ ♅♈	3:39 pm	**12:39 pm**
☽♐ □ ⚷♓	4:29 pm	**1:29 pm**
☽♐ ☌ ☉♐	7:22 pm	**4:22 pm**

3 Tue

1st ♐

☽♐ ⚻ ♃♋	8:51 am	**5:51 am**
☿♏ ⚹ ♂♍	11:35 am	**8:35 am**
☽♐ □ ♂♍	10:45 pm	**7:45 pm** ☽ v/c
☽ enters ♑		**10:49 pm**

4 Wed

1st ♐

☽ enters ♑	1:49 am	
☽♑ ⚹ ♆♓	6:08 am	**3:08 am**
☽♑ □ ♅♈	3:38 pm	**12:38 pm**
☽♑ ⚹ ⚷♓	4:33 pm	**1:33 pm**
☽♑ ☌ ♇♑	6:18 pm	**3:18 pm**
☿ enters ♐	9:42 pm	**6:42 pm**

5 Thu

1st ♑

Hanukkah ends

OP: After Moon sextiles Saturn until v/c Moon today/Friday. We can get a lot done—even new ideas might work out now.

☽♑ ⚹ ♄♏	5:59 am	**2:59 am**
☽♑ ☍ ♃♋	8:29 am	**5:29 am**
☽♑ ☌ ♀♑	4:46 pm	**1:46 pm**
☽♑ △ ♂♍		**9:31 pm** ☽ v/c
☽ enters ♒		**10:53 pm**

☽♑ △ ♂♍ 12:31 am ☽ v/c
☽ enters ♒ 1:53 am
☽♒ ✶ ☿♐ 5:09 am **2:09 am**
☽♒ ✶ ♅♈ 3:58 pm **12:58 pm**
☿♐ □ ♆♓ 4:31 pm **1:31 pm**

FRI 6
1st ♑

☽♒ ✶ ☉♐ 3:03 am **12:03 am**
☽♒ □ ♄♏ 7:11 am **4:11 am** ☽ v/c
☽♒ ⊼ ♃♋ 9:06 am **6:06 am**
♂ enters ♎ 3:41 pm **12:41 pm**

SAT 7
1st ♒

☽ enters ♓ 3:34 am **12:34 am**
☽♓ ⊼ ♂♎ 4:01 am **1:01 am**
☽♓ ☌ ♆♓ 8:16 am **5:16 am**
☽♓ □ ☿♐ 1:07 pm **10:07 am**
☽♓ ☌ ⚷♓ 7:32 pm **4:32 pm**
☽♓ ✶ ♇♑ 9:33 pm **6:33 pm**

SUN 8
1st ♒

Eastern Time plain / **Pacific Time bold**

NOVEMBER

S	M	T	W	T	F	S
					1	2
3	4	5	6	7	8	9
10	11	12	13	14	15	16
17	18	19	20	21	22	23
24	25	26	27	28	29	30

DECEMBER

S	M	T	W	T	F	S
1	2	3	4	5	6	7
8	9	10	11	12	13	14
15	16	17	18	19	20	21
22	23	24	25	26	27	28
29	30	31				

JANUARY 2014

S	M	T	W	T	F	S
			1	2	3	4
5	6	7	8	9	10	11
12	13	14	15	16	17	18
19	20	21	22	23	24	25
26	27	28	29	30	31	

December

9 Mon

1st ♓

◐ 17 ♓ 43

OP: After Moon squares Sun today until Moon enters Aries on Tuesday. Good for artistic matters, meditation, and helping others.

☽♓ □ ☉♐	10:12 am	**7:12 am**	
☽♓ △ ♄♏	10:53 am	**7:53 am**	
☽♓ △ ♃♋	12:08 pm	**9:08 am**	
☽♓ ⚹ ♀♑		**10:41 pm**	☽ v/c

10 Tue

2nd ♓

☽♓ ⚹ ♀♑	1:41 am		☽ v/c
☽ enters ♈	8:06 am	**5:06 am**	
☉♐ ⚻ ♃♋	9:56 am	**6:56 am**	
☽♈ ☍ ♂♎	10:40 am	**7:40 am**	
☿♐ △ ♅♈	12:05 pm	**9:05 am**	
☿♐ □ ⚷♓	11:31 pm	**8:31 pm**	
☽♈ ☌ ♅♈	11:45 pm	**8:45 pm**	
☽♈ △ ☿♐		**10:19 pm**	

11 Wed

2nd ♈

☽♈ △ ☿♐	1:19 am	
☽♈ □ ♇♑	3:18 am	**12:18 am**
☽♈ ⚻ ♄♏	5:45 pm	**2:45 pm**
☽♈ □ ♃♋	6:10 pm	**3:10 pm**
☽♈ △ ☉♐	9:13 pm	**6:13 pm**

12 Thu

2nd ♈

☽♈ □ ♀♑	10:37 am	**7:37 am**	☽ v/c
☽ enters ♉	3:40 pm	**12:40 pm**	
♃♋ △ ♄♏	7:01 pm	**4:01 pm**	
☽♉ ⚻ ♂♎	8:42 pm	**5:42 pm**	
☽♉ ⚹ ♆♓	9:02 pm	**6:02 pm**	

FRI 13
2nd ♉

♂♎ ⚻ ♆♓	5:20 am	**2:20 am**
☽♉ ⚹ ⚷♓	9:38 am	**6:38 am**
☽♉ △ ♇♑	11:59 am	**8:59 am**
☽♉ ⚻ ☿♐	5:46 pm	**2:46 pm**
☽♉ ⚹ ♃♋		**11:52 pm**

SAT 14
2nd ♉

☽♉ ⚹ ♃♋	2:52 am	
☽♉ ☍ ♄♏	3:25 am	**12:25 am**
☽♉ ⚻ ☉♐	11:41 am	**8:41 am**
☽♉ △ ♀♑	9:54 pm	**6:54 pm** ☽ v/c
☽ enters ♊		**10:40 pm**

OP: After Moon opposes Saturn today until Moon enters Gemini today/Sunday. A lovely day, whether you choose to do Christmas shopping or not.

SUN 15
2nd ♉

☽ enters ♊	1:40 am	
☽♊ □ ♆♓	7:19 am	**4:19 am**
☽♊ △ ♂♎	9:22 am	**6:22 am**
☽♊ ⚹ ♅♈	6:37 pm	**3:37 pm**
☽♊ □ ⚷♓	8:20 pm	**5:20 pm**
☽♊ ⚻ ♇♑	10:48 pm	**7:48 pm**

OP: After Moon sextiles Uranus today until v/c Moon on Tuesday. Lots of mental energy.

Eastern Time plain / **Pacific Time bold**

NOVEMBER

S	M	T	W	T	F	S
					1	2
3	4	5	6	7	8	9
10	11	12	13	14	15	16
17	18	19	20	21	22	23
24	25	26	27	28	29	30

DECEMBER

S	M	T	W	T	F	S
1	2	3	4	5	6	7
8	9	10	11	12	13	14
15	16	17	18	19	20	21
22	23	24	25	26	27	28
29	30	31				

JANUARY 2014

S	M	T	W	T	F	S
			1	2	3	4
5	6	7	8	9	10	11
12	13	14	15	16	17	18
19	20	21	22	23	24	25
26	27	28	29	30	31	

December

16 Mon

2nd ♊

OP: After Moon sextiles Uranus on Sunday until v/c Moon on Tuesday. Lots of mental energy.

☽♊ ☍ ☿♐	1:17 pm	**10:17 am**
☿♐ ⚻ ♃♋	2:02 pm	**11:02 am**
☽♊ ⚻ ♄♏	3:02 pm	**12:02 pm**

17 Tue

2nd ♊

○ Full Moon 25 ♊ 36

☽♊ ☍ ☉♐	4:28 am	**1:28 am**	☽ v/c
☽♊ ⚻ ♀♑	10:31 am	**7:31 am**	
♅♈ D	12:40 pm	**9:40 am**	
☽ enters ♋	1:17 pm	**10:17 am**	
☽♋ △ ♆♓	7:07 pm	**4:07 pm**	
☽♋ □ ♂♎	11:42 pm	**8:42 pm**	

18 Wed

3rd ♋

OP: After Moon opposes Pluto today until Moon enters Leo on Thursday/Friday. Another great time for Christmas shopping.

☽♋ □ ♅♈	6:33 am	**3:33 am**
☽♋ △ ⚷♓	8:26 am	**5:26 am**
☽♋ ☍ ♇♑	10:59 am	**7:59 am**
☽♋ ☌ ♃♋		**10:02 pm**

19 Thu

3rd ♋

☽♋ ☌ ♃♋	1:02 am		
☽♋ △ ♄♏	3:49 am	**12:49 am**	
☽♋ ⚻ ☿♐	10:37 am	**7:37 am**	
☽♋ ⚻ ☉♐	10:34 pm	**7:34 pm**	
☽♋ ☍ ♀♑	11:37 pm	**8:37 pm**	☽ v/c
☽ enters ♌		**10:48 pm**	

☽ enters ♌ 1:48 am
☽♌ ⚻ ♆♓ 7:47 am **4:47 am**
☽♌ ✶ ♂♎ 2:53 pm **11:53 am**
☽♌ △ ♅♈ 7:11 pm **4:11 pm**
☽♌ ⚻ ⚷♓ 9:13 pm **6:13 pm**
☽♌ ⚻ ♇♑ 11:48 pm **8:48 pm**

FRI 20
3rd ♋

☉ enters ♑ 12:11 pm **9:11 am**
♀♑℞ 4:53 pm **1:53 pm**
☽♌ □ ♄♏ 5:00 pm **2:00 pm**

SAT 21
3rd ♌
WINTER SOLSTICE
YULE
SUN ENTERS CAPRICORN

OP: After Moon squares Saturn today until v/c Moon on Sunday. Get some much-needed rest.

☽♌ △ ☿♐ 8:25 am **5:25 am** ☽ v/c
☽♌ ⚻ ♀♑ 12:15 pm **9:15 am**
☽ enters ♍ 2:19 pm **11:19 am**
☽♍ △ ☉♑ 4:44 pm **1:44 pm**
☽♍ ☍ ♆♓ 8:20 pm **5:20 pm**

SUN 22
3rd ♌

Eastern Time plain / **Pacific Time bold**

NOVEMBER

S	M	T	W	T	F	S
					1	2
3	4	5	6	7	8	9
10	11	12	13	14	15	16
17	18	19	20	21	22	23
24	25	26	27	28	29	30

DECEMBER

S	M	T	W	T	F	S
1	2	3	4	5	6	7
8	9	10	11	12	13	14
15	16	17	18	19	20	21
22	23	24	25	26	27	28
29	30	31				

JANUARY 2014

S	M	T	W	T	F	S
			1	2	3	4
5	6	7	8	9	10	11
12	13	14	15	16	17	18
19	20	21	22	23	24	25
26	27	28	29	30	31	

December

23 Mon

3rd ♍

OP: After Moon trines Pluto today until v/c Moon on Tuesday. A fortunate last chance for Christmas shopping.

☽♍ ⚻ ♅♈	7:28 am	**4:28 am**
☽♍ ☍ ⚷♓	9:36 am	**6:36 am**
☽♍ △ ♇♑	12:09 pm	**9:09 am**
☽♍ ⚹ ♃♋		**9:19 pm**

24 Tue

3rd ♍

Christmas Eve

☽♍ ⚹ ♃♋	12:19 am	
☿ enters ♑	5:12 am	**2:12 am**
☽♍ ⚹ ♄♏	5:13 am	**2:13 am**
☉♑⚹ ♆♓	12:05 pm	**9:05 am**
☽♍ △ ♀♑	10:55 pm	**7:55 pm** ☽ v/c
☽ enters ♎		**10:17 pm**

25 Wed

3rd ♍

◑ 3 ♎ 56

Christmas Day

☽ enters ♎	1:17 am	
♂♎☍ ♅♈	3:33 am	**12:33 am**
☽♎□ ☿♑	4:11 am	**1:11 am**
☽♎⚻ ♆♓	7:09 am	**4:09 am**
☽♎□ ☉♑	8:48 am	**5:48 am**
☽♎☍ ♅♈	5:41 pm	**2:41 pm**
☽♎☌ ♂♎	6:12 pm	**3:12 pm**
☽♎⚻ ⚷♓	7:49 pm	**4:49 pm**
☽♎□ ♇♑	10:15 pm	**7:15 pm**

26 Thu

4th ♎

Kwanzaa begins

☿♑ ⚹ ♆♓	4:03 am	**1:03 am**
☽♎□ ♃♋	9:01 am	**6:01 am**

Fri 27
4th ♎

Aspect	Eastern	Pacific
☽♎□ ♀♑	6:00 am	**3:00 am** ☽ v/c
☽ enters ♏	8:58 am	**5:58 am**
☽♏△ ♆♓	2:32 pm	**11:32 am**
♂♎⚻ ⚷♓	6:12 pm	**3:12 pm**
☽♏✶ ☿♑	7:02 pm	**4:02 pm**
☽♏✶ ☉♑	8:26 pm	**5:26 pm**
☽♏⚻ ♅♈		**9:14 pm**
☽♏△ ⚷♓		**11:20 pm**

Sat 28
4th ♏

Aspect	Eastern	Pacific
☽♏⚻ ♅♈	12:14 am	
☽♏△ ⚷♓	2:20 am	
☽♏✶ ♇♑	4:35 am	**1:35 am**
☽♏△ ♃♋	1:56 pm	**10:56 am**
☽♏☌ ♄♏	7:58 pm	**4:58 pm**
☉♑☌ ☿♑		**10:27 pm**

OP: After Moon conjoins Saturn today until v/c Moon on Sunday. Have a pleasant and relaxing Saturday night.

Sun 29
4th ♏

Aspect	Eastern	Pacific
☉♑☌ ☿♑	1:27 am	
☽♏✶ ♀♑	8:54 am	**5:54 am** ☽ v/c
☽ enters ♐	12:37 pm	**9:37 am**
☿♑□ ♅♈	3:48 pm	**12:48 pm**
☽♐□ ♆♓	5:52 pm	**2:52 pm**
☉♑□ ♅♈		**9:05 pm**
☽♐△ ♅♈		**11:51 pm**

Eastern Time plain / **Pacific Time bold**

NOVEMBER

S	M	T	W	T	F	S
					1	2
3	4	5	6	7	8	9
10	11	12	13	14	15	16
17	18	19	20	21	22	23
24	25	26	27	28	29	30

DECEMBER

S	M	T	W	T	F	S
1	2	3	4	5	6	7
8	9	10	11	12	13	14
15	16	17	18	19	20	21
22	23	24	25	26	27	28
29	30	31				

JANUARY 2014

S	M	T	W	T	F	S
			1	2	3	4
5	6	7	8	9	10	11
12	13	14	15	16	17	18
19	20	21	22	23	24	25
26	27	28	29	30	31	

30 MON

4th ♐

OP: After Moon sextiles Mars today until Moon enters Capricorn on Tuesday. Take care of business during this break between holidays, but be aware that the Moon becomes Balsamic this afternoon.

☉♑□ ♅♈	12:05 am		
☽♐△ ♅♈	2:51 am		
☽♐□ ⚷♓	4:53 am	**1:53 am**	
☽♐ ⚹ ♂♎	6:36 am	**3:36 am**	☽ v/c
☿♑ ⚹ ⚷♓	10:47 am	**7:47 am**	
☽♐ ⚻ ♃♋	3:10 pm	**12:10 pm**	
♂♎□ ♇♑	8:22 pm	**5:22 pm**	

31 TUE

4th ♐

NEW YEAR'S EVE

☿♑ ☌ ♇♑	6:26 am	**3:26 am**	
☉♑ ⚹ ⚷♓	6:36 am	**3:36 am**	
☿♑□ ♂♎	9:59 am	**6:59 am**	
☽ enters ♑	1:01 pm	**10:01 am**	
☽♑ ⚹ ♆♓	6:06 pm	**3:06 pm**	
☽♑□ ♅♈		**11:40 pm**	

1 WED

4th ♑

NEW YEAR'S DAY

● New Moon 10 ♑ 57

KWANZAA ENDS

☽♑□ ♅♈	2:40 am		
☽♑ ⚹ ⚷♓	4:43 am	**1:43 am**	
☽♑ ☌ ☉♑	6:14 am	**3:14 am**	
☽♑ ☌ ♇♑	6:44 am	**3:44 am**	
☽♑□ ♂♎	7:41 am	**4:41 am**	
☽♑ ☌ ☿♑	9:32 am	**6:32 am**	
☉♑ ☌ ♇♑	1:57 pm	**10:57 am**	
☽♑ ☍ ♃♋	2:09 pm	**11:09 am**	
☽♑ ⚹ ♄♏	9:06 pm	**6:06 pm**	

2 THU

1st ♑

☽♑ ☌ ♀♑	6:12 am	**3:12 am**	☽ v/c
☽ enters ♒	12:03 pm	**9:03 am**	
☉♑□♂♎	7:14 pm	**4:14 pm**	
☽♒ ⚹ ♅♈		**10:46 pm**	
☿♑ ☍ ♃♋		**11:11 pm**	

Blank Horoscope Chart

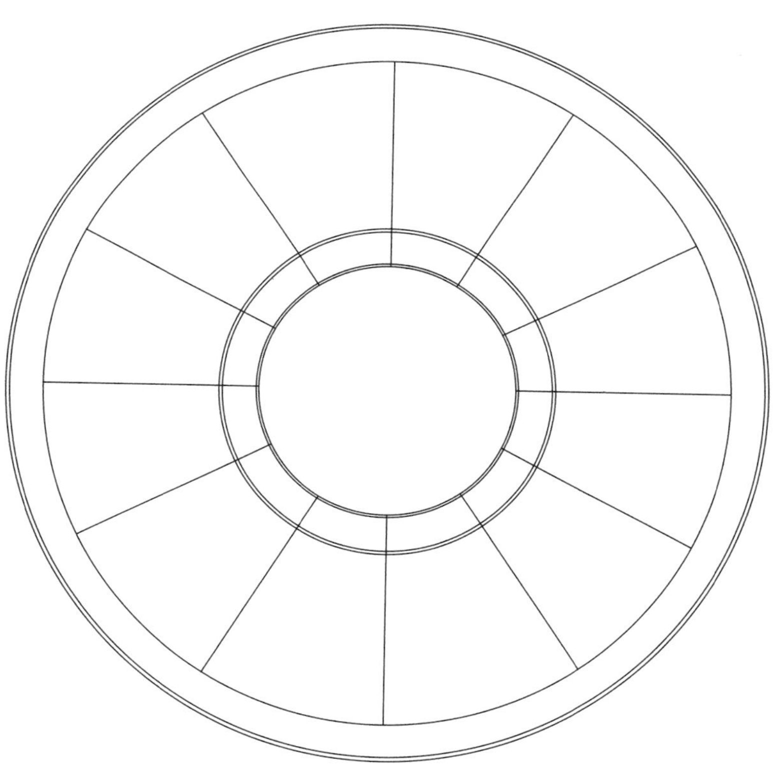

World Time Zones

Compared to Eastern Standard Time

(R) EST (used in *Guide*)
(S) CST/Subtract 1 hour
(Q) Add 1 hour
(P) Add 2 hours
(O) Add 3 hours
(Z) Add 5 hours
(T) MST/Subtract 2 hours
(U) PST/Subtract 3 hours
(U*) Subtract 3.5 hours
(V) Subtract 4 hours
(V*) Subtract 4.5 hours
(W) Subtract 5 hours
(X) Subtract 6 hours
(Y) Subtract 7 hours
(A) Add 6 hours
(B) Add 7 hours
(C) Add 8 hours
(C*) Add 8.5 hours
(D) Add 9 hours
(D*) Add 9.5 hours
(E) Add 10 hours
(E*) Add 10.5 hours
(F) Add 11 hours
(F*) Add 11.5 hours
(G) Add 12 hours
(H) Add 13 hours
(I) Add 14 hours
(I*) Add 14.5 hours
(K) Add 15 hours
(K*) Add 15.5 hours
(L) Add 16 hours
(L*) Add 16.5 hours
(M) Add 17 hours
(M*) Add 18 hours
(P*) Add 2.5 hours

Eastern Standard Time = Universal Time (Greenwich Mean Time) + or – the value from the table.

World Map of Time Zones

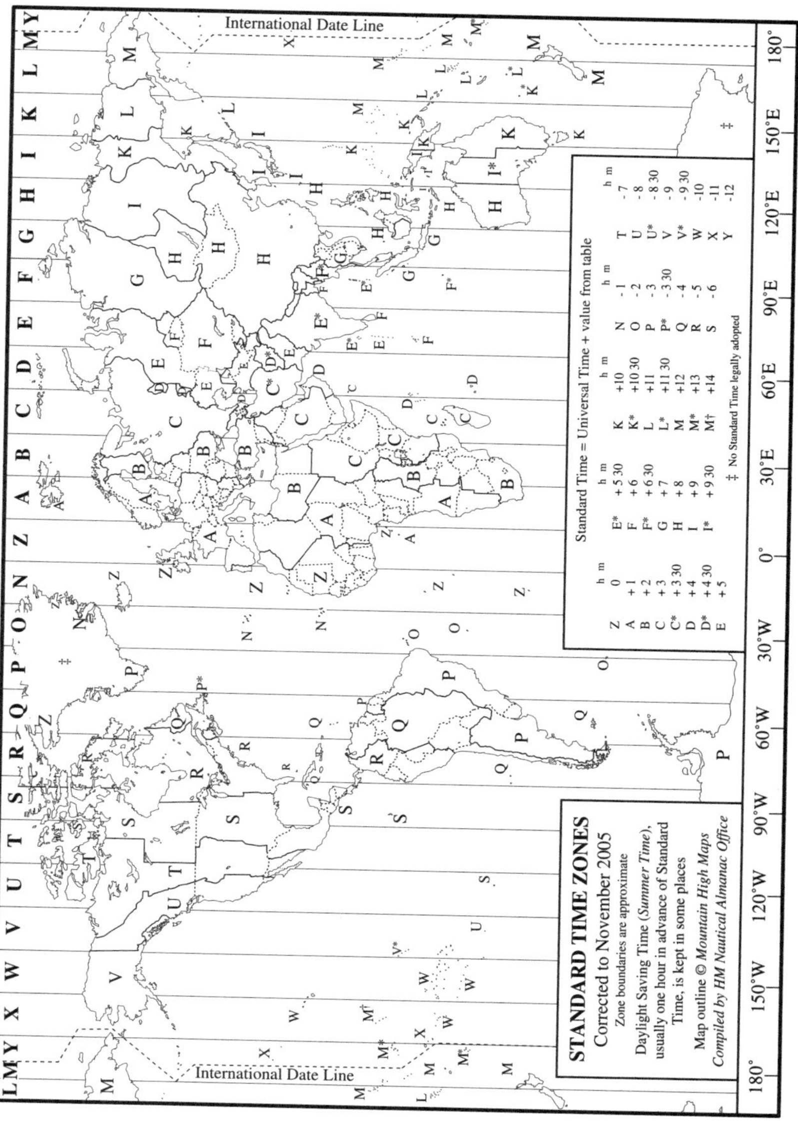

2013 Ephemeris Tables

January 2013

DATE	SID.TIME	SUN	MOON	N.NODE	MERCURY	VENUS	MARS	JUPITER	SATURN	URANUS	NEPTUNE	PLUTO	CERES	PALLAS	JUNO	VESTA	CHIRON
1 T	6:43:15	10♑43 48	20 ♌ 46	25 ♏ 01	0 ♑ 38	19 ♐ 46	4 ♒ 41	7 ♊ 46	9 ♏ 33	4 ♈ 46	1 ♓ 04	9 ♑ 19	23 ♊ 43	27 ♓ 33	4 ♑ 42	12 ♊ 18	6 ♓ 02
2 W	6:47:11	11 44 56	3 ♍ 24	24 53 ℞	2 11	21 01	5 28	7 41 ℞	9 37	4 47	1 06	9 21	23 30 ℞	27 47	5 04	12 07 ℞	6 05
3 Th	6:51:08	12 46 05	16 15	24 48	3 44	22 16	6 15	7 35	9 42	4 48	1 08	9 24	23 18	28 01	5 26	11 56	6 08
4 F	6:55:04	13 47 14	29 21	24 45	5 18	23 31	7 02	7 30	9 46	4 49	1 09	9 26	23 06	28 16	5 48	11 46	6 10
5 Sa	6:59:01	14 48 23	12 ♎ 44	24 43 D	6 51	24 46	7 50	7 25	9 51	4 50	1 11	9 28	22 54	28 31	6 10	11 36	6 13
6 Su	7:02:57	15 49 32	26 26	24 44	8 26	26 01	8 37	7 20	9 55	4 51	1 13	9 30	22 42	28 46	6 32	11 27	6 16
7 M	7:06:54	16 50 42	10 ♏ 29	24 45 ℞	10 00	27 17	9 24	7 15	9 59	4 52	1 14	9 32	22 31	29 01	6 54	11 18	6 19
8 T	7:10:50	17 51 52	24 51	24 45	11 35	28 32	10 11	7 11	10 03	4 54	1 16	9 34	22 20	29 17	7 16	11 09	6 21
9 W	7:14:47	18 53 02	9 ♐ 32	24 45	13 10	29 47	10 59	7 06	10 07	4 55	1 18	9 36	22 09	29 32	7 38	11 01	6 24
10 Th	7:18:44	19 54 12	24 26	24 41	14 46	1 ♑ 02	11 46	7 02	10 11	4 56	1 20	9 38	21 59	29 48	8 00	10 53	6 27
11 F	7:22:40	20 55 21	9 ♑ 27	24 36	16 22	2 17	12 33	6 58	10 15	4 58	1 22	9 40	21 49	0 ♈ 05	8 22	10 46	6 30
12 Sa	7:26:37	21 56 31	24 25	24 27	17 59	3 32	13 21	6 54	10 19	4 59	1 23	9 43	21 39	0 21	8 44	10 39	6 33
13 Su	7:30:33	22 57 40	9 ♒ 11	24 18	19 36	4 48	14 08	6 51	10 23	5 01	1 25	9 45	21 30	0 38	9 06	10 33	6 36
14 M	7:34:30	23 58 49	23 38	24 08	21 14	6 03	14 55	6 47	10 26	5 02	1 27	9 47	21 21	0 55	9 28	10 27	6 39
15 T	7:38:26	24 59 57	7 ♓ 38	23 59	22 52	7 18	15 43	6 44	10 30	5 04	1 29	9 49	21 12	1 12	9 50	10 21	6 42
16 W	7:42:23	26 01 05	21 10	23 51	24 30	8 33	16 30	6 41	10 33	5 05	1 31	9 51	21 04	1 29	10 12	10 16	6 46
17 Th	7:46:19	27 02 11	4 ♈ 15	23 46	26 09	9 48	17 17	6 38	10 37	5 07	1 33	9 53	20 56	1 47	10 34	10 12	6 49
18 F	7:50:16	28 03 17	16 53	23 44 D	27 49	11 04	18 05	6 36	10 40	5 09	1 35	9 55	20 48	2 05	10 56	10 08	6 52
19 Sa	7:54:13	29 04 22	29 11	23 43	29 29	12 19	18 52	6 33	10 43	5 11	1 37	9 57	20 41	2 22	11 18	10 04	6 55
20 Su	7:58:09	0♒05 26	11 ♉ 13	23 43	1 ♒ 10	13 34	19 40	6 31	10 46	5 12	1 39	9 59	20 35	2 41	11 40	10 01	6 59
21 M	8:02:06	1 06 30	23 05	23 44 ℞	2 51	14 49	20 27	6 29	10 49	5 14	1 41	10 01	20 28	2 59	12 02	9 58	7 02
22 T	8:06:02	2 07 32	4 ♊ 52	23 43	4 33	16 04	21 15	6 27	10 52	5 16	1 43	10 03	20 22	3 18	12 24	9 56	7 05
23 W	8:09:59	3 08 34	16 39	23 41	6 15	17 20	22 02	6 25	10 55	5 18	1 45	10 05	20 17	3 36	12 46	9 54	7 09
24 Th	8:13:55	4 09 35	28 31	23 35	7 58	18 35	22 49	6 24	10 57	5 20	1 47	10 07	20 12	3 55	13 07	9 52	7 12
25 F	8:17:52	5 10 34	10 ♋ 30	23 27	9 41	19 50	23 37	6 23	11 00	5 22	1 49	10 09	20 07	4 14	13 29	9 51	7 15
26 Sa	8:21:48	6 11 33	22 39	23 16	11 25	21 05	24 24	6 22	11 02	5 24	1 51	10 11	20 03	4 34	13 51	9 51 D	7 19
27 Su	8:25:45	7 12 31	5 ♌ 00	23 04	13 09	22 20	25 12	6 21	11 05	5 26	1 53	10 13	19 59	4 53	14 13	9 51	7 22
28 M	8:29:42	8 13 28	17 33	22 50	14 54	23 35	25 59	6 20	11 07	5 29	1 55	10 15	19 56	5 13	14 35	9 51	7 26
29 T	8:33:38	9 14 24	0 ♍ 18	22 37	16 39	24 51	26 47	6 20	11 09	5 31	1 58	10 17	19 53	5 33	14 57	9 52	7 29
30 W	8:37:35	10 15 19	13 14	22 25	18 24	26 06	27 34	6 20 D	11 11	5 33	2 00	10 19	19 51	5 53	15 18	9 53	7 33
31 Th	8:41:31	11 16 13	26 22	22 16	20 10	27 21	28 21	6 20	11 13	5 35	2 02	10 21	19 49	6 13	15 40	9 55	7 36

February 2013

DATE	SID.TIME	SUN	MOON	N.NODE	MERCURY	VENUS	MARS	JUPITER	SATURN	URANUS	NEPTUNE	PLUTO	CERES	PALLAS	JUNO	VESTA	CHIRON
1 F	8:45:28	12♒17 07	9 ♎ 40	22 ♏ 09	21 ♒ 55	28 ♑ 36	29 ♒ 09	6 ♊ 20	11 ♏ 15	5 ♈ 38	2 ♓ 04	10 ♑ 22	19 ♊ 47	6 ♈ 34	16 ♑ 02	9 ♊ 57	7 ♓ 40
2 Sa	8:49:24	13 18 00	23 10	22 06 ℞	23 41	29 51	29 56	6 20	11 17	5 40	2 06	10 24	19 46 ℞	6 54	16 23	9 59	7 44
3 Su	8:53:21	14 18 52	6 ♏ 51	22 04 D	25 26	1 ♒ 06	0 ♓ 44	6 21	11 19	5 42	2 08	10 26	19 45	7 15	16 45	10 02	7 47
4 M	8:57:17	15 19 43	20 45	22 04 ℞	27 11	2 22	1 31	6 22	11 20	5 45	2 11	10 28	19 45 D	7 36	17 07	10 06	7 51
5 T	9:01:14	16 20 33	4 ♐ 52	22 04	28 56	3 37	2 18	6 23	11 22	5 47	2 13	10 30	19 45	7 57	17 28	10 09	7 55
6 W	9:05:11	17 21 23	19 12	22 02	0 ♓ 39	4 52	3 06	6 24	11 23	5 50	2 15	10 32	19 45	8 18	17 50	10 13	7 58
7 Th	9:09:07	18 22 12	3 ♑ 41	21 58	2 21	6 07	3 53	6 25	11 24	5 52	2 17	10 33	19 46	8 39	18 11	10 18	8 02
8 F	9:13:04	19 23 00	18 17	21 50	4 02	7 22	4 41	6 27	11 26	5 55	2 19	10 35	19 47	9 01	18 33	10 23	8 06
9 Sa	9:17:00	20 23 46	2 ♒ 52	21 40	5 41	8 37	5 28	6 29	11 27	5 58	2 22	10 37	19 49	9 23	18 54	10 28	8 09
10 Su	9:20:57	21 24 32	17 20	21 28	7 17	9 53	6 15	6 31	11 28	6 00	2 24	10 39	19 51	9 45	19 16	10 34	8 13
11 M	9:24:53	22 25 16	1 ♓ 34	21 15	8 51	11 08	7 03	6 33	11 28	6 03	2 26	10 40	19 54	10 07	19 37	10 40	8 17
12 T	9:28:50	23 25 58	15 28	21 03	10 21	12 23	7 50	6 36	11 29	6 06	2 28	10 42	19 57	10 29	19 58	10 46	8 21
13 W	9:32:46	24 26 39	28 58	20 53	11 46	13 38	8 37	6 38	11 30	6 08	2 31	10 44	20 00	10 51	20 20	10 53	8 25
14 Th	9:36:43	25 27 19	12 ♈ 04	20 46	13 07	14 53	9 25	6 41	11 30	6 11	2 33	10 45	20 04	11 14	20 41	11 00	8 28
15 F	9:40:40	26 27 57	24 45	20 41	14 23	16 08	10 12	6 44	11 31	6 14	2 35	10 47	20 08	11 36	21 02	11 08	8 32
16 Sa	9:44:36	27 28 33	7 ♉ 06	20 39	15 32	17 23	10 59	6 47	11 31	6 17	2 37	10 49	20 13	11 59	21 23	11 16	8 36
17 Su	9:48:33	28 29 08	19 10	20 38	16 35	18 38	11 47	6 51	11 31	6 20	2 40	10 50	20 18	12 22	21 44	11 24	8 40
18 M	9:52:29	29 29 40	1 ♊ 04	20 38	17 30	19 53	12 34	6 54	11 32 ℞	6 22	2 42	10 52	20 23	12 45	22 05	11 33	8 44
19 T	9:56:26	0♓30 11	12 53	20 38	18 17	21 08	13 21	6 58	11 32	6 25	2 44	10 53	20 29	13 08	22 26	11 42	8 48
20 W	10:00:22	1 30 40	24 41	20 35	18 55	22 24	14 08	7 02	11 31	6 28	2 47	10 55	20 35	13 32	22 47	11 51	8 51
21 Th	10:04:19	2 31 08	6 ♋ 35	20 31	19 24	23 39	14 56	7 06	11 31	6 31	2 49	10 56	20 41	13 55	23 08	12 01	8 55
22 F	10:08:15	3 31 33	18 39	20 24	19 43	24 54	15 43	7 10	11 31	6 34	2 51	10 58	20 48	14 19	23 29	12 10	8 59
23 Sa	10:12:12	4 31 57	0 ♌ 56	20 14	19 52 ℞	26 09	16 30	7 15	11 31	6 37	2 53	10 59	20 55	14 42	23 50	12 21	9 03
24 Su	10:16:09	5 32 19	13 28	20 02	19 51	27 24	17 17	7 19	11 30	6 40	2 56	11 00	21 02	15 06	24 11	12 31	9 07
25 M	10:20:05	6 32 39	26 17	19 49	19 40	28 39	18 04	7 24	11 30	6 43	2 58	11 02	21 10	15 30	24 32	12 42	9 11
26 T	10:24:02	7 32 57	9 ♍ 22	19 36	19 19	29 54	18 51	7 29	11 29	6 46	3 00	11 03	21 19	15 54	24 52	12 53	9 15
27 W	10:27:58	8 33 14	22 41	19 25	18 50	1 ♓ 09	19 38	7 35	11 28	6 49	3 03	11 05	21 27	16 18	25 13	13 05	9 19
28 Th	10:31:55	9 33 29	6 ♎ 12	19 16	18 12	2 24	20 25	7 40	11 27	6 53	3 05	11 06	21 36	16 43	25 33	13 17	9 22

March 2013

DATE	SID.TIME	SUN	MOON	N.NODE	MERCURY	VENUS	MARS	JUPITER	SATURN	URANUS	NEPTUNE	PLUTO	CERES	PALLAS	JUNO	VESTA	CHIRON
1 F	10:35:51	10♓33 42	19 ♎ 54	19 ♏ 10	17 ♓ 27	3 ♓ 38	21 ♓ 12	7 ♊ 45	11 ♏ 26	6 ♈ 56	3 ♓ 07	11 ♑ 07	21 ♊ 45	17 ♈ 07	25 ♑ 54	13 ♊ 29	9 ♓ 26
2 Sa	10:39:48	11 33 54	3 ♏ 43	19 07 ℞	16 35 ℞	4 53	21 59	7 51	11 25 ℞	6 59	3 09	11 08	21 55	17 32	26 14	13 41	9 30
3 Su	10:43:44	12 34 04	17 39	19 06 D	15 39	6 08	22 46	7 57	11 24	7 02	3 12	11 10	22 05	17 57	26 34	13 54	9 34
4 M	10:47:41	13 34 13	1 ♐ 39	19 06 ℞	14 40	7 23	23 33	8 03	11 22	7 05	3 14	11 11	22 15	18 21	26 55	14 06	9 38
5 T	10:51:37	14 34 20	15 44	19 06	13 38	8 38	24 20	8 09	11 21	7 09	3 16	11 12	22 25	18 46	27 15	14 20	9 42
6 W	10:55:34	15 34 26	29 52	19 06	12 36	9 53	25 07	8 16	11 20	7 12	3 18	11 13	22 36	19 12	27 35	14 33	9 46
7 Th	10:59:31	16 34 30	14 ♑ 02	19 03	11 36	11 08	25 54	8 22	11 18	7 15	3 21	11 14	22 47	19 37	27 55	14 47	9 50
8 F	11:03:27	17 34 33	28 13	18 57	10 37	12 23	26 41	8 29	11 16	7 18	3 23	11 15	22 58	20 02	28 15	15 01	9 53
9 Sa	11:07:24	18 34 34	12 ♒ 20	18 49	9 42	13 38	27 27	8 36	11 14	7 22	3 25	11 17	23 10	20 28	28 35	15 15	9 57
10 Su	11:11:20	19 34 33	26 21	18 40	8 51	14 53	28 14	8 43	11 13	7 25	3 27	11 18	23 22	20 53	28 55	15 29	10 01
11 M	11:15:17	20 34 31	10 ♓ 10	18 29	8 05	16 08	29 01	8 50	11 11	7 28	3 29	11 19	23 34	21 19	29 15	15 44	10 05
12 T	11:19:13	21 34 26	23 44	18 20	7 25	17 22	29 47	8 57	11 09	7 31	3 32	11 20	23 47	21 45	29 35	15 59	10 09
13 W	11:23:10	22 34 20	6 ♈ 59	18 12	6 51	18 37	0 ♈ 34	9 04	11 06	7 35	3 34	11 21	24 00	22 10	29 54	16 14	10 13
14 Th	11:27:06	23 34 11	19 55	18 06	6 24	19 52	1 21	9 12	11 04	7 38	3 36	11 21	24 13	22 36	0 ♒ 14	16 30	10 16
15 F	11:31:03	24 34 01	2 ♉ 32	18 02	6 03	21 07	2 07	9 20	11 02	7 41	3 38	11 22	24 26	23 03	0 33	16 45	10 20
16 Sa	11:35:00	25 33 48	14 51	18 01 D	5 48	22 22	2 54	9 28	10 59	7 45	3 40	11 23	24 40	23 29	0 52	17 01	10 24
17 Su	11:38:56	26 33 33	26 56	18 01	5 40 D	23 36	3 40	9 36	10 57	7 48	3 42	11 24	24 54	23 55	1 12	17 17	10 28
18 M	11:42:53	27 33 16	8 ♊ 51	18 02	5 38	24 51	4 27	9 44	10 54	7 52	3 45	11 25	25 08	24 22	1 31	17 33	10 31
19 T	11:46:49	28 32 57	20 41	18 03 ℞	5 42	26 06	5 13	9 52	10 51	7 55	3 47	11 26	25 22	24 48	1 50	17 50	10 35
20 W	11:50:46	29 32 36	2 ♋ 31	18 03	5 52	27 21	6 00	10 00	10 49	7 58	3 49	11 26	25 37	25 15	2 09	18 07	10 39
21 Th	11:54:42	0♈32 12	14 26	18 02	6 07	28 35	6 46	10 09	10 46	8 02	3 51	11 27	25 52	25 41	2 28	18 24	10 43
22 F	11:58:39	1 31 46	26 31	17 59	6 27	29 50	7 33	10 18	10 43	8 05	3 53	11 28	26 07	26 08	2 47	18 41	10 46
23 Sa	12:02:35	2 31 18	8 ♌ 51	17 54	6 52	1 ♈ 05	8 19	10 26	10 40	8 09	3 55	11 28	26 22	26 35	3 05	18 58	10 50
24 Su	12:06:32	3 30 47	21 29	17 47	7 22	2 19	9 05	10 35	10 37	8 12	3 57	11 29	26 38	27 02	3 24	19 15	10 54
25 M	12:10:29	4 30 15	4 ♍ 28	17 40	7 56	3 34	9 51	10 44	10 34	8 15	3 59	11 30	26 54	27 29	3 43	19 33	10 57
26 T	12:14:25	5 29 40	17 47	17 33	8 35	4 48	10 37	10 54	10 30	8 19	4 01	11 30	27 10	27 57	4 01	19 51	11 01
27 W	12:18:22	6 29 02	1 ♎ 25	17 26	9 17	6 03	11 24	11 03	10 27	8 22	4 03	11 31	27 26	28 24	4 19	20 09	11 04
28 Th	12:22:18	7 28 23	15 20	17 21	10 03	7 18	12 10	11 12	10 24	8 26	4 05	11 31	27 42	28 51	4 38	20 27	11 08
29 F	12:26:15	8 27 42	29 28	17 18	10 52	8 32	12 56	11 22	10 20	8 29	4 07	11 32	27 59	29 19	4 56	20 46	11 12
30 Sa	12:30:11	9 26 59	13 ♏ 45	17 16 D	11 44	9 47	13 42	11 31	10 17	8 33	4 09	11 32	28 16	29 47	5 14	21 04	11 15
31 Su	12:34:08	10 26 14	28 05	17 17	12 40	11 01	14 28	11 41	10 13	8 36	4 11	11 33	28 33	0 ♉ 14	5 31	21 23	11 19

April 2013

DATE	SID.TIME	SUN	MOON	N.NODE	MERCURY	VENUS	MARS	JUPITER	SATURN	URANUS	NEPTUNE	PLUTO	CERES	PALLAS	JUNO	VESTA	CHIRON
1 M	12:38:04	11 ♈ 25 27	12 ♐ 25	17 ♏ 18	13 ♓ 38	12 ♈ 16	15 ♈ 14	11 ♊ 51	10 ♏ 09	8 ♈ 39	4 ♓ 13	11 ♑ 33	28 ♊ 50	0 ♉ 42	5 ♒ 49	21 ♊ 42	11 ♓ 22
2 T	12:42:01	12 24 39	26 41	17 19	14 40	13 30	16 00	12 01	10 06 ℞	8 43	4 15	11 33	29 08	1 10	6 07	22 01	11 25
3 W	12:45:58	13 23 49	10 ♑ 52	17 20 ℞	15 43	14 45	16 45	12 11	10 02	8 46	4 17	11 34	29 25	1 38	6 24	22 20	11 29
4 Th	12:49:54	14 22 57	24 56	17 20	16 50	15 59	17 31	12 21	9 58	8 50	4 19	11 34	29 43	2 06	6 42	22 40	11 32
5 F	12:53:51	15 22 04	8 ♒ 52	17 18	17 59	17 14	18 17	12 31	9 54	8 53	4 20	11 34	0 ♋ 01	2 34	6 59	22 59	11 36
6 Sa	12:57:47	16 21 08	22 37	17 15	19 10	18 28	19 03	12 42	9 50	8 57	4 22	11 34	0 20	3 03	7 16	23 19	11 39
7 Su	13:01:44	17 20 11	6 ♓ 12	17 10	20 23	19 42	19 48	12 52	9 46	9 00	4 24	11 35	0 38	3 31	7 33	23 39	11 42
8 M	13:05:40	18 19 12	19 34	17 06	21 38	20 57	20 34	13 03	9 42	9 03	4 26	11 35	0 57	3 59	7 50	23 59	11 46
9 T	13:09:37	19 18 11	2 ♈ 42	17 01	22 55	22 11	21 20	13 13	9 38	9 07	4 28	11 35	1 15	4 28	8 07	24 19	11 49
10 W	13:13:33	20 17 08	15 36	16 57	24 15	23 26	22 05	13 24	9 34	9 10	4 29	11 35	1 34	4 57	8 23	24 39	11 52
11 Th	13:17:30	21 16 03	28 15	16 55	25 36	24 40	22 51	13 35	9 30	9 13	4 31	11 35	1 53	5 25	8 40	25 00	11 55
12 F	13:21:26	22 14 56	10 ♉ 40	16 54 D	26 59	25 54	23 36	13 46	9 26	9 17	4 33	11 35 ℞	2 13	5 54	8 56	25 20	11 58
13 Sa	13:25:23	23 13 48	22 52	16 54	28 24	27 09	24 21	13 57	9 21	9 20	4 34	11 35	2 32	6 23	9 12	25 41	12 02
14 Su	13:29:20	24 12 37	4 ♊ 53	16 55	29 50	28 23	25 07	14 08	9 17	9 24	4 36	11 35	2 52	6 52	9 28	26 02	12 05
15 M	13:33:16	25 11 23	16 47	16 56	1 ♈ 19	29 37	25 52	14 19	9 13	9 27	4 38	11 35	3 11	7 21	9 44	26 23	12 08
16 T	13:37:13	26 10 08	28 37	16 58	2 49	0 ♉ 51	26 37	14 31	9 08	9 30	4 39	11 35	3 31	7 50	10 00	26 44	12 11
17 W	13:41:09	27 08 51	10 ♋ 27	16 59	4 21	2 06	27 23	14 42	9 04	9 34	4 41	11 35	3 51	8 19	10 16	27 05	12 14
18 Th	13:45:06	28 07 31	22 22	17 00 ℞	5 54	3 20	28 08	14 54	9 00	9 37	4 42	11 35	4 12	8 49	10 31	27 27	12 17
19 F	13:49:02	29 06 09	4 ♌ 26	17 00	7 30	4 34	28 53	15 05	8 55	9 40	4 44	11 35	4 32	9 18	10 46	27 48	12 20
20 Sa	13:52:59	0 ♉ 04 45	16 46	16 59	9 07	5 48	29 38	15 17	8 51	9 43	4 45	11 34	4 52	9 48	11 01	28 10	12 23
21 Su	13:56:55	1 03 19	29 23	16 58	10 45	7 02	0 ♉ 23	15 28	8 46	9 47	4 47	11 34	5 13	10 17	11 16	28 31	12 25
22 M	14:00:52	2 01 50	12 ♍ 23	16 56	12 25	8 16	1 08	15 40	8 42	9 50	4 48	11 34	5 34	10 47	11 31	28 53	12 28
23 T	14:04:49	3 00 19	25 47	16 54	14 07	9 30	1 53	15 52	8 37	9 53	4 50	11 34	5 55	11 16	11 46	29 15	12 31
24 W	14:08:45	3 58 47	9 ♎ 35	16 52	15 51	10 45	2 38	16 04	8 33	9 56	4 51	11 33	6 16	11 46	12 00	29 37	12 34
25 Th	14:12:42	4 57 12	23 45	16 51	17 36	11 59	3 22	16 16	8 28	10 00	4 52	11 33	6 37	12 16	12 14	29 59	12 36
26 F	14:16:38	5 55 35	8 ♏ 13	16 50 D	19 23	13 13	4 07	16 28	8 24	10 03	4 54	11 33	6 58	12 46	12 28	0 ♋ 22	12 39
27 Sa	14:20:35	6 53 57	22 54	16 50	21 12	14 27	4 52	16 40	8 19	10 06	4 55	11 32	7 20	13 16	12 42	0 44	12 42
28 Su	14:24:31	7 52 17	7 ♐ 41	16 51	23 02	15 41	5 36	16 52	8 14	10 09	4 56	11 32	7 41	13 46	12 56	1 06	12 44
29 M	14:28:28	8 50 35	22 27	16 51	24 54	16 55	6 21	17 05	8 10	10 12	4 58	11 31	8 03	14 16	13 09	1 29	12 47
30 T	14:32:24	9 48 52	7 ♑ 05	16 52	26 48	18 09	7 06	17 17	8 05	10 15	4 59	11 31	8 25	14 47	13 23	1 52	12 49

May 2013

DATE	SID.TIME	SUN	MOON	N.NODE	MERCURY	VENUS	MARS	JUPITER	SATURN	URANUS	NEPTUNE	PLUTO	CERES	PALLAS	JUNO	VESTA	CHIRON
1 W	14:36:21	10♉47 07	21 ♑ 31	16 ♏ 53	28 ♈ 44	19 ♉ 23	7 ♉ 50	17 ♊ 29	8 ♏ 01	10 ♈ 18	5 ♓ 00	11 ♑ 30	8 ♋ 47	15 ♉ 17	13 ♒ 36	2 ♋ 14	12 ♓ 52
2 Th	14:40:18	11 45 21	5 ♒ 41	16 53 ℞	0 ♉ 41	20 37	8 35	17 42	7 56 ℞	10 21	5 01	11 30 ℞	9 09	15 47	13 49	2 37	12 54
3 F	14:44:14	12 43 33	19 33	16 53	2 40	21 50	9 19	17 54	7 52	10 24	5 02	11 29	9 31	16 18	14 01	3 00	12 56
4 Sa	14:48:11	13 41 44	3 ♓ 08	16 53	4 41	23 04	10 03	18 07	7 47	10 27	5 03	11 28	9 53	16 48	14 14	3 23	12 59
5 Su	14:52:07	14 39 53	16 25	16 52	6 43	24 18	10 48	18 19	7 43	10 30	5 04	11 28	10 15	17 19	14 26	3 46	13 01
6 M	14:56:04	15 38 01	29 26	16 52	8 47	25 32	11 32	18 32	7 38	10 33	5 06	11 27	10 38	17 50	14 38	4 09	13 03
7 T	15:00:00	16 36 08	12 ♈ 12	16 52 D	10 52	26 46	12 16	18 45	7 34	10 36	5 07	11 26	11 00	18 21	14 50	4 33	13 05
8 W	15:03:57	17 34 12	24 45	16 52	12 58	28 00	13 00	18 57	7 29	10 39	5 08	11 26	11 23	18 51	15 02	4 56	13 07
9 Th	15:07:53	18 32 16	7 ♉ 06	16 52 ℞	15 06	29 14	13 44	19 10	7 25	10 42	5 08	11 25	11 46	19 22	15 13	5 20	13 10
10 F	15:11:50	19 30 18	19 17	16 52	17 15	0 ♊ 28	14 28	19 23	7 20	10 45	5 09	11 24	12 09	19 53	15 24	5 43	13 12
11 Sa	15:15:47	20 28 18	1 ♊ 19	16 52	19 25	1 41	15 12	19 36	7 16	10 48	5 10	11 23	12 32	20 25	15 35	6 07	13 14
12 Su	15:19:43	21 26 17	13 15	16 52	21 35	2 55	15 56	19 49	7 12	10 50	5 11	11 23	12 55	20 56	15 46	6 31	13 16
13 M	15:23:40	22 24 14	25 06	16 51	23 46	4 09	16 40	20 02	7 07	10 53	5 12	11 22	13 18	21 27	15 56	6 54	13 17
14 T	15:27:36	23 22 10	6 ♋ 55	16 50	25 57	5 23	17 24	20 15	7 03	10 56	5 13	11 21	13 41	21 58	16 07	7 18	13 19
15 W	15:31:33	24 20 03	18 46	16 49	28 07	6 36	18 08	20 28	6 59	10 59	5 14	11 20	14 05	22 30	16 17	7 42	13 21
16 Th	15:35:29	25 17 55	0 ♌ 41	16 48	0 ♊ 18	7 50	18 52	20 41	6 54	11 01	5 14	11 19	14 28	23 01	16 26	8 06	13 23
17 F	15:39:26	26 15 46	12 45	16 48	2 28	9 04	19 35	20 54	6 50	11 04	5 15	11 18	14 52	23 33	16 36	8 31	13 24
18 Sa	15:43:22	27 13 34	25 02	16 47 D	4 37	10 17	20 19	21 08	6 46	11 07	5 16	11 17	15 15	24 04	16 45	8 55	13 26
19 Su	15:47:19	28 11 21	7 ♍ 37	16 48	6 45	11 31	21 02	21 21	6 42	11 09	5 16	11 16	15 39	24 36	16 54	9 19	13 28
20 M	15:51:16	29 09 06	20 32	16 48	8 51	12 45	21 46	21 34	6 38	11 12	5 17	11 15	16 03	25 07	17 02	9 43	13 29
21 T	15:55:12	0♊06 50	3 ♎ 52	16 49	10 55	13 58	22 29	21 47	6 34	11 14	5 18	11 14	16 27	25 39	17 11	10 08	13 31
22 W	15:59:09	1 04 32	17 38	16 50	12 58	15 12	23 13	22 01	6 30	11 17	5 18	11 13	16 51	26 11	17 19	10 32	13 32
23 Th	16:03:05	2 02 13	1 ♏ 51	16 51	14 59	16 25	23 56	22 14	6 26	11 19	5 19	11 12	17 15	26 43	17 27	10 57	13 33
24 F	16:07:02	2 59 52	16 27	16 52 ℞	16 57	17 39	24 39	22 28	6 22	11 22	5 19	11 11	17 39	27 15	17 34	11 21	13 35
25 Sa	16:10:58	3 57 29	1 ♐ 22	16 51	18 53	18 52	25 23	22 41	6 19	11 24	5 20	11 10	18 03	27 47	17 42	11 46	13 36
26 Su	16:14:55	4 55 06	16 28	16 50	20 46	20 06	26 06	22 54	6 15	11 26	5 20	11 09	18 27	28 19	17 49	12 11	13 37
27 M	16:18:51	5 52 42	1 ♑ 35	16 48	22 36	21 19	26 49	23 08	6 11	11 29	5 20	11 08	18 52	28 51	17 55	12 36	13 38
28 T	16:22:48	6 50 16	16 36	16 45	24 24	22 33	27 32	23 21	6 08	11 31	5 21	11 06	19 16	29 23	18 02	13 00	13 40
29 W	16:26:45	7 47 49	1 ♒ 20	16 43	26 09	23 46	28 15	23 35	6 04	11 33	5 21	11 05	19 40	29 56	18 08	13 25	13 41
30 Th	16:30:41	8 45 22	15 44	16 41	27 52	25 00	28 58	23 49	6 01	11 36	5 21	11 04	20 05	0 ♊ 28	18 13	13 50	13 42
31 F	16:34:38	9 42 54	29 43	16 40 D	29 31	26 13	29 41	24 02	5 57	11 38	5 22	11 03	20 30	1 01	18 19	14 15	13 43

June 2013

DATE	SID.TIME	SUN	MOON	N.NODE	MERCURY	VENUS	MARS	JUPITER	SATURN	URANUS	NEPTUNE	PLUTO	CERES	PALLAS	JUNO	VESTA	CHIRON
1 Sa	16:38:34	10 ♊ 40 25	13 ♓ 17	16 ♏ 39	1 ♋ 08	27 ♊ 26	0 ♊ 24	24 ♊ 16	5 ♏ 54	11 ♈ 40	5 ♓ 22	11 ♑ 02	20 ♋ 54	1 ♊ 33	18 ♒ 24	14 ♋ 40	13 ♓ 43
2 Su	16:42:31	11 37 55	26 28	16 40	2 41	28 40	1 07	24 29	5 51 ℞	11 42	5 22	11 00 ℞	21 19	2 06	18 29	15 06	13 44
3 M	16:46:27	12 35 24	9 ♈ 18	16 41	4 12	29 53	1 49	24 43	5 47	11 44	5 22	10 59	21 44	2 38	18 33	15 31	13 45
4 T	16:50:24	13 32 53	21 50	16 43	5 39	1 ♋ 07	2 32	24 57	5 44	11 46	5 22	10 58	22 09	3 11	18 37	15 56	13 46
5 W	16:54:20	14 30 20	4 ♉ 08	16 44	7 04	2 20	3 15	25 10	5 41	11 48	5 22	10 56	22 34	3 44	18 41	16 21	13 46
6 Th	16:58:17	15 27 48	16 15	16 45 ℞	8 25	3 33	3 57	25 24	5 38	11 50	5 22	10 55	22 59	4 16	18 45	16 47	13 47
7 F	17:02:14	16 25 14	28 15	16 44	9 43	4 47	4 40	25 38	5 35	11 52	5 22 ℞	10 54	23 24	4 49	18 48	17 12	13 48
8 Sa	17:06:10	17 22 40	10 ♊ 09	16 42	10 59	6 00	5 23	25 51	5 33	11 54	5 22	10 52	23 49	5 22	18 51	17 38	13 48
9 Su	17:10:07	18 20 05	21 59	16 39	12 11	7 13	6 05	26 05	5 30	11 56	5 22	10 51	24 14	5 55	18 53	18 03	13 49
10 M	17:14:03	19 17 29	3 ♋ 49	16 34	13 19	8 26	6 47	26 19	5 27	11 57	5 22	10 50	24 39	6 28	18 55	18 29	13 49
11 T	17:18:00	20 14 52	15 39	16 28	14 25	9 40	7 30	26 33	5 25	11 59	5 22	10 48	25 05	7 01	18 57	18 54	13 49
12 W	17:21:56	21 12 14	27 32	16 22	15 27	10 53	8 12	26 46	5 22	12 01	5 22	10 47	25 30	7 34	18 58	19 20	13 50
13 Th	17:25:53	22 09 36	9 ♌ 30	16 16	16 25	12 06	8 54	27 00	5 20	12 02	5 22	10 46	25 56	8 07	18 59	19 46	13 50
14 F	17:29:49	23 06 56	21 37	16 11	17 20	13 19	9 36	27 14	5 17	12 04	5 22	10 44	26 21	8 41	19 00	20 12	13 50
15 Sa	17:33:46	24 04 16	3 ♍ 54	16 07	18 11	14 32	10 19	27 28	5 15	12 06	5 22	10 43	26 47	9 14	19 00 ℞	20 37	13 50
16 Su	17:37:43	25 01 34	16 26	16 06 D	18 59	15 45	11 01	27 41	5 13	12 07	5 21	10 41	27 12	9 47	19 00	21 03	13 50 ℞
17 M	17:41:39	25 58 52	29 17	16 05	19 42	16 59	11 43	27 55	5 11	12 09	5 21	10 40	27 38	10 21	19 00	21 29	13 50
18 T	17:45:36	26 56 09	12 ♎ 30	16 06	20 22	18 12	12 25	28 09	5 09	12 10	5 21	10 38	28 04	10 54	18 59	21 55	13 50
19 W	17:49:32	27 53 25	26 09	16 07	20 58	19 25	13 07	28 23	5 07	12 11	5 20	10 37	28 29	11 28	18 58	22 21	13 50
20 Th	17:53:29	28 50 40	10 ♏ 14	16 08 ℞	21 29	20 38	13 48	28 36	5 05	12 13	5 20	10 35	28 55	12 01	18 56	22 47	13 50
21 F	17:57:25	29 47 55	24 45	16 08	21 57	21 51	14 30	28 50	5 04	12 14	5 19	10 34	29 21	12 35	18 54	23 13	13 49
22 Sa	18:01:22	0 ♋ 45 09	9 ♐ 39	16 06	22 20	23 04	15 12	29 04	5 02	12 15	5 19	10 33	29 47	13 08	18 52	23 39	13 49
23 Su	18:05:18	1 42 23	24 49	16 02	22 38	24 17	15 54	29 18	5 00	12 17	5 19	10 31	0 ♌ 13	13 42	18 49	24 05	13 49
24 M	18:09:15	2 39 36	10 ♑ 06	15 57	22 52	25 30	16 35	29 32	4 59	12 18	5 18	10 30	0 39	14 16	18 46	24 32	13 48
25 T	18:13:12	3 36 49	25 19	15 50	23 01	26 42	17 17	29 45	4 58	12 19	5 17	10 28	1 05	14 49	18 43	24 58	13 48
26 W	18:17:08	4 34 02	10 ♒ 18	15 43	23 06 ℞	27 55	17 59	29 59	4 56	12 20	5 17	10 27	1 31	15 23	18 39	25 24	13 48
27 Th	18:21:05	5 31 14	24 55	15 37	23 06	29 08	18 40	0 ♋ 13	4 55	12 21	5 16	10 25	1 57	15 57	18 35	25 50	13 47
28 F	18:25:01	6 28 26	9 ♓ 04	15 32	23 02	0 ♌ 21	19 22	0 26	4 54	12 22	5 16	10 24	2 23	16 31	18 30	26 17	13 46
29 Sa	18:28:58	7 25 39	22 44	15 29	22 53	1 34	20 03	0 40	4 53	12 23	5 15	10 22	2 49	17 05	18 25	26 43	13 46
30 Su	18:32:54	8 22 51	5 ♈ 56	15 28 D	22 40	2 47	20 44	0 54	4 52	12 24	5 14	10 21	3 15	17 39	18 20	27 10	13 45

July 2013

DATE	SID.TIME	SUN	MOON	N.NODE	MERCURY	VENUS	MARS	JUPITER	SATURN	URANUS	NEPTUNE	PLUTO	CERES	PALLAS	JUNO	VESTA	CHIRON
1 M	18:36:51	9 ♋ 20 04	18 ♈ 44	15 ♏ 28	22 ♋ 23	3 ♌ 59	21 ♊ 26	1 ♋ 08	4 ♏ 52	12 ♈ 25	5 ♓ 14	10 ♑ 19	3 ♌ 42	18 ♊ 13	18 ♒ 14	27 ♋ 36	13 ♓ 44
2 T	18:40:47	10 17 17	1 ♉ 10	15 29	22 01 R	5 12	22 07	1 21	4 51 R	12 25	5 13 R	10 18 R	4 08	18 47	18 08 R	28 03	13 43 R
3 W	18:44:44	11 14 30	13 22	15 30 R	21 36	6 25	22 48	1 35	4 50	12 26	5 12	10 16	4 34	19 21	18 01	28 29	13 42
4 Th	18:48:41	12 11 43	25 21	15 29	21 08	7 38	23 29	1 49	4 50	12 27	5 11	10 14	5 01	19 55	17 54	28 56	13 42
5 F	18:52:37	13 08 56	7 ♊ 14	15 27	20 36	8 50	24 10	2 02	4 50	12 27	5 10	10 13	5 27	20 30	17 47	29 22	13 41
6 Sa	18:56:34	14 06 10	19 04	15 22	20 03	10 03	24 51	2 16	4 49	12 28	5 10	10 11	5 54	21 04	17 39	29 49	13 40
7 Su	19:00:30	15 03 24	0 ♋ 52	15 15	19 27	11 16	25 32	2 29	4 49	12 29	5 09	10 10	6 20	21 38	17 31	0 ♌ 16	13 38
8 M	19:04:27	16 00 37	12 43	15 05	18 50	12 28	26 13	2 43	4 49 D	12 29	5 08	10 08	6 47	22 12	17 23	0 42	13 37
9 T	19:08:23	16 57 51	24 37	14 54	18 12	13 41	26 54	2 56	4 49	12 29	5 07	10 07	7 13	22 47	17 14	1 09	13 36
10 W	19:12:20	17 55 05	6 ♌ 36	14 43	17 34	14 53	27 35	3 10	4 49	12 30	5 06	10 05	7 40	23 21	17 05	1 36	13 35
11 Th	19:16:16	18 52 19	18 42	14 31	16 57	16 06	28 16	3 24	4 49	12 30	5 05	10 04	8 06	23 56	16 56	2 03	13 34
12 F	19:20:13	19 49 34	0 ♍ 55	14 22	16 20	17 19	28 57	3 37	4 50	12 31	5 04	10 02	8 33	24 30	16 46	2 29	13 32
13 Sa	19:24:10	20 46 48	13 19	14 14	15 46	18 31	29 37	3 50	4 50	12 31	5 03	10 01	9 00	25 05	16 36	2 56	13 31
14 Su	19:28:06	21 44 02	25 55	14 09	15 14	19 43	0 ♋ 18	4 04	4 51	12 31	5 02	10 00	9 26	25 39	16 25	3 23	13 29
15 M	19:32:03	22 41 16	8 ♎ 46	14 06	14 45	20 56	0 59	4 17	4 51	12 31	5 01	9 58	9 53	26 14	16 15	3 50	13 28
16 T	19:35:59	23 38 30	21 56	14 05 D	14 20	22 08	1 39	4 31	4 52	12 31	5 00	9 57	10 20	26 48	16 04	4 17	13 26
17 W	19:39:56	24 35 44	5 ♏ 27	14 05 R	13 59	23 21	2 20	4 44	4 53	12 31 R	4 58	9 55	10 47	27 23	15 52	4 44	13 25
18 Th	19:43:52	25 32 59	19 22	14 05	13 42	24 33	3 00	4 57	4 54	12 31	4 57	9 54	11 13	27 57	15 41	5 11	13 23
19 F	19:47:49	26 30 14	3 ♐ 40	14 04	13 30	25 45	3 40	5 10	4 55	12 31	4 56	9 52	11 40	28 32	15 29	5 38	13 21
20 Sa	19:51:45	27 27 28	18 22	14 01	13 23 D	26 57	4 21	5 24	4 56	12 31	4 55	9 51	12 07	29 07	15 17	6 05	13 20
21 Su	19:55:42	28 24 44	3 ♑ 22	13 55	13 22	28 10	5 01	5 37	4 57	12 31	4 54	9 49	12 34	29 41	15 04	6 32	13 18
22 M	19:59:39	29 21 59	18 32	13 46	13 26	29 22	5 41	5 50	4 58	12 31	4 52	9 48	13 01	0 ♋ 16	14 52	6 59	13 16
23 T	20:03:35	0 ♌ 19 15	3 ♒ 43	13 36	13 36	0 ♍ 34	6 22	6 03	5 00	12 31	4 51	9 47	13 28	0 51	14 39	7 26	13 14
24 W	20:07:32	1 16 31	18 43	13 26	13 51	1 46	7 02	6 16	5 01	12 30	4 50	9 45	13 55	1 25	14 26	7 53	13 12
25 Th	20:11:28	2 13 49	3 ♓ 25	13 16	14 13	2 58	7 42	6 29	5 03	12 30	4 49	9 44	14 22	2 00	14 13	8 20	13 10
26 F	20:15:25	3 11 06	17 40	13 08	14 40	4 10	8 22	6 42	5 05	12 30	4 47	9 42	14 49	2 35	13 59	8 48	13 08
27 Sa	20:19:21	4 08 25	1 ♈ 25	13 02	15 14	5 22	9 02	6 55	5 06	12 29	4 46	9 41	15 16	3 10	13 45	9 15	13 06
28 Su	20:23:18	5 05 45	14 42	12 59	15 53	6 34	9 42	7 08	5 08	12 29	4 45	9 40	15 43	3 44	13 32	9 42	13 04
29 M	20:27:14	6 03 06	27 32	12 58 D	16 38	7 46	10 22	7 21	5 10	12 28	4 43	9 38	16 10	4 19	13 18	10 09	13 02
30 T	20:31:11	7 00 27	9 ♉ 59	12 58 R	17 29	8 58	11 02	7 33	5 12	12 28	4 42	9 37	16 37	4 54	13 03	10 37	13 00
31 W	20:35:08	7 57 50	22 09	12 57	18 26	10 10	11 41	7 46	5 14	12 27	4 40	9 36	17 04	5 29	12 49	11 04	12 58

August 2013

DATE	SID.TIME	SUN	MOON	N.NODE	MERCURY	VENUS	MARS	JUPITER	SATURN	URANUS	NEPTUNE	PLUTO	CERES	PALLAS	JUNO	VESTA	CHIRON
1 Th	20:39:04	8 ♌ 55 14	4 ♊ 07	12 ♏ 56	19 ♋ 28	11 ♍ 22	12 ♋ 21	7 ♋ 59	5 ♏ 17	12 ♈ 26	4 ♓ 39	9 ♑ 35	17 ♌ 31	6 ♋ 04	12 ♒ 35	11 ♌ 31	12 ♓ 56
2 F	20:43:01	9 52 39	15 59	12 53 ℞	20 36	12 33	13 01	8 12	5 19	12 26 ℞	4 37 ℞	9 33 ℞	17 58	6 39	12 20 ℞	11 58	12 54 ℞
3 Sa	20:46:57	10 50 06	27 47	12 47	21 49	13 45	13 41	8 24	5 21	12 25	4 36	9 32	18 26	7 13	12 06	12 26	12 51
4 Su	20:50:54	11 47 33	9 ♋ 37	12 38	23 07	14 57	14 20	8 37	5 24	12 24	4 35	9 31	18 53	7 48	11 51	12 53	12 49
5 M	20:54:50	12 45 01	21 32	12 27	24 31	16 08	15 00	8 49	5 27	12 23	4 33	9 30	19 20	8 23	11 37	13 21	12 47
6 T	20:58:47	13 42 31	3 ♌ 32	12 14	25 59	17 20	15 39	9 02	5 29	12 22	4 32	9 28	19 47	8 58	11 22	13 48	12 44
7 W	21:02:43	14 40 01	15 41	12 00	27 32	18 32	16 19	9 14	5 32	12 22	4 30	9 27	20 14	9 33	11 07	14 15	12 42
8 Th	21:06:40	15 37 32	27 58	11 47	29 09	19 43	16 58	9 26	5 35	12 21	4 29	9 26	20 42	10 08	10 53	14 43	12 39
9 F	21:10:37	16 35 05	10 ♍ 25	11 35	0 ♌ 50	20 55	17 38	9 39	5 38	12 20	4 27	9 25	21 09	10 43	10 38	15 10	12 37
10 Sa	21:14:33	17 32 38	23 01	11 26	2 35	22 06	18 17	9 51	5 41	12 18	4 25	9 24	21 36	11 17	10 23	15 38	12 34
11 Su	21:18:30	18 30 12	5 ♎ 49	11 19	4 23	23 18	18 56	10 03	5 44	12 17	4 24	9 23	22 03	11 52	10 09	16 05	12 32
12 M	21:22:26	19 27 47	18 49	11 15	6 14	24 29	19 35	10 15	5 47	12 16	4 22	9 22	22 31	12 27	9 55	16 33	12 29
13 T	21:26:23	20 25 23	2 ♏ 04	11 14 D	8 08	25 40	20 15	10 27	5 51	12 15	4 21	9 21	22 58	13 02	9 40	17 00	12 27
14 W	21:30:19	21 23 00	15 34	11 14 ℞	10 04	26 51	20 54	10 39	5 54	12 14	4 19	9 20	23 25	13 37	9 26	17 28	12 24
15 Th	21:34:16	22 20 38	29 23	11 14	12 02	28 03	21 33	10 51	5 58	12 13	4 18	9 19	23 53	14 12	9 12	17 55	12 22
16 F	21:38:12	23 18 17	13 ♐ 30	11 12	14 01	29 14	22 12	11 02	6 01	12 11	4 16	9 18	24 20	14 46	8 58	18 23	12 19
17 Sa	21:42:09	24 15 57	27 55	11 09	16 01	0 ♎ 25	22 51	11 14	6 05	12 10	4 14	9 17	24 47	15 21	8 44	18 50	12 16
18 Su	21:46:06	25 13 38	12 ♑ 36	11 03	18 02	1 36	23 30	11 26	6 09	12 08	4 13	9 16	25 15	15 56	8 31	19 18	12 14
19 M	21:50:02	26 11 20	27 27	10 55	20 03	2 47	24 09	11 37	6 12	12 07	4 11	9 15	25 42	16 31	8 17	19 45	12 11
20 T	21:53:59	27 09 03	12 ♒ 20	10 45	22 05	3 58	24 48	11 49	6 16	12 06	4 09	9 14	26 09	17 05	8 04	20 13	12 08
21 W	21:57:55	28 06 48	27 07	10 35	24 06	5 09	25 26	12 00	6 20	12 04	4 08	9 13	26 37	17 40	7 51	20 41	12 05
22 Th	22:01:52	29 04 33	11 ♓ 39	10 25	26 07	6 19	26 05	12 11	6 24	12 02	4 06	9 12	27 04	18 15	7 38	21 08	12 03
23 F	22:05:48	0 ♍ 02 20	25 49	10 16	28 07	7 30	26 44	12 23	6 28	12 01	4 05	9 11	27 31	18 49	7 26	21 36	12 00
24 Sa	22:09:45	1 00 09	9 ♈ 34	10 10	0 ♍ 07	8 41	27 22	12 34	6 33	11 59	4 03	9 11	27 59	19 24	7 13	22 03	11 57
25 Su	22:13:41	1 58 00	22 52	10 07	2 06	9 51	28 01	12 45	6 37	11 58	4 01	9 10	28 26	19 59	7 01	22 31	11 54
26 M	22:17:38	2 55 52	5 ♉ 44	10 06 D	4 04	11 02	28 40	12 56	6 41	11 56	4 00	9 09	28 53	20 33	6 50	22 59	11 51
27 T	22:21:35	3 53 46	18 14	10 06	6 00	12 12	29 18	13 07	6 46	11 54	3 58	9 08	29 21	21 08	6 38	23 26	11 49
28 W	22:25:31	4 51 41	0 ♊ 26	10 06 ℞	7 56	13 23	29 57	13 18	6 50	11 52	3 56	9 08	29 48	21 42	6 27	23 54	11 46
29 Th	22:29:28	5 49 39	12 26	10 06	9 51	14 33	0 ♌ 35	13 28	6 55	11 51	3 55	9 07	0 ♍ 16	22 17	6 16	24 22	11 43
30 F	22:33:24	6 47 38	24 18	10 04	11 44	15 44	1 13	13 39	6 59	11 49	3 53	9 06	0 43	22 51	6 06	24 49	11 40
31 Sa	22:37:21	7 45 40	6 ♋ 09	10 01	13 36	16 54	1 52	13 50	7 04	11 47	3 51	9 06	1 10	23 25	5 56	25 17	11 37

September 2013

DATE	SID.TIME	SUN	MOON	N.NODE	MERCURY	VENUS	MARS	JUPITER	SATURN	URANUS	NEPTUNE	PLUTO	CERES	PALLAS	JUNO	VESTA	CHIRON
1 Su	22:41:17	8♍43 43	18 ♋ 01	9 ♏ 54	15 ♍ 27	18 ♎ 04	2 ♌ 30	14 ♋ 00	7 ♏ 09	11 ♈ 45	3 ♓ 50	9 ♑ 05	1 ♍ 38	24 ♋ 00	5 ♒ 46	25 ♌ 45	11 ♓ 34
2 M	22:45:14	9 41 48	0 ♌ 00	9 46 ℞	17 17	19 14	3 08	14 10	7 14	11 43 ℞	3 48 ℞	9 05 ℞	2 05	24 34	5 36 ℞	26 12	11 32 ℞
3 T	22:49:10	10 39 54	12 07	9 36	19 05	20 24	3 47	14 21	7 19	11 41	3 47	9 04	2 32	25 08	5 27	26 40	11 29
4 W	22:53:07	11 38 03	24 26	9 25	20 52	21 34	4 25	14 31	7 24	11 39	3 45	9 04	3 00	25 43	5 19	27 08	11 26
5 Th	22:57:04	12 36 13	6 ♍ 57	9 15	22 38	22 44	5 03	14 41	7 29	11 37	3 43	9 03	3 27	26 17	5 10	27 36	11 23
6 F	23:01:00	13 34 25	19 40	9 06	24 23	23 54	5 41	14 51	7 34	11 35	3 42	9 03	3 55	26 51	5 02	28 03	11 20
7 Sa	23:04:57	14 32 39	2 ♎ 36	8 58	26 07	25 04	6 19	15 00	7 39	11 33	3 40	9 02	4 22	27 25	4 55	28 31	11 17
8 Su	23:08:53	15 30 54	15 43	8 54	27 49	26 13	6 57	15 10	7 44	11 31	3 38	9 02	4 49	27 59	4 48	28 59	11 15
9 M	23:12:50	16 29 11	29 02	8 51 D	29 30	27 23	7 35	15 20	7 50	11 29	3 37	9 01	5 17	28 33	4 41	29 26	11 12
10 T	23:16:46	17 27 30	12 ♏ 32	8 51	1 ♎ 10	28 32	8 12	15 29	7 55	11 27	3 35	9 01	5 44	29 07	4 35	29 54	11 09
11 W	23:20:43	18 25 50	26 13	8 52	2 49	29 42	8 50	15 39	8 00	11 25	3 34	9 01	6 11	29 40	4 29	0 ♍ 22	11 06
12 Th	23:24:39	19 24 12	10 ♐ 05	8 53 ℞	4 27	0 ♏ 51	9 28	15 48	8 06	11 22	3 32	9 01	6 39	0 ♌ 14	4 23	0 49	11 03
13 F	23:28:36	20 22 35	24 08	8 53	6 04	2 01	10 06	15 57	8 12	11 20	3 31	9 00	7 06	0 48	4 18	1 17	11 00
14 Sa	23:32:33	21 21 00	8 ♑ 22	8 52	7 39	3 10	10 43	16 06	8 17	11 18	3 29	9 00	7 33	1 22	4 13	1 45	10 58
15 Su	23:36:29	22 19 26	22 44	8 48	9 14	4 19	11 21	16 15	8 23	11 16	3 27	9 00	8 00	1 55	4 09	2 13	10 55
16 M	23:40:26	23 17 54	7 ♒ 11	8 43	10 47	5 28	11 58	16 24	8 29	11 14	3 26	9 00	8 28	2 29	4 06	2 40	10 52
17 T	23:44:22	24 16 23	21 38	8 37	12 19	6 37	12 36	16 33	8 34	11 11	3 24	9 00	8 55	3 02	4 02	3 08	10 49
18 W	23:48:19	25 14 55	5 ♓ 59	8 30	13 51	7 45	13 13	16 41	8 40	11 09	3 23	8 59	9 22	3 35	3 59	3 36	10 47
19 Th	23:52:15	26 13 28	20 09	8 23	15 21	8 54	13 51	16 50	8 46	11 07	3 21	8 59	9 49	4 08	3 57	4 03	10 44
20 F	23:56:12	27 12 02	4 ♈ 03	8 18	16 50	10 03	14 28	16 58	8 52	11 04	3 20	8 59 D	10 17	4 42	3 55	4 31	10 41
21 Sa	0:00:08	28 10 39	17 36	8 14	18 18	11 11	15 05	17 06	8 58	11 02	3 18	8 59	10 44	5 15	3 53	4 59	10 38
22 Su	0:04:05	29 09 18	0 ♉ 47	8 13 D	19 45	12 20	15 42	17 14	9 04	11 00	3 17	8 59	11 11	5 48	3 52	5 26	10 36
23 M	0:08:01	0♎07 59	13 37	8 12	21 11	13 28	16 20	17 22	9 10	10 57	3 16	8 59	11 38	6 21	3 51	5 54	10 33
24 T	0:11:58	1 06 42	26 07	8 14	22 36	14 36	16 57	17 30	9 16	10 55	3 14	9 00	12 05	6 53	3 51 D	6 21	10 31
25 W	0:15:55	2 05 28	8 ♊ 21	8 15	23 59	15 44	17 34	17 37	9 22	10 53	3 13	9 00	12 32	7 26	3 51	6 49	10 28
26 Th	0:19:51	3 04 15	20 22	8 17	25 22	16 52	18 11	17 45	9 29	10 50	3 11	9 00	12 59	7 59	3 51	7 17	10 25
27 F	0:23:48	4 03 05	2 ♋ 16	8 17 ℞	26 43	18 00	18 48	17 52	9 35	10 48	3 10	9 00	13 26	8 31	3 52	7 44	10 23
28 Sa	0:27:44	5 01 58	14 08	8 17	28 03	19 07	19 25	17 59	9 41	10 45	3 09	9 00	13 54	9 04	3 54	8 12	10 20
29 Su	0:31:41	6 00 52	26 02	8 15	29 22	20 15	20 02	18 06	9 48	10 43	3 07	9 00	14 21	9 36	3 55	8 40	10 18
30 M	0:35:37	6 59 49	8 ♌ 03	8 12	0 ♏ 40	21 22	20 38	18 13	9 54	10 41	3 06	9 01	14 48	10 08	3 58	9 07	10 15

October 2013

DATE	SID.TIME	SUN	MOON	N.NODE	MERCURY	VENUS	MARS	JUPITER	SATURN	URANUS	NEPTUNE	PLUTO	CERES	PALLAS	JUNO	VESTA	CHIRON
1 T	0:39:34	7 ♎ 58 48	20 ♌ 15	8 ♏ 08	1 ♏ 56	22 ♏ 30	21 ♌ 15	18 ♋ 20	10 ♏ 00	10 ♈ 38	3 ♓ 05	9 ♑ 01	15 ♍ 15	10 ♌ 40	4 ♒ 00	9 ♍ 35	10 ♓ 13
2 W	0:43:30	8 57 49	2 ♍ 41	8 03 ℞	3 11	23 37	21 52	18 27	10 07	10 36 ℞	3 04 ℞	9 01	15 42	11 12	4 03	10 02	10 10 ℞
3 Th	0:47:27	9 56 52	15 23	7 58	4 24	24 44	22 28	18 33	10 13	10 33	3 02	9 02	16 09	11 44	4 07	10 30	10 08
4 F	0:51:24	10 55 57	28 22	7 54	5 35	25 51	23 05	18 40	10 20	10 31	3 01	9 02	16 35	12 16	4 11	10 57	10 06
5 Sa	0:55:20	11 55 05	11 ♎ 37	7 51	6 45	26 58	23 42	18 46	10 27	10 28	3 00	9 03	17 02	12 48	4 15	11 25	10 03
6 Su	0:59:17	12 54 14	25 08	7 49 D	7 53	28 04	24 18	18 52	10 33	10 26	2 59	9 03	17 29	13 19	4 20	11 52	10 01
7 M	1:03:13	13 53 26	8 ♏ 52	7 48	8 58	29 11	24 54	18 58	10 40	10 24	2 58	9 04	17 56	13 51	4 25	12 20	9 59
8 T	1:07:10	14 52 39	22 47	7 49	10 02	0 ♐ 17	25 31	19 03	10 47	10 21	2 56	9 04	18 23	14 22	4 30	12 47	9 57
9 W	1:11:06	15 51 55	6 ♐ 50	7 50	11 03	1 23	26 07	19 09	10 53	10 19	2 55	9 05	18 50	14 53	4 36	13 15	9 55
10 Th	1:15:03	16 51 12	20 58	7 51	12 02	2 29	26 43	19 14	11 00	10 16	2 54	9 05	19 16	15 24	4 42	13 42	9 52
11 F	1:18:59	17 50 31	5 ♑ 09	7 52 ℞	12 57	3 35	27 19	19 19	11 07	10 14	2 53	9 06	19 43	15 55	4 49	14 09	9 50
12 Sa	1:22:56	18 49 52	19 22	7 53	13 50	4 40	27 56	19 24	11 14	10 12	2 52	9 06	20 10	16 25	4 56	14 37	9 48
13 Su	1:26:53	19 49 14	3 ♒ 33	7 52	14 39	5 46	28 32	19 29	11 21	10 09	2 51	9 07	20 36	16 56	5 03	15 04	9 46
14 M	1:30:49	20 48 38	17 40	7 51	15 25	6 51	29 08	19 34	11 27	10 07	2 50	9 08	21 03	17 26	5 11	15 31	9 44
15 T	1:34:46	21 48 04	1 ♓ 42	7 49	16 06	7 56	29 43	19 38	11 34	10 04	2 49	9 09	21 29	17 57	5 19	15 59	9 42
16 W	1:38:42	22 47 32	15 34	7 47	16 43	9 01	0 ♍ 19	19 43	11 41	10 02	2 48	9 09	21 56	18 27	5 28	16 26	9 41
17 Th	1:42:39	23 47 01	29 16	7 45	17 15	10 05	0 55	19 47	11 48	10 00	2 47	9 10	22 22	18 57	5 37	16 53	9 39
18 F	1:46:35	24 46 32	12 ♈ 44	7 44	17 41	11 09	1 31	19 51	11 55	9 57	2 47	9 11	22 49	19 27	5 46	17 20	9 37
19 Sa	1:50:32	25 46 06	25 57	7 43 D	18 02	12 13	2 06	19 54	12 02	9 55	2 46	9 12	23 15	19 56	5 56	17 47	9 35
20 Su	1:54:28	26 45 41	8 ♉ 54	7 43	18 16	13 17	2 42	19 58	12 09	9 53	2 45	9 13	23 41	20 26	6 06	18 14	9 34
21 M	1:58:25	27 45 18	21 34	7 43	18 23 ℞	14 21	3 18	20 02	12 16	9 51	2 44	9 14	24 08	20 55	6 16	18 42	9 32
22 T	2:02:21	28 44 58	4 ♊ 00	7 44	18 22	15 24	3 53	20 05	12 23	9 48	2 43	9 15	24 34	21 24	6 27	19 09	9 30
23 W	2:06:18	29 44 40	16 11	7 44	18 14	16 27	4 28	20 08	12 30	9 46	2 43	9 15	25 00	21 53	6 38	19 36	9 29
24 Th	2:10:15	0 ♏ 44 24	28 13	7 45	17 57	17 30	5 04	20 11	12 38	9 44	2 42	9 16	25 26	22 22	6 49	20 03	9 27
25 F	2:14:11	1 44 10	10 ♋ 07	7 46	17 31	18 33	5 39	20 13	12 45	9 42	2 41	9 17	25 52	22 50	7 01	20 30	9 26
26 Sa	2:18:08	2 43 58	21 59	7 46	16 55	19 35	6 14	20 16	12 52	9 39	2 41	9 19	26 18	23 19	7 13	20 56	9 24
27 Su	2:22:04	3 43 49	3 ♌ 53	7 46 ℞	16 11	20 37	6 49	20 18	12 59	9 37	2 40	9 20	26 44	23 47	7 25	21 23	9 23
28 M	2:26:01	4 43 41	15 53	7 46	15 19	21 38	7 24	20 20	13 06	9 35	2 39	9 21	27 10	24 15	7 38	21 50	9 22
29 T	2:29:57	5 43 36	28 05	7 46	14 18	22 40	7 59	20 22	13 13	9 33	2 39	9 22	27 36	24 43	7 50	22 17	9 21
30 W	2:33:54	6 43 33	10 ♍ 32	7 46	13 10	23 41	8 34	20 24	13 20	9 31	2 38	9 23	28 02	25 11	8 04	22 44	9 19
31 Th	2:37:50	7 43 32	23 17	7 46 D	11 57	24 41	9 09	20 25	13 28	9 29	2 38	9 24	28 28	25 38	8 17	23 11	9 18

November 2013

DATE	SID.TIME	SUN	MOON	N.NODE	MERCURY	VENUS	MARS	JUPITER	SATURN	URANUS	NEPTUNE	PLUTO	CERES	PALLAS	JUNO	VESTA	CHIRON
1 F	2:41:47	8 ♏ 43 34	6 ♎ 24	7 ♏ 46	10 ♏ 40	25 ♐ 42	9 ♍ 44	20 ♋ 27	13 ♏ 35	9 ♈ 27	2 ♓ 37	9 ♑ 25	28 ♍ 54	26 ♌ 05	8 ♒ 31	23 ♍ 37	9 ♓ 17
2 Sa	2:45:44	9 43 37	19 54	7 46	9 22 ℞	26 41	10 18	20 28	13 42	9 25 ℞	2 37 ℞	9 27	29 19	26 32	8 45	24 04	9 16 ℞
3 Su	2:49:40	10 43 42	3 ♏ 44	7 46 ℞	8 06	27 41	10 53	20 29	13 49	9 23	2 37	9 28	29 45	26 59	9 00	24 30	9 15
4 M	2:53:37	11 43 49	17 53	7 46	6 53	28 40	11 28	20 30	13 56	9 21	2 36	9 29	0 ♎ 10	27 25	9 14	24 57	9 14
5 T	2:57:33	12 43 58	2 ♐ 16	7 46	5 45	29 39	12 02	20 30	14 03	9 19	2 36	9 31	0 36	27 52	9 29	25 23	9 13
6 W	3:01:30	13 44 09	16 48	7 45	4 46	0 ♑ 37	12 36	20 31	14 11	9 17	2 36	9 32	1 01	28 18	9 45	25 50	9 13
7 Th	3:05:26	14 44 22	1 ♑ 23	7 45	3 56	1 35	13 11	20 31 ℞	14 18	9 15	2 36	9 33	1 27	28 44	10 00	26 16	9 12
8 F	3:09:23	15 44 36	15 54	7 44	3 17	2 32	13 45	20 31	14 25	9 13	2 35	9 35	1 52	29 09	10 16	26 43	9 11
9 Sa	3:13:19	16 44 51	0 ♒ 18	7 43	2 50	3 29	14 19	20 30	14 32	9 12	2 35	9 36	2 17	29 35	10 32	27 09	9 10
10 Su	3:17:16	17 45 08	14 31	7 43 D	2 34 D	4 26	14 53	20 30	14 39	9 10	2 35	9 38	2 42	0 ♍ 00	10 49	27 35	9 10
11 M	3:21:13	18 45 26	28 30	7 43	2 30	5 21	15 27	20 29	14 47	9 08	2 35	9 39	3 07	0 25	11 05	28 01	9 09
12 T	3:25:09	19 45 46	12 ♓ 14	7 43	2 36	6 17	16 01	20 28	14 54	9 07	2 35	9 40	3 32	0 49	11 22	28 27	9 09
13 W	3:29:06	20 46 07	25 45	7 44	2 54	7 11	16 34	20 27	15 01	9 05	2 35 D	9 42	3 57	1 13	11 40	28 53	9 08
14 Th	3:33:02	21 46 29	9 ♈ 01	7 46	3 21	8 05	17 08	20 26	15 08	9 03	2 35	9 43	4 22	1 37	11 57	29 19	9 08
15 F	3:36:59	22 46 53	22 03	7 47	3 56	8 59	17 42	20 25	15 15	9 02	2 35	9 45	4 47	2 01	12 15	29 45	9 08
16 Sa	3:40:55	23 47 19	4 ♉ 53	7 47 ℞	4 40	9 52	18 15	20 23	15 23	9 00	2 35	9 47	5 11	2 25	12 33	0 ♎ 11	9 08
17 Su	3:44:52	24 47 46	17 31	7 47	5 31	10 44	18 48	20 21	15 30	8 59	2 35	9 48	5 36	2 48	12 51	0 37	9 07
18 M	3:48:48	25 48 14	29 57	7 46	6 28	11 35	19 22	20 19	15 37	8 57	2 35	9 50	6 00	3 11	13 09	1 02	9 07
19 T	3:52:45	26 48 44	12 ♊ 12	7 44	7 30	12 26	19 55	20 17	15 44	8 56	2 35	9 51	6 25	3 33	13 28	1 28	9 07 D
20 W	3:56:42	27 49 16	24 18	7 41	8 37	13 16	20 28	20 14	15 51	8 55	2 35	9 53	6 49	3 56	13 47	1 54	9 07
21 Th	4:00:38	28 49 49	6 ♋ 17	7 37	9 48	14 05	21 01	20 12	15 58	8 53	2 36	9 55	7 13	4 18	14 06	2 19	9 07
22 F	4:04:35	29 50 24	18 11	7 33	11 03	14 54	21 34	20 09	16 05	8 52	2 36	9 57	7 37	4 40	14 25	2 45	9 07
23 Sa	4:08:31	0 ♐ 51 01	0 ♌ 02	7 30	12 21	15 41	22 07	20 06	16 12	8 51	2 36	9 58	8 01	5 01	14 45	3 10	9 08
24 Su	4:12:28	1 51 39	11 54	7 27	13 41	16 28	22 39	20 03	16 19	8 50	2 37	10 00	8 25	5 22	15 04	3 35	9 08
25 M	4:16:24	2 52 19	23 52	7 26 D	15 03	17 14	23 12	19 59	16 26	8 48	2 37	10 02	8 49	5 43	15 24	4 00	9 08
26 T	4:20:21	3 53 00	6 ♍ 00	7 25	16 27	17 58	23 44	19 56	16 33	8 47	2 37	10 03	9 13	6 03	15 45	4 25	9 08
27 W	4:24:17	4 53 43	18 23	7 26	17 53	18 42	24 17	19 52	16 40	8 46	2 38	10 05	9 36	6 23	16 05	4 50	9 09
28 Th	4:28:14	5 54 28	1 ♎ 05	7 28	19 20	19 25	24 49	19 48	16 47	8 45	2 38	10 07	10 00	6 43	16 26	5 15	9 09
29 F	4:32:11	6 55 14	14 10	7 29	20 48	20 06	25 21	19 44	16 54	8 44	2 39	10 09	10 23	7 02	16 46	5 40	9 10
30 Sa	4:36:07	7 56 01	27 41	7 31 ℞	22 16	20 47	25 53	19 39	17 01	8 43	2 39	10 11	10 47	7 21	17 07	6 05	9 10

December 2013

DATE	SID.TIME	SUN	MOON	N.NODE	MERCURY	VENUS	MARS	JUPITER	SATURN	URANUS	NEPTUNE	PLUTO	CERES	PALLAS	JUNO	VESTA	CHIRON
1 Su	4:40:04	8 ♐ 56 51	11 ♏ 38	7 ♏ 31	23 ♏ 46	21 ♑ 26	26 ♍ 25	19 ♋ 35	17 ♏ 08	8 ♈ 42	2 ♓ 40	10 ♑ 13	11 ♎ 10	7 ♍ 40	17 ♒ 29	6 ♎ 30	9 ♓ 11
2 M	4:44:00	9 57 41	26 02	7 30 ℞	25 16	22 05	26 57	19 30 ℞	17 15	8 42 ℞	2 40	10 14	11 33	7 58	17 50	6 54	9 12
3 T	4:47:57	10 58 33	10 ♐ 46	7 27	26 47	22 41	27 28	19 25	17 22	8 41	2 41	10 16	11 56	8 16	18 12	7 19	9 13
4 W	4:51:53	11 59 26	25 43	7 22	28 18	23 17	28 00	19 20	17 28	8 40	2 42	10 18	12 19	8 34	18 33	7 43	9 13
5 Th	4:55:50	13 00 20	10 ♑ 46	7 17	29 50	23 51	28 31	19 15	17 35	8 40	2 42	10 20	12 42	8 51	18 55	8 07	9 14
6 F	4:59:46	14 01 15	25 44	7 11	1 ♐ 21	24 24	29 02	19 10	17 42	8 39	2 43	10 22	13 04	9 07	19 18	8 31	9 15
7 Sa	5:03:43	15 02 11	10 ♒ 30	7 06	2 54	24 55	29 33	19 04	17 49	8 38	2 44	10 24	13 27	9 24	19 40	8 55	9 16
8 Su	5:07:40	16 03 07	24 56	7 03	4 26	25 25	0 ♎ 04	18 59	17 55	8 38	2 45	10 26	13 49	9 39	20 03	9 19	9 17
9 M	5:11:36	17 04 04	9 ♓ 00	7 01 D	5 58	25 53	0 35	18 53	18 02	8 37	2 46	10 28	14 11	9 55	20 25	9 43	9 18
10 T	5:15:33	18 05 02	22 41	7 01	7 31	26 19	1 06	18 47	18 08	8 37	2 47	10 30	14 33	10 10	20 48	10 07	9 19
11 W	5:19:29	19 06 00	6 ♈ 01	7 02	9 03	26 44	1 36	18 41	18 15	8 37	2 47	10 32	14 55	10 24	21 11	10 30	9 21
12 Th	5:23:26	20 06 59	19 01	7 03	10 36	27 06	2 07	18 34	18 22	8 36	2 48	10 34	15 17	10 38	21 35	10 54	9 22
13 F	5:27:22	21 07 58	1 ♉ 45	7 04 ℞	12 09	27 27	2 37	18 28	18 28	8 36	2 49	10 36	15 39	10 52	21 58	11 17	9 23
14 Sa	5:31:19	22 08 58	14 16	7 04	13 42	27 46	3 07	18 21	18 34	8 36	2 50	10 38	16 00	11 05	22 22	11 40	9 25
15 Su	5:35:15	23 09 59	26 36	7 02	15 15	28 03	3 37	18 15	18 41	8 36	2 51	10 40	16 22	11 18	22 45	12 03	9 26
16 M	5:39:12	24 11 00	8 ♊ 47	6 58	16 49	28 18	4 07	18 08	18 47	8 35	2 52	10 42	16 43	11 30	23 09	12 26	9 28
17 T	5:43:09	25 12 02	20 52	6 51	18 22	28 30	4 36	18 01	18 53	8 35 D	2 54	10 44	17 04	11 42	23 33	12 49	9 29
18 W	5:47:05	26 13 04	2 ♋ 51	6 42	19 55	28 41	5 06	17 54	19 00	8 35	2 55	10 46	17 25	11 53	23 57	13 12	9 31
19 Th	5:51:02	27 14 08	14 46	6 32	21 29	28 49	5 35	17 47	19 06	8 35	2 56	10 48	17 46	12 04	24 22	13 34	9 32
20 F	5:54:58	28 15 11	26 39	6 21	23 03	28 55	6 04	17 40	19 12	8 35	2 57	10 50	18 06	12 15	24 46	13 56	9 34
21 Sa	5:58:55	29 16 16	8 ♌ 30	6 11	24 37	28 58 ℞	6 33	17 32	19 18	8 36	2 58	10 52	18 27	12 24	25 11	14 19	9 36
22 Su	6:02:51	0 ♑ 17 21	20 23	6 03	26 11	28 59	7 02	17 25	19 24	8 36	3 00	10 54	18 47	12 34	25 36	14 41	9 38
23 M	6:06:48	1 18 27	2 ♍ 21	5 56	27 45	28 57	7 30	17 18	19 30	8 36	3 01	10 56	19 07	12 42	26 01	15 03	9 39
24 T	6:10:45	2 19 33	14 26	5 52	29 20	28 54	7 59	17 10	19 36	8 36	3 02	10 59	19 27	12 51	26 26	15 24	9 41
25 W	6:14:41	3 20 40	26 44	5 50 D	0 ♑ 54	28 47	8 27	17 02	19 42	8 37	3 03	11 01	19 47	12 58	26 51	15 46	9 43
26 Th	6:18:38	4 21 48	9 ♎ 19	5 50	2 29	28 38	8 55	16 55	19 48	8 37	3 05	11 03	20 07	13 05	27 17	16 08	9 45
27 F	6:22:34	5 22 57	22 16	5 50	4 05	28 27	9 23	16 47	19 53	8 38	3 06	11 05	20 26	13 12	27 42	16 29	9 47
28 Sa	6:26:31	6 24 05	5 ♏ 39	5 51 ℞	5 40	28 13	9 50	16 39	19 59	8 38	3 08	11 07	20 45	13 18	28 08	16 50	9 49
29 Su	6:30:27	7 25 15	19 31	5 50	7 16	27 57	10 18	16 31	20 05	8 39	3 09	11 09	21 04	13 23	28 34	17 11	9 52
30 M	6:34:24	8 26 25	3 ♐ 52	5 47	8 52	27 38	10 45	16 23	20 10	8 39	3 11	11 11	21 23	13 28	29 00	17 32	9 54
31 T	6:38:20	9 27 36	18 39	5 41	10 28	27 17	11 12	16 15	20 16	8 40	3 12	11 13	21 42	13 32	29 26	17 52	9 56

The Planetary Hours

The selection of an auspicious time for starting any activity is an important matter. Its existence tends to take on a nature corresponding to the conditions under which it was begun. Each hour is ruled by a planet, and the nature of any hour corresponds to the nature of the planet ruling it. The nature of the planetary hours is the same as the description of each of the planets. Uranus, Neptune, and Pluto are considered here as higher octaves of Mercury, Venus, and Mars.

Sunrise Hour	Sun	Mon	Tue	Wed	Thu	Fri	Sat
1	☉	☽	♂	☿	♃	♀	♄
2	♀	♄	☉	☽	♂	☿	♃
3	☿	♃	♀	♄	☉	☽	♂
4	☽	♂	☿	♃	♀	♄	☉
5	♄	☉	☽	♂	☿	♃	♀
6	♃	♀	♄	☉	☽	♂	☿
7	♂	☿	♃	♀	♄	☉	☽
8	☉	☽	♂	☿	♃	♀	♄
9	♀	♄	☉	☽	♂	☿	♃
10	☿	♃	♀	♄	☉	☽	♂
11	☽	♂	☿	♃	♀	♄	☉
12	♄	☉	☽	♂	☿	♃	♀

Sunset Hour	Sun	Mon	Tue	Wed	Thu	Fri	Sat
1	♃	♀	♄	☉	☽	♂	☿
2	♂	☿	♃	♀	♄	☉	☽
3	☉	☽	♂	☿	♃	♀	♄
4	♀	♄	☉	☽	♂	☿	♃
5	☿	♃	♀	♄	☉	☽	♂
6	☽	♂	☿	♃	♀	♄	☉
7	♄	☉	☽	♂	☿	♃	♀
8	♃	♀	♄	☉	☽	♂	☿
9	♂	☿	♃	♀	♄	☉	☽
10	☉	☽	♂	☿	♃	♀	♄
11	♀	♄	☉	☽	♂	☿	♃
12	☿	♃	♀	♄	☉	☽	♂

Table of Rising and Setting Signs

To find your approximate Ascendant, locate your Sun sign in the left column and determine the approximate time of your birth. Line up your Sun sign with birth time to find Ascendant. Note: This table will give you the approximate Ascendant only. To obtain your exact Ascendant you must consult your natal chart.

Sun Sign	6–8 am	8–10 am	10 am–12 pm	12–2 pm	2–4 pm	4–6 pm
Aries	Taurus	Gemini	Cancer	Leo	Virgo	Libra
Taurus	Gemini	Cancer	Leo	Virgo	Libra	Scorpio
Gemini	Cancer	Leo	Virgo	Libra	Scorpio	Sagittarius
Cancer	Leo	Virgo	Libra	Scorpio	Sagittarius	Capricorn
Leo	Virgo	Libra	Scorpio	Sagittarius	Capricorn	Aquarius
Virgo	Libra	Scorpio	Sagittarius	Capricorn	Aquarius	Pisces
Libra	Scorpio	Sagittarius	Capricorn	Aquarius	Pisces	Aries
Scorpio	Sagittarius	Capricorn	Aquarius	Pisces	Aries	Taurus
Sagittarius	Capricorn	Aquarius	Pisces	Aries	Taurus	Gemini
Capricorn	Aquarius	Pisces	Aries	Taurus	Gemini	Cancer
Aquarius	Pisces	Aries	Taurus	Gemini	Cancer	Leo
Pisces	Aries	Taurus	Gemini	Cancer	Leo	Virgo

Sun Sign	6–8 pm	8–10 pm	10 pm–12 am	12–2 am	2–4 am	4–6 am
Aries	Scorpio	Sagittarius	Capricorn	Aquarius	Pisces	Aries
Taurus	Sagittarius	Capricorn	Aquarius	Pisces	Aries	Taurus
Gemini	Capricorn	Aquarius	Pisces	Aries	Taurus	Gemini
Cancer	Aquarius	Pisces	Aries	Taurus	Gemini	Cancer
Leo	Pisces	Aries	Taurus	Gemini	Cancer	Leo
Virgo	Aries	Taurus	Gemini	Cancer	Leo	Virgo
Libra	Taurus	Gemini	Cancer	Leo	Virgo	Libra
Scorpio	Gemini	Cancer	Leo	Virgo	Libra	Scorpio
Sagittarius	Cancer	Leo	Virgo	Libra	Scorpio	Sagittarius
Capricorn	Leo	Virgo	Libra	Scorpio	Sagittarius	Capricorn
Aquarius	Virgo	Libra	Scorpio	Sagittarius	Capricorn	Aquarius
Pisces	Libra	Scorpio	Sagittarius	Capricorn	Aquarius	Pisces

Address Book

Name

Address

City, State, Zip

Phone Phone

E-mail

Name

Address

City, State, Zip

Phone Phone

E-mail

Name

Address

City, State, Zip

Phone Phone

E-mail

Name

Address

City, State, Zip

Phone Phone

E-mail

Name

Address

City, State, Zip

Phone Phone

E-mail

Address Book

Name

Address

City, State, Zip

Phone Phone

E-mail

Name

Address

City, State, Zip

Phone Phone

E-mail

Name

Address

City, State, Zip

Phone Phone

E-mail

Name

Address

City, State, Zip

Phone Phone

E-mail

Name

Address

City, State, Zip

Phone Phone

E-mail

Notes